Contents

ST JOHN'S CO-CATHEDRAL, VALETTA P51

COVID-19

We have re-checked every business in this book before publication to ensure that it is still open after the COVID-19 outbreak. However, the economic and social impacts of COVID-19 will continue to be felt long after the outbreak has been contained, and many businesses, services and events referenced in this guide may experience ongoing restrictions. Some businesses may be temporarily closed, have changed their opening hours and services, or require bookings; some unfortunately could have closed permanently. We suggest you check with venues before visiting for the latest information.

Right: The Inland Sea, Gozo (p141)

EMMA SHAW/LONELY PLANET ©

WELCOME TO

Malta & Gozo

Malta is the most surprising destination in the Mediterranean. I love exploring Valletta's improbable historic fortress before discovering the city's cosmopolitan bars and galleries. Malta's coastline conceals coves perfect both for swimming and to whet the appetite for a cuisine packed with historical influences. Across on Gozo, massive churches rise from sun-caressed landscapes, with clifftop paths running past historical monuments to hidden bays. All this and more, an easy day trip from anywhere in the country.

By Brett Atkinson, Writer

@travelwriternz travelwriternz

For more about our writers, see p192

Malta & Gozo

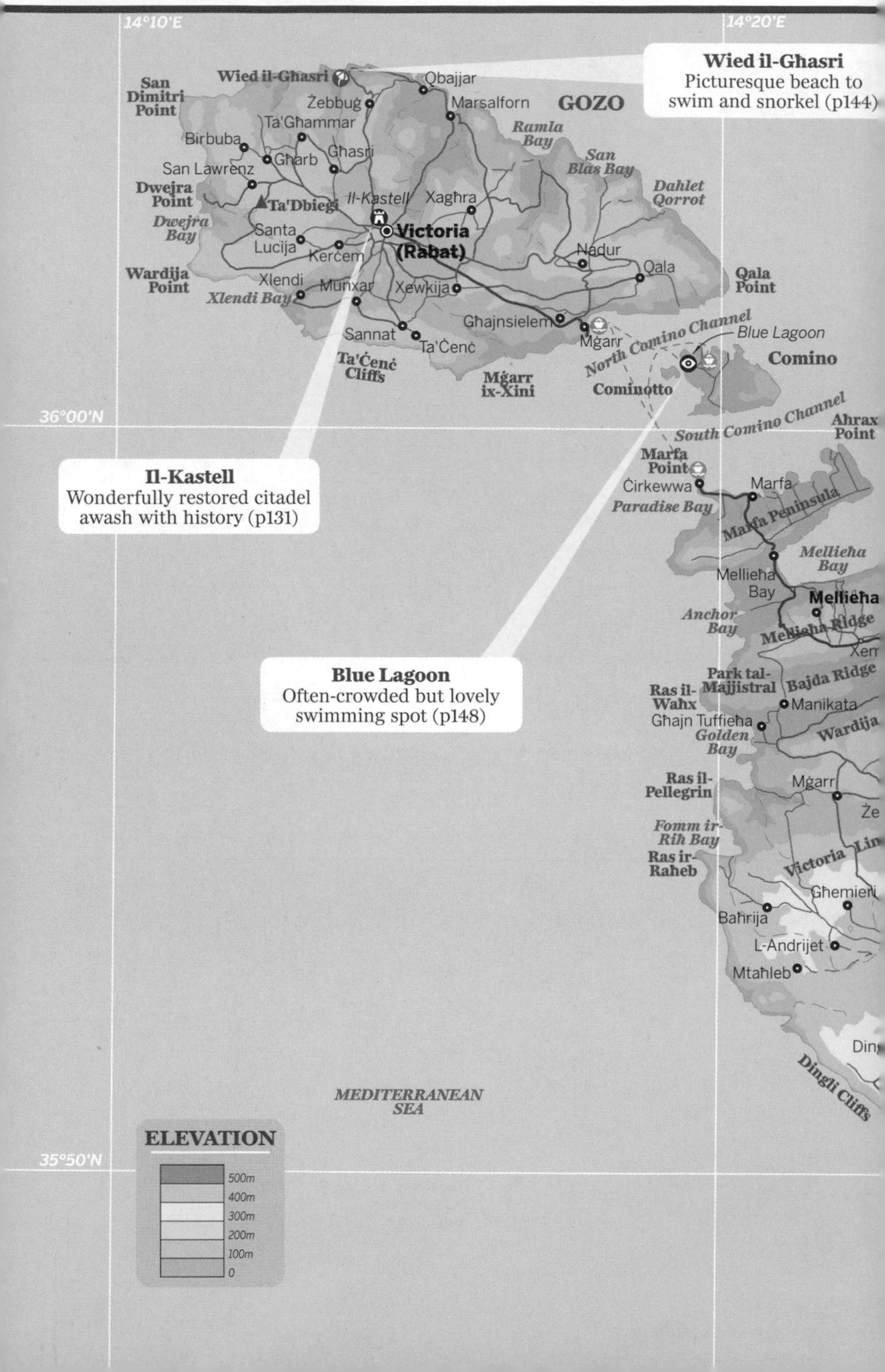

Wied il-Għasri
Picturesque beach to swim and snorkel (p144)
Il-Kastell
Wonderfully restored citadel awash with history (p131)
Blue Lagoon
Often-crowded but lovely swimming spot (p148)
14°10'E
14°20'E
36°00'N
35°50'N
GOZO
Wied il-Għasri
San Dimitri Point
Qbajjar
Żebbuġ
Marsalforn
Ta'Għammar
Birbuba
Għarb
Għasri
San Lawrenz
Dwejra Point
Dwejra Bay
Ta'Dbiegi
Il-Kastell
Xagħra
Victoria (Rabat)
Santa Lucija
Kerċem
Wardija Point
Xlendi
Xlendi Bay
Munxar
Xewkija
Sannat
Ta'Ċenċ
Ta'Ċenċ Cliffs
Mġarr ix-Xini
Għajnsielem
Mġarr
Nadur
Qala
Qala Point
Ramla Bay
San Blas Bay
Dahlet Qorrot
North Comino Channel
Blue Lagoon
Comino
Cominotto
South Comino Channel
Aħrax Point
Marfa Point
Ċirkewwa
Marfa
Paradise Bay
Marfa Peninsula
Mellieħa Bay
Mellieħa Bay
Mellieħa
Anchor Bay
Mellieħa Ridge
Park tal-Majjistral
Bajda Ridge
Ras il-Waħx
Manikata
Għajn Tuffieħa
Golden Bay
Wardija
Ras il-Pellegrin
Mġarr
Fomm ir-Riħ Bay
Ras ir-Raħeb
Victoria Lines
Għemieri
Baħrija
L-Andrijet
Mtaħleb
Dingli Cliffs
MEDITERRANEAN SEA
ELEVATION
500m
400m
300m
200m
100m
0

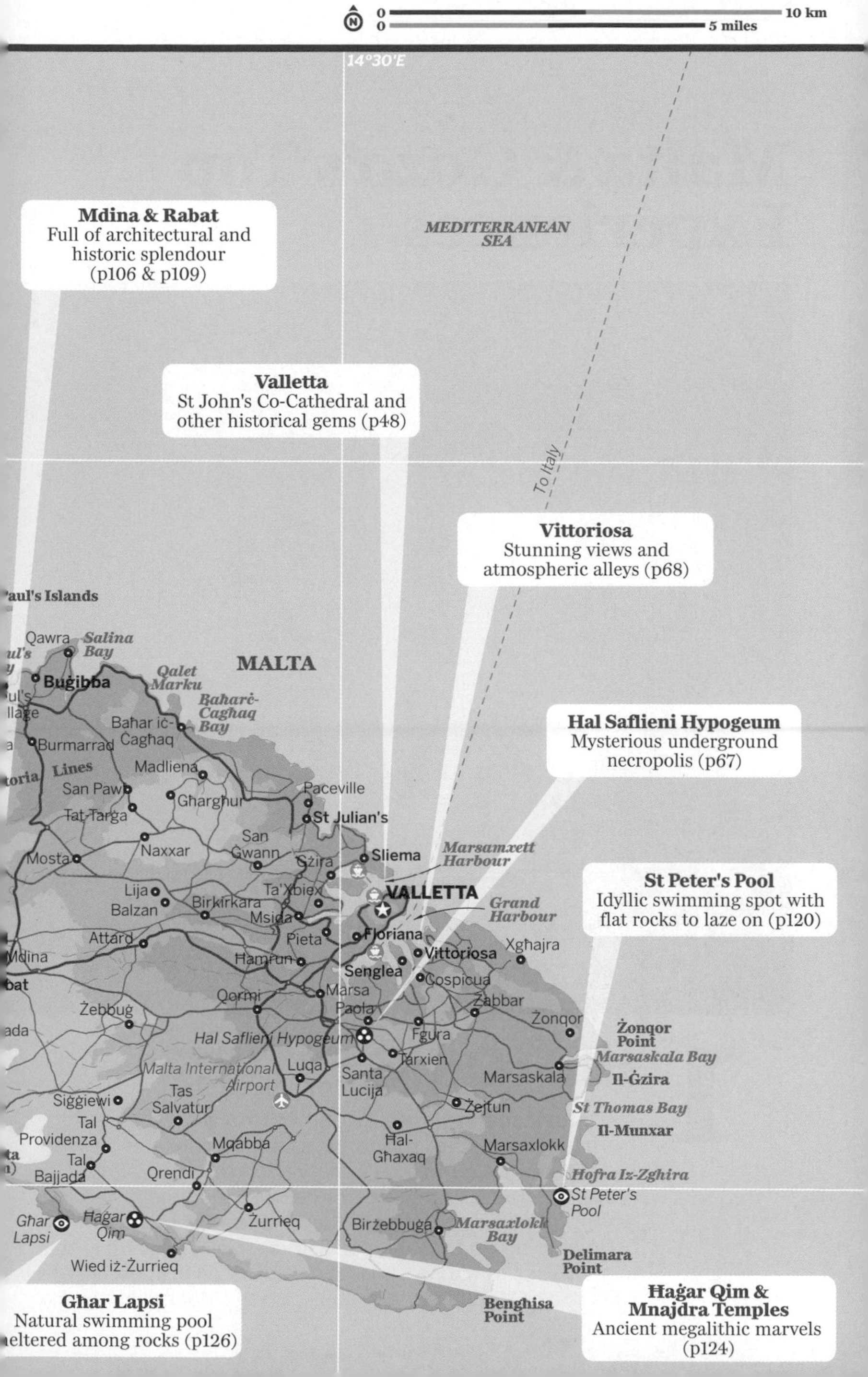

0 10 km
0 5 miles
14°30'E
Mdina & Rabat
Full of architectural and historic splendour (p106 & p109)
MEDITERRANEAN SEA
Valletta
St John's Co-Cathedral and other historical gems (p48)
To Italy
Vittoriosa
Stunning views and atmospheric alleys (p68)
Hal Saflieni Hypogeum
Mysterious underground necropolis (p67)
St Peter's Pool
Idyllic swimming spot with flat rocks to laze on (p120)
Għar Lapsi
Natural swimming pool
ıeltered among rocks (p126)
Ħaġar Qim & Mnajdra Temples
Ancient megalithic marvels (p124)
MALTA
Qawra
Salina Bay
Buġibba
Qalet Marku
Baħar iċ-Caghaq Bay
Baħar iċ-Ċagħaq
Burmarrad
Madliena
San Pawl
Għargħur
Paceville
St Julian's
Tat-Targa
Naxxar
San Ġwann
Mosta
Sliema
Marsamxett Harbour
Gżira
Ta'Xbiex
Lija
Balzan
Birkirkara
VALLETTA
Grand Harbour
Msida
Pieta
Floriana
Attard
Mdina
Ħamrun
Vittoriosa
Xgħajra
Senglea
Cospicua
Qormi
Marsa
Żabbar
Żebbuġ
Paola
Żonqor
Żonqor Point
Hal Saflieni Hypogeum
Fgura
Tarxien
Marsaskala Bay
Malta International Airport
Luqa
Santa Lucija
Marsaskala
Il-Ġzira
Siġġiewi
Tas Salvatur
Żejtun
St Thomas Bay
Tal Providenza
Il-Munxar
Mqabba
Ħal-Għaxaq
Marsaxlokk
Tal Bajjada
Qrendi
Hofra Iz-Zghira
St Peter's Pool
Għar Lapsi
Ħaġar Qim
Żurrieq
Birżebbuġa
Marsaxlokk Bay
Wied iż-Żurrieq
Delimara Point
Benghisa Point

Malta & Gozo's Top Experiences

1 HISTORIC CITIES

A strategic hub from ancient times to WWII, Malta has been fought over for millennia, and the echoes of diverse civilisations linger in the country's fortresses. Valletta is endowed with stunning architecture including the astounding St John's Cathedral, a legacy of the Knights of St John in defending against Ottoman invasion, while the inland cities of Mdina and Gozo's Il-Kastell first emerged from rocky Mediterranean soils during Phoenician times.

Above: Valletta (p49)

ROMAN BABAKIN/SHUTTERSTOCK ©

Valletta

Measuring only 1km by 600m, with every street leading to the sea, Valletta's walls contain stunning 16th- and 17th-century townhouses fronted by traditional balconies. Recently, Valletta has bloomed with exciting restaurants, new galleries and museums, and an emerging nightlife scene. p49

Right: Valletta's old town

ANIBAL TREJO/SHUTTERSTOCK ©

KRIVINIS/SHUTTERSTOCK ©

Mdina

A compact, hilltop walled city, Mdina is studded with beautiful honey-coloured buildings. During the day it's a treasure trove of museums, artefacts and churches, while at night Mdina is appealingly mysterious: everything is closed and the 'Silent City' is atmospherically lit and virtually empty. p106

Above: St Paul's Cathedral, Mdina

Il-Kastell

The 15th-century fortifications of Victoria's fortress town were used to shelter Gozo's entire population during Turkish raids, a defiant history that's illuminated in the Ċittadella Visitors' Centre. Elsewhere, centuries-old marble and limestone backstreets lead to the beautiful Cathedral of the Assumption. p131

Above: Il-Kastell, Victoria

2 ECHOES OF PREHISTORY

Located at the heart of the Mediterranean, Malta dates back more than 5000 years, and punctuating the country are poignant and alluring reminders of some of Europe's earliest civilisations. Temples and towers built amid coastal views provide evidence of the surprising architectural sophistication of prehistoric cultures, while a subterranean necropolis carved out of ancient rock offers a fascinating insight into the historic mists of early millennia.

SERG ZASTAVKIN/SHUTTERSTOCK ©

HELOVI/GETTY IMAGES ©

Ħaġar Qim & Mnajdra Temples

Malta's finest prehistoric structures are breathtakingly located high on the edge of coastal cliffs. p124

Top left: South Temple, Mnajdra Temples

Ġgantija Temples

Dating from 3600 to 3000 BC, Gozo's megalithic Ġgantija Temples are some of Malta's oldest prehistoric structures. p143

Bottom left: Ġgantija Temples

Hal Saflieni Hypogeum

Ancient underground burial chambers c 5000 years old offer an enigmatic window to a mystical and storied time. p67

Above: Hal Saflieni Hypogeum

3 SENSATIONAL SWIMMING

SOSN-A/SHUTTERSTOCK ©

ZGPHOTOGRAPHY/SHUTTERSTOCK ©

St Peter's Pool

On Malta's southeastern coast, the searingly beautiful St Peter's Pool is a great place to leap into the wild Mediterranean blue. p120

Left: St Peter's Pool, near Marsaxlokk

Gozo's Secret Cove

A rocky staircase cut into coastal cliffs is the best way to access Wied il-Għasri's narrow and sheltered gorge. p144

Comino's Surprise

Comino's most extraordinary feature is the other-worldly Blue Lagoon, a serene sea pool so blue it looks like an over-saturated photograph. p148

Left: Blue Lagoon

Blessed by fine weather and warm waters for most of the year, Malta is a brilliant place for a dip in the ocean. Arcing sandy beaches are definitely a sparkling highlight of the islands, but even more enjoyable and exciting are the rocky coves and natural pools dotting Malta's serried coastlines. Often it's a mini-adventure just getting to the best spots.

4 ISLAND ADVENTURES

For a small country, Malta packs in an exciting diversity of opportunities for active travellers. Mediterranean underwater seascapes await snorkellers and divers, SUP and kayak enthusiasts can explore bays and coves, and the islands' rocky landscapes are often best negotiated while hiking or mountain biking. Windsurfing, rock climbing and horseriding are also popular ways to lure travellers away from the considerable charms of Malta's beaches.

Mediterranean Rambles

Spectacular spots for coastal walking include Gozo's Xlendi Walk and the rugged headland of Ras il-Qammieħ on Malta. p35 & p94

Below: Rock-hewn stairs, Gozo

MJUP/SHUTTERSTOCK ©

Diverse Diving

Malta and Gozo arguably offer Europe's best diving, with warm seas, astounding underwater architecture and thrilling WWII shipwrecks. p26

Above: Wreck diving

Gozo's Wild Side

Kayaking, climbing, mountain biking and hiking with Gozo Adventures are all great ways to experience Malta's second island. p130

Right: Rock climbing, Mġarr ix-Xini (p136)

5 CULINARY FUSION

Above: A traditional Maltese plate featuring *ġbejna* (p37)

From the everyday snack of the *pastizzi* to innovative dishes served in elegant dining rooms, Maltese flavours and ingredients reflect centuries of conquest and cultural interaction, and are popular throughout the country. Italian, French, British and Arabic influences all blend to emerge as the flavourful synthesis making up traditional Maltese cuisine.

Farm-to-Table Surprises

The use of local, often organic, produce is growing in importance in Maltese restaurants, including Diar il-Bniet near the spectacular Dingli Cliffs. p112

Fine Dining in Valletta

Stylish openings such as Noni and 59 Republic have added a contemporary and cosmopolitan sheen to Valletta's restaurant scene. p60

Rabat's Emerging Scene

Standout dining opportunities enlivening and modernising Rabat's labyrinthine heritage include Root 81 and Townhouse No 3. p110

Need to Know

For more information, see Survival Guide (p171)

Currency
euro (€)

Language
Malti, English

Visas
Malta is in the Schengen area. Also, visas are not required for citizens of EU and EEA countries. Other nationalities should check www.identitymalta.com/schengen.

Money
ATMs are widespread. Credit cards are used in larger hotels and upmarket restaurants, but some smaller hotels and restaurants only accept cash.

Mobile Phones
Malta uses the GSM900 mobile network (not compatible with the USA's and Canada's GSM1900).

Time
Central European Time (GMT/UTC plus one hour)

When to Go

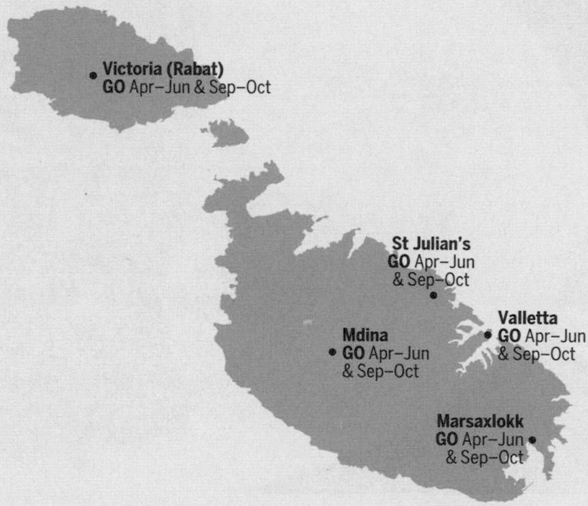

Warm to hot summers, mild winters

High Season
(Jun–Aug)

- Many resort hotels are booked solid; beaches are busy.
- Daytime temperatures in July and August can reach more than 35°C.
- Main season for village festas (feast days) and music festivals.

Shoulder
(Apr–Jun, Sep–Oct)

- Warm and sunny; occasional rainfall or hot and humid wind.
- Sea is warmer in autumn than in spring.
- Accommodation prices can increase during Easter's Holy Week.

Low Season
(Nov–Mar)

- November and December temperatures average 12°C to 18°C.
- January and February are coldest; a northeasterly wind *(grigal)* occasionally disrupts the Gozo ferry service.
- Christmas to New Year is a mini high season.

Useful Websites

Lonely Planet (www.lonelyplanet.com/malta) Destination information, hotel bookings, traveller forum and more.

Malta Tourism Authority (www.visitmalta.com) Huge official site with lots of useful information.

Gozo (www.visitgozo.com) All about Gozo.

Restaurants Malta (www.restaurantsmalta.com) Helpful, reliable survey-based restaurant guide. Also produces the fab restaurant guide the *Definitive(ly) Good Guide to Restaurants in Malta & Gozo.*

What's on Malta (www.whatson.com.mt) Music, art, festivals, theatre and clubbing listings.

Malta Uncovered (www.maltauncovered.com) Comprehensive and informative site by an expat resident.

Important Numbers

International access code	☎00
Country code	☎356
Directory enquiries	☎1182
Directory enquiries (Go Mobile)	☎1187
Directory enquiries (Vodafone)	☎1189
Emergency	☎112

Exchange Rates

Australia	A$1	€0.62
Canada	C$1	€0.67
Japan	¥100	€0.76
New Zealand	NZ$1	€0.57
UK	£1	€1.12
US	US$1	€0.86

For current exchange rates, see www.xe.com.

Daily Costs

Budget: Less than €80

- Dorm bed: €15–20
- Double room in budget hotel: €40–60
- Sandwiches, pizza or pasta: €6–12
- 12-journey bus pass: €15

Midrange: €80–140

- Double room in midrange hotel: €70–140
- Car rental: average per day €25
- Meal in restaurant: €20–30

Top End: More than €140

- Double room in top-end hotel: €140–300
- Meal in top restaurant: €50–100
- Private yacht hire: per day €400

Opening Hours

The following are high-season opening hours; hours are sometimes shorter in the low season.

Banks 8.30am–12.30pm Monday to Friday, sometimes to 2pm Friday, 8.30am–noon Saturday

Bars 8pm–4am

Cafes 9am–10pm

Museums 9am–5pm daily (last entry at 4.30pm)

Pharmacies 9am–1pm and 4–7pm Monday to Saturday. Duty pharmacies that open late and on Sunday or public holidays are listed in local newspapers.

Restaurants noon–3pm and 7–11pm, usually closed Sunday or Monday

Shops 9am–1pm and 4–7pm Monday to Saturday

Arriving in Malta & Gozo

Malta International Airport (Valletta) Six express (X) services and other buses run from the airport to all of Malta's main towns from around 5am to midnight. MaltaTransfer operates airport shuttle services to major hotels; booking ahead online is recommended. For a taxi, the fixed price from the airport to Valletta is €20 (15 to 25 minutes).

Valletta Sea Passenger Terminal A taxi to Valletta or the main bus station in Floriana is around €15. For Sliema or St Julian's the cost is around €25.

Etiquette

With a strong Roman Catholic heritage, Maltese society remains largely conservative.

Clothing Cover shoulders and avoid wearing shorts when visiting churches.

Sunbathing Don't go topless at the beach.

Eating Avoid eating meat on Friday, traditionally the day Roman Catholics eat fish.

Greetings When meeting someone for the first time, a handshake is appropriate.

What to Pack

- Walking shoes for Valletta's hilly streets and Gozo's walking tracks.
- An effective sun hat – Malta and Gozo can be very sunny in spring and summer.
- Carry a cover-up with you – for example, a sarong – so you're properly attired when entering churches and cathedrals.

For much more on **getting around**, see p20 & p178

What's New

Following 10 years of consistent tourism growth leading to Valletta's time as one of 2018's European Capitals of Culture, the significant impediments of 2020 and 2021 are being addressed by Malta's consistent and coordinated approach to supporting tourism businesses and overcoming the country's economic and health challenges.

Malta & Covid-19

After a peak in case numbers in early 2021, Malta managed the rollout of Covid-19 vaccinations more efficiently than many other European Union nations. This was due to an existing and effective network of community health centres across the country. At the time of writing, it was expected Malta and Gozo would be open with minimal restrictions to allow travellers to visit during the 2021 summer tourist season.

Driving Tourism's Regeneration

Tourism is a vital component of the Maltese economy, contributing 13% of the country's GDP, and Valletta's time as a European Capital of Culture throughout 2018 saw visitor numbers increase from 2.27 million in 2017 to 2.73 million in 2019. The Maltese Tourism Authority launched several key initiatives to inspire tourism's re-emergence following the challenges of Covid-19. Incentive programs and subsidies were provided to restaurant, cafe and accommodation owners, and in the summer of 2021, MTA's 'Incentives For Free Independent Travellers' scheme provided cash bonuses of up to €200 per person for visitors to the island.

The Legacy of Valletta 2018

During the city's European Capital of Culture spotlight in 2018, Vallettta was endowed with new and revitalised infrastructure projects and cultural assets. The most important of these was the November 2018 opening of MUŻA (p56), and in 2021, the National Museum of Fine Arts at MUŻA was further enhanced by the opening of the Preti Hall showcasing Italian Barqoue artist Mattia Preti who lived and worked in Malta for 40 years. Other lega-

LOCAL KNOWLEDGE

WHAT'S HAPPENING IN MALTA

Brett Atkinson, Lonely Planet Writer

It's been a challenging few years in Malta. After basking in global admiration and awareness as one of Europe's high-profile destinations in 2018 – that continued with record visitor numbers throughout 2019 – the challenges of 2020 and 2021 were strongly felt in a country focused on rolling out a welcome mat to travellers.

Across recent years, cruise liners have been visiting Malta more regularly, and the enforced hiatus of 2020 prompted conversations about a more sustainable future for Maltese tourism, reflecting trends including a growth in farm-to-table dining, low-impact outdoor activities and sustainably focused accommodation.

Maltese politics remained complex and tangled, with fallout from the 2017 assassination of journalist and anti-corruption activist Daphne Caruana Galizia continuing throughout the trial of those complicit in her death, eventually impacting on prominent business people and forcing the resignation of the nation's prime minister in 2020.

cies of Valletta 2018 include the restoration of the Triton Fountain (p58), the redevelopment of the Valletta Ditch to include public gardens, and the addition of a museum annex featuring the work of Caravaggio at St John's Co-Cathedral (p51). In early 2021, Victoria on Gozo and Vittoriosa on Malta both applied to be a European Capital of Culture in 2031, with the Valletta Cultural Agency set to mentor the towns during the two-year application process.

Michelin-Starred Eateries

Michelin's first guide to Malta's fine-dining scene was published in 2020, and the 2021 edition awarded Michelin stars to five restaurants including Noni (p62) in Valletta and Bahia (p115) in the central Maltese town of Lija. Awarded a Michelin Green Star for significant achievement in sustainable practices were Noni and Valletta's Harbour Club (p62), De Mondion (p107) in Mdina, and Tmun Mġarr (p136) in the harbourside town of Mġarr on Gozo.

A Modern Museum in a Centuries-old Building

Formerly a 16th-century hospital of the Order of St John, the museum at Sacra Infermeria (p58) at the northern end of Valletta's compact peninsula has been further enhanced by the opening of new augmented reality (AR) and holographic displays showcasing the country's storied past. The Holographic Display room allows visitors to interact with a digital life-size version of Grandmaster De Valette, the Great Siege-winning 49th Grand Master of the Order of Malta, while 18 AR displays accessed by visitors' tablets or smartphones showcase the building's history and the Maltese experience during WWII.

Valletta to Gozo by Fast Ferry

A fast passenger ferry linking Gozo directly to Valletta has been considered for several decades, and in early 2021 it was announced two competing companies would commence offering the service from mid-2021.

The catamaran services linking Mġarr harbour on Gozo and Valletta's Grand Harbour will take around 45 minutes, and provide a convenient option for travellers to Malta and also commuters living on Gozo, but working or shopping in Valletta.

Restoring a Royal Villa

From 1949 to 1951, Villa Guardamangia on thc outskirts of Valletta was the residence of Princess Elizabeth (later Queen Elizabeth II), and Prince Philip, while the Prince was stationed in Malta as a British naval officer. Their stay in Malta was described by the Queen as one of the best periods of her life, as it was the only time she was able to live 'normally'. In early 2021, Heritage Malta announced a significant five-year restoration of the villa, after which it will be open for public viewing.

LISTEN, WATCH AND FOLLOW

For inspiration and up-to-date news, visit www.lonelyplanet.com/malta/articles.

Lovin Malta (www.lovinmalta.com) News, articles and restaurant reviews.

GuideMeMalta (www.guidememalta.com) Maltese news, articles and restaurant openings.

Facebook www.facebook.com/visitmalta Official Facebook page of Malta's national tourism authority.

Insta @VisitMalta Official Instagram page for Visit Malta.

FAST FACTS

Food Trend Village restaurants with their own small farms.

Movies & TV series filmed in Malta More than 140 (and counting)

Churches An estimated 365

Population 441,543

Population density 1380 per km^2

Accommodation

Accommodation Types

Guesthouses

Guesthouses in Malta are usually small, family-run places and are good value at around €40 to €50 per person. A simple breakfast is normally included in the price. Facilities usually don't include air-con or a swimming pool, but there are a few exceptions.

B&Bs

The B&B is a relatively recent concept in Malta, but there are some lovely options around the islands. Some have just two or three rooms, and guests can expect excellent attention to detail and delicious breakfasts. There are terrific B&Bs in the Three Cities, central Malta around Naxxar, and on Gozo.

Hostels

A development in Malta in recent years is the number of excellent hostel options clustered in Sliema and St Julian's, usually small-scale and with smart, attractive rooms and facilities at very reasonable prices. These attract a wide mix of tourists and students of all ages, and are sociable, friendly places to stay.

Hotels

Hotels in Malta range from simple seaside options to five-star palaces overlooking private marinas. There are also places to stay offering boutique style, especially in Valletta and on Gozo. For more traditional larger hotels, consider the St Julian's and Sliema districts.

Rental Accommodation

Buġibba, St Paul's Bay and Qawra have hundreds of good-value self-catering apartments. More stylish self-catering apartments are on offer in Valletta and the Three Cities. For the most outdoor space and laid-back family holidays, rent a farmhouse on Gozo.

Booking Accommodation

Malta-specific hotel booking sites include the following. Visit Malta (www.visitmalta.com) and www.lonelyplanet.com/hotels are also excellent online resources.

- www.holiday-malta.com
- www.malta-hotels.com

For farmhouse stays on Gozo:

- www.gozo.com/gozodirectory/farmhouses.php
- www.gozofarmhouses.com
- www.gozoescape.com

Malta and Gozo are small so most of the islands' attractions can be visited on day trips from a single accommodation base.

Top Choices

Best Boutique Lodging

- **Valletta Vintage** (www.vallettavintage.com; d €110-150) Stylish retro decor in the heart of Valletta.
- **Thirtyseven, Gozo** (www.thirtysevengozo.com; r €180-200, ste €250-300) Superbly luxurious in a quiet Gozitan village.
- **19 Rooms, Valletta** (www.19rooms.com.mt; d €150-210, apt €210-250) Modern designer ambience in a restored Valletta townhouse.

SCIMMERY/SHUTTERSTOCK ©

GOZO FARMHOUSES

One of the best accommodation options on Gozo is to rent a farmhouse. Dozens have been converted into accommodation spaces, and many of these retain the beautiful stone arches, wooden beams and flagstone floors dating from their original construction (some are up to 400 years old). Most properties are equipped with a kitchen, a swimming pool, an outdoor terrace and a barbecue, laundry facilities and cable TV.

They can sleep from two to 16 people, so are perfect for families or groups of friends, and the costs are very reasonable – from around €800 per week for two people in the high season (most high-season rentals are weekly), or from €70 per night for two people in the low season.

Best Luxury Apartments

➡ **Indulgence Divine, Vittoriosa** (www.indulgencedivine.com; apt low/high season €106/140) Concealed in the beautiful backstreets of the Three Cities.

➡ **Valletta G-House** (www.vallettahouse.com; 2-person apt low/high season €99/145) Character-filled and romantic heritage.

➡ **Valletta Suites – Maison La Vallette** (www.vallettasuites.com; d low/high season €119/149) Convenience and historic charm.

Best B&Bs

➡ **Ghand in-Nanna, Mellieħa** (www.ghandin-nanna.com; d low/high season €60/80) Friendly hosts with plenty of local recommendations.

➡ **Julesys's B&B** (www.julesysbnb.com; r low/high season €159/189) In a restored 18th-century Three Cities townhouse.

➡ **Maple Farm Bed & Breakfast, Rabat** (www.maplefarmbedandbreakfast.com; d low/high season €70/95) Well located with rural views.

Best for Families

➡ **Port View Guesthouse, Marsaxlokk** (www.portview.com; d low/high season from €55/77) Well-located for exploring Marsaxlokk.

➡ **Akwador Guesthouse, Marsaskala** (www.akwador.com; d low/high season from €55/75) Including a roof terrace and town views.

➡ **San Antonio Guesthouse, Xlendi** (www.clubgozo.com.mt; d from €62) Excellent poolside views on Gozo.

Best on a Budget

➡ **Maria Townhouse, Victoria** (jos.attard44@gmail.com; d €40-50, apt €60) Superb value in Victoria's heritage old town.

➡ **Inhawi, St Julian's & Paceville** (www.inhawi.com; dm low/high season from €14/23) Malta's most stylish and interesting hostel.

➡ **Splendid Guesthouse, Mellieħa** (www.splendidmalta.com; d low/high season €40/70) Ethnic style and a rooftop chill-out space.

Getting Around Malta & Gozo

For more information, see Transport (p177)

Travelling by Car

Car Hire

Car hire in Malta is very affordable and having your own vehicle is an excellent way of exploring Malta and Gozo in-depth and at your own pace. Due to the compact size of the country and the fact that many roads are narrow and winding, this is one country where renting a compact car is highly recommended.

Driving Conditions

With a high population density, many of Malta's roads are busy and crowded, especially around more heavily populated areas such as Mosta, Birkirkara & the Three Villages and the Buġibba, Qawra & St Paul's Bay area. Roads off the main arterial routes can be cracked and potholed, but overall road conditions are adequate. While road rules are the same as the rest of Europe, local Maltese drivers are not always consistent at respecting them. Always drive defensively, and don't always assume other drivers will give way at roundabouts or intersections. The frequency of signposting can also be inconsistent and having a good printed road map is recommended.

Note that some rural roads are not accurately recorded as one-way routes in GPS mapping apps so additional care should be taken.

RESOURCES

Automobile Associations

If you're renting a car, you'll be provided with a telephone number to contact in the event of mechanical difficulties or breakdown. If you're bringing your own vehicle, it's a good idea to take out European breakdown cover (offered in the UK by both the RAC and the AA). For roadside assistance in Malta, contact **RMF** (☎2124 2222; www.rmfmalta.com) or **MTC** (☎2143 3333; www.mtctowingmalta.com).

Car Hire

As well as all the major international companies, such as Avis, Budget and Hertz, there are dozens of local car-hire agencies. Most hire companies will drop off and collect cars at your accommodation.

Billy's (☎2152 3676; www.billyscarhire.com; 113 Triq Ġorġ Borg Olivier, Mellieħa) Excellent local option on Malta.

Mayjo Car Rentals (☎2155 6678; www.mayjocarhire.com; Triq Fortunato Mizzi; per day around €22; ⌚8.30am-4.30pm Mon-Fri, to 12.30pm Sat) Gozo's widest range of cars.

Wembleys (☎2137 4141, 2137 4242; http://wembleys.com; 50 Triq San Ġorġ) Malta-based and also a good taxi service.

Parking

Parking in Malta can be a challenge, especially in the busy and built-up Sliema-St Julian's and Buġibba, Qawra & St Paul's Bay areas. Parking within Valletta's city walls is largely reserved for residents, and using the underground car park in nearby Floriana is the recommended option.

Catching the Ferry to Gozo

Gozo Channel operates car ferries that shuttle regularly between Ċirkewwa on Malta's northern coast and Mġarr harbour on Gozo. Note that Friday afternoon and Saturday morning sailings from Ċirkewwa can be busy, so try and schedule ferry crossings on alternative times and days if possible. Definitely expect long queues around Easter and other holiday weekends throughout the year.

If you're planning on visiting both Malta and Gozo, it's best to rent a vehicle on Malta and use it to explore both islands. Cars are available to rent on Gozo if that is your sole focus. If you're renting a car on Gozo during the busy months of July and August, it's prudent to book ahead to secure a vehicle.

Public Transport

Bus

Bus services throughout Malta – and to a lesser degree on Gozo – offer comprehensive coverage to most parts of the islands. The service is extremely well priced and frequency of departures convenient. Note that timetables tend to fall behind time later in the day.

Boat

Regular passenger ferries link Valletta with the Three Cities and Sliema, and car and passenger ferries provide transport from northern Malta across the Comino Channel to Gozo.

Bicycle

Due to how busy many of Malta's roads are, cycling around the country is only recommended for experienced cyclists. Across on Gozo, roads are considerably quieter, and cycling is a good way to explore the island's compact terrain. Around Sliema and St Julian's, and around St Paul's Bay and Buġibba, short-term rental bicycles from nextbike (p179) are a good option for exploring the area's waterfront areas.

Train

There are no train services in Malta.

DRIVING FAST FACTS

Right or left?: Left

Manual or automatic: Manual

Top speed limit: 80km/h

Legal driving age: 18

Signature car: Toyota Aygo (for Malta's narrow roads)

Alternative vehicle: Hyundai Getz (bigger but still compact)

ROAD DISTANCES (KM)

	Valletta	Mellieħa	Buġibba	Mdina
Mellieħa	23			
Buġibba	17	8		
Mdina	12	15	9	
Victoria (Rabat)*	40	16	24	37

*Distance to Victoria, Gozo includes ferry journey.

Month by Month

TOP EVENTS

Carnival February

Holy Week March/April

Malta Arts Festival July

BirguFest October

Christmas December

February

As winter draws to a close, the islands celebrate Carnival with notable verve. It's definitely still too cold to swim, and cultural attractions remain the focus.

Carnival

A week of celebrations preceding Lent, with traditional processions of floats, fancy dress and grotesque masks. Carnival (www.visitmalta.com/carnival) is celebrated throughout the islands but with particular flair in Valletta and Nadur.

March

Holy Week sees Malta's most spectacular and important celebrations and it's an exciting time to visit. Weather-wise, the Mediterranean spring is kicking off.

Good Friday

Life-size statues depicting scenes from the Passion of the Christ are carried shoulder high in processions through towns and villages.

Easter Sunday

In contrast to the solemnity of Good Friday, this is a day of joy. Early in the morning, processions bear the statue of the Risen Christ – in the three harbour towns of Vittoriosa, Senglea and Cospicua, the statue-bearers *run* with the statue.

April

Temperatures begin to warm and wildflowers carpet the countryside. It's too cold to swim for all but the hardiest, but spring is a glorious time to be in Malta.

Fireworks Festival

A noisy and colourful festival of fireworks, folk music and entertainment (www.visitmalta.com/malta-fireworks-festival) in Valletta's Grand Harbour and across Malta and Gozo.

Medieval Mdina

A weekend of medieval events, including human chess, birds of prey, archery and cookery at the Medieval Mdina Festival (www.medievalmdina.eu).

May

Malta's weather reaches a lovely pitch in May, with warm sunshine making the occasional dip inviting. Sights remain uncrowded and there's a musical buzz in the air.

Lost & Found

Malta's spring and summer music festival season kicks off with this annual celebration of dance, house and techno. It's held at venues across Malta and Gozo. (p163)

June

Early summer is the perfect time to visit for piercing blue skies and quieter beaches. The ocean is still relatively bracing, but perfect for lazy days on the sand.

Valletta Film Festival

An international competition (www.vallettafilmfestival.com), with films showing at St James's Cavalier as well as outdoors at Pjazza Teatru Rjal, Fort St Elmo and Pjazza San Ġorg.

Għanafest

Traditional Maltese folk songs are celebrated with three days of live music in Floriana's Argotti Gardens (www.ghanafest.com).

Isle of MTV

This huge concert held in Floriana stars big-name DJs and pop acts, setting the scene for Malta Music Week on subsequent days. (p163)

July

High summer might be the hottest and busiest period, but it's also a joyous time of year, packed with interesting festivals showcasing everything from music to dance.

Malta Arts Festival

For three weeks from early July, the Malta Arts Festival (www.maltaartsfestival.org) incorporates music, dance, theatre and literature performances, and art exhibitions at various Valletta venues and Argotti Gardens in Floriana.

August

There are fewer events this month as temperatures reach their height and crowds flop onto the beaches. Village and community feasts are the main focus.

Feast of Santa Marija

Also known as the Feast of the Assumption, 15 August marks the ascent into heaven of the Virgin Mary and is celebrated in Għaxaq, Gudja, Ħ'Attard, Mosta, Mqabba and Qrendi in Malta, and Victoria in Gozo.

September

In autumn the crowds ebb, the dust settles, occasional storms quench the land and temperatures cool; the sea has been warmed over the summer, so it's better for swimming than in the spring.

Malta International Air Show

A weekend of visiting aircraft and aerial displays in late September at the Luqa airfield (www.maltairshow.com).

October

Malta's autumnal months are an ideal time to visit, with greenery returning to the parched landscape, and sunny weather. Vintage-car buffs should definitely head to Mdina.

Malta Classic

This classic-car racing event (www.maltaclassic.com) takes place in the stunning location of Mdina and Rabat.

BirguFest

BirguFest is three days of music, dance and pageantry in Vittoriosa, culminating in 'Birgu by Candlelight', when the streets are lit by candles. (p71)

November

There tends to be more rain in late autumn, but it's still a great time of year for some guaranteed sunshine, few crowds and low prices.

Mediterranea

Mediterranea (www.mediterranea.com.mt), a 10-day festival of culture on Gozo, celebrates the history, art, crafts, opera and music of the island.

Mdina Cathedral Contemporary Art Biennale

From November to January every two years, this festival (www.mdinabiennale.com) exhibits works by international artists in Mdina.

December

Although it's cold and damp at this time of year, the Christmas period is an enchanting time to visit, and there's an enjoyable focus on family and tradition.

Christmas

Christmas is celebrated with fervour. Nativity scenes are set up all over the islands, most spectacularly in Għajnsielem (www.ghajnsielem.com/bethlehem) in Gozo, which has a 150-strong living nativity.

Itineraries

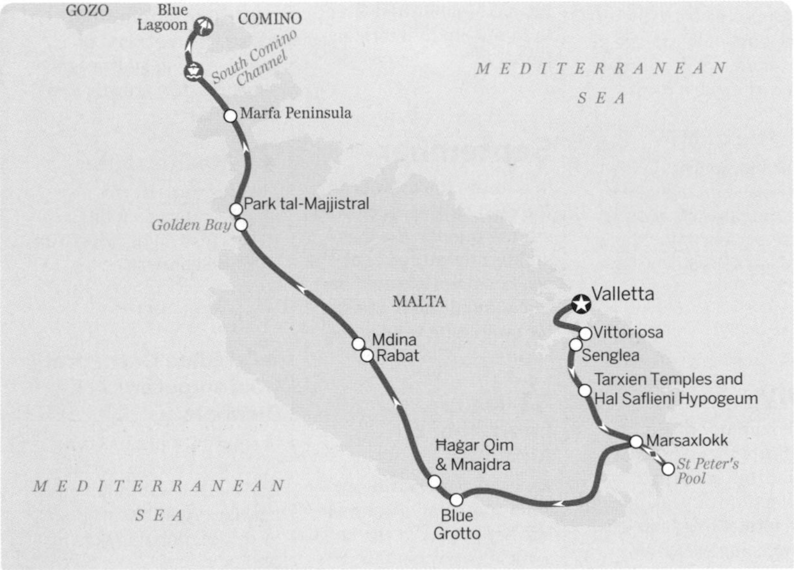

1 WEEK Essential Malta

Malta's diminutive dimensions (27km by 14.5km) mean having your own car is an asset; otherwise, base yourself in Valletta, Naxxar, Sliema or St Julian's for the easiest bus connections.

Begin in **Valletta** – explore the narrow streets and fortifications, admire views across the Grand Harbour, and visit MUŻA, St John's Co-Cathedral and the Grand Master's Palace. On the second day, experience Fort St Elmo, visiting the National War Museum, before a ferry ride across the harbour to **Vittoriosa** and **Senglea**. On day three visit the **Tarxien Temples** and **Hal Saflieni Hypogeum**, en route south for a seafood lunch at **Marsaxlokk**. Spend the afternoon at **St Peter's Pool**, a rocky bay with flat rocks for sunbathing.

On day four take a boat trip to the **Blue Grotto**, explore the clifftop temples of **Ħaġar Qim & Mnajdra**, and then spend the afternoon in **Mdina** and **Rabat**. Allocate day five to relaxing on a beach, such as **Golden Bay**, recharging for physical activity on day six – a walk around **Park tal-Majjistral** or maybe scuba diving around the **Marfa Peninsula**. End on a high with a day trip to Comino's **Blue Lagoon**.

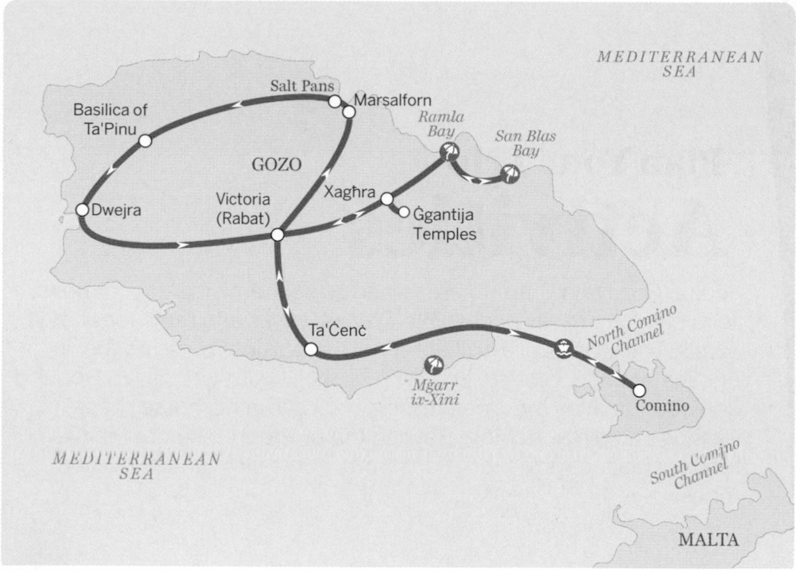

5 DAYS Gozo

The island of Gozo (14km by 7km) is much smaller than Malta but you still need time to do it justice. Because of its modest size, you can base yourself almost anywhere, particularly if you have your own set of wheels (recommended).

Another great way to get around is to hire a bicycle (available on Gozo) or an electric bike (to help with the hills) – the latter must be collected on Malta and brought to Gozo on the ferry. To get the most out of your stay, rent a rambling, idyllic Gozitan farmhouse.

Start your visit by spending a morning exploring **Victoria (Rabat)**, wandering around recently restored Il-Kastell, with its astounding views, and the narrow lanes of Il-Borgo. Take a trip over to the huddled seaside resort town of **Marsalforn** for a lazy lunch with sea views and then visit the dramatically set **salt pans** just outside the town. On day two, head to the grand pilgrimage centre of **Basilica of Ta'Pinu** with its poignant votive offerings, to pay your respects, then while away the rest of the day walking, swimming and snorkelling amid the fantastical moonscape scenery of **Dwejra**.

Set aside day three for walking around the soul-stirring clifftop scenery of **Ta'Ċenċ**, and for seeking out a lesser-known spot for swimming and snorkelling (nearby Mġarr ix-Xini is lovely, and a great place for a leisurely lunch).

Begin day four with a visit to the extraordinary prehistoric **Ġgantija Temples** and other attractions of **Xagħra**, then spend the afternoon reclining on **Ramla Bay** or more remote **San Blas Bay**, both of which are beautiful beaches where red sands meet blue water.

It's even easier to visit the tiny island of **Comino** from Gozo than it is from Malta, so arrange your boat trip and spend an afternoon paddling around the Blue Lagoon.

There's five days covered, but why not allocate a week and spend a few days relaxing poolside or on the beach?

Plan Your Trip
Activities

Malta, Gozo and Comino are famed as scuba-diving destinations, with plenty of easily accessible wrecks, caves and reefs for all skill levels. The islands are brilliant for other outdoor pursuits too, including boating, windsurfing and snorkelling, as well as land-bound activities such as mountain biking, rock climbing, horse riding, walking and birdwatching. Beyond the outdoors, explore Malta's food scene and movie locations from iconic films and television series.

Best Time to Go

- Diving – year-round
- Sailing – April and November
- Kayaking – April to October
- Walking – October to June
- Rock climbing – October to June
- Birdwatching – year-round
- Horse riding – October to June

Best Dive Sites for Beginners

- HMS *Maori*, Valletta
- Għar Lapsi, Southern Malta
- Anchor Bay, Northern Malta
- Ċirkewwa Arch, Northern Malta

Best Sites for Experienced Divers

- Blenheim Bomber, Southern Malta
- Fessej Rock, Southern Gozo
- Double Arch Reef, Northern Gozo
- Bristol Beaufighter, Valletta & St Julian's area

Best Sites for Snorkelling

- Wied il-Għasri, Northern Gozo
- San Dimitri Point, Western Gozo
- Blue Hole & Chimney, Western Gozo
- Aħrax Point, Northern Malta

Diving

The calm, non-tidal nature of the sea surrounding Malta and Gozo makes for excellent visibility (25m to 30m on average). The islands are particularly renowned for their wrecks but there is a fantastic range of interesting dive sites, including caves and reefs.

These sites are also remarkably easy to reach, with many accessible from the shore. If you're here for a week you could potentially dive off all three islands.

The climate is pleasant and the water warm; the main season is April to November, but you can dive all year around – in winter the water temperature rarely drops below 13°C.

There are also a large number of dive schools with qualified, professional, multilingual instructors to choose from. The following organisations' websites offer information about diving and dive qualifications, plus details of accredited diving schools:

- British Sub-Aqua Club (www.bsac.com)
- Confédération Mondiale des Activités Subaquatiques (www.cmas.org)
- Professional Association of Diving Instructors (www.padi.com)

Malta's Marine Life

Malta's marine life is richer than in many other parts of the Mediterranean, though it has suffered from the effects of boat traffic and over-fishing in recent years.

You're likely to see crabs, lobsters, octopuses, swordfish, sea bream, sea bass, grouper, red mullet, wrasse, dogfish and stingray.

Migratory shoals of sardine, sprat, bluefin tuna, bonito, mackerel and dolphin fish (*lampuka*) are common in late summer and autumn.

Many divers hope to see the maned seahorse; potential spots are the HMS *Maori* and Mġarr ix-Xini.

Ċirkewwa is a good place to spot barracuda, amberjack, tuna and squid, while Comino's Santa Marija Caves are good for seeing saddled bream and cow bream. San Dimitri Point off Gozo is noted for big schools of barracuda, plus dentex, grouper and rays.

The loggerhead turtle is occasionally sighted in Maltese waters. In 2012 a turtle laid eggs at Ġnejna Bay, the first time this had occurred for 100 years. Nature Trust Malta runs a turtle rescue program at the San Lucjan Aquaculture Research Centre.

The common dolphin (*denfil* in Malti) and the bottlenose dolphin are sometimes sighted on boat trips.

In April 1987 a great white shark caught by local fisherman Alfredo Cutajar off Filfla measured around 7m. Nowadays shark sightings in inshore waters are extremely unlikely.

Dive Schools

There are around 50 dive school operators in Malta, all of which are licensed by the Malta Tourism Authority. The majority are also members of the Professional Diving Schools Association (www.pdsa.org.mt), an organisation dedicated to promoting high standards of safety and professionalism.

All of the dive schools we recommend provide a similarly comprehensive menu of PADI-, BSAC- or CMAS-approved training and education courses, guided diving and the rental of scuba equipment to experienced divers. All are suitable for beginners, and most also offer technical diving.

If you're interested in wrecks, it's best to choose a centre in Malta rather than Gozo, as there's a much wider choice of wrecks here. If you're travelling with non-divers in the low season, you may also want to choose Malta, because there's more for them to do here while you're diving. If you just want to dive, Gozo is a good choice.

Nautic Team (☎2155 8507; www.nautict-eam.com; Triq il-Vulcan; introductory dives from €37) diving centre in Gozo specialises in diving for people with disabilities.

Sliema & St Julian's Area

Dive Systems (p79)

Diveshack (p79)

Divewise (p82)

Northern Malta

Buddies Dive Cove (p99)

Dive Deep Blue (p99)

Sea Shell Dive Centre (p93)

Paradise Diving (☎2157 4116; www.paradisediving.com; Paradise Bay Resort Hotel, Ċirkewwa; introductory dives from €40)

BEST DIVE SITES FOR...

Caves

- Coral Cave, Western Gozo
- Wied iż-Żurrieq, Southeast Malta
- St Marija Caves, Comino

Wrecks

- HMS *Maori*, Valletta
- P29, Northwest Malta
- Tugboat Rozi, Northwest Malta

Dramatic Scenery

- Ċirkewwa Arch, Northwest Malta
- Marfa Point, Northwest Malta
- Delimara Point, Southeast Malta

Colourful Coral & Sea Life

- Xatt l'Aħmar, Southern Gozo
- Lantern Point, Comino
- Reqqa Point, Northern Gozo

Seahorses

- HMS *Maori*, Valletta
- Wied il-Għasri, Northern Gozo
- Mġarr ix-Xini, Southern Gozo

Gozo

Atlantis (p143)

Calypso (p143)

Nautic Team (p27)

Gozo Diving (☎7900 9575; www.gozodiving.com; Triq Mġarr, Xewkija; introductory dives from €50)

Moby Dives (p138)

St Andrews Divers Cove (p138)

Comino

Diveshack Comino (p148)

Courses & Qualifications

Most schools offer a 'taster course' or 'beginner's dive' (around €50), which includes one or two hours of shore-based instruction, instruction in breathing underwater in a pool or shallow bay, and a 30-minute dive in the sea.

A two- or three-day resort-based scuba course (around €280) gives you shore-based instruction plus open-water dives accompanied by an instructor. Such a course would qualify you up to 12m, and with two days' more instruction you can upgrade it to an open-water diving qualification.

A course that will give you an entry-level diving qualification (CMAS One-Star Diver, PADI Open Water Diver, BSAC Ocean Diver) takes three to five days and costs from around €400.

For certified divers, guided dives usually cost around €40 for one dive (including all equipment), but multidive packages are better value, costing around €220 for six dives (price dependent on the amount of gear included). Transport to dive sites may be included in these packages, but if you're staying in Malta, boat trips to Gozo or Comino will often be an additional cost.

An unaccompanied six-day dive package that includes use of cylinder, weight belt and unlimited air fills costs from around €150.

Requirements

Operators usually teach junior open-water diving from 10 years of age; those under 18 must have written parental consent. Most dive schools operate PADI 'Bubblemaker' programs designed to introduce kids aged eight and nine to breathing underwater.

If you have a medical condition that may restrict your diving practices, you will be requested to have a medical to determine your fitness. The medical can be organised by the dive school, usually at a cost of €20 to €25. You should also heed medical warnings and not fly within 24 hours of your last dive.

Qualified divers wishing to lead their own groups must do so through a licensed

RESPONSIBLE DIVING

The popularity of diving is placing immense pressure on many sites – more than 60,000 divers a year visit the Maltese Islands. If you dive responsibly you will help preserve the ecology and beauty of Malta's underwater world.

- Avoid touching living marine organisms with your body or dragging equipment across rocks. Be conscious of your fins – even without contact the surge from heavy fin strokes can damage delicate organisms.
- Never feed fish. You may disturb their normal eating habits, encourage aggressive behaviour or feed them something detrimental to their health.
- Minimise your disturbance of marine animals; for example, never touch turtles.
- Take great care in underwater caves. Spend as little time within them as possible because your air bubbles can be caught within the roof, leaving previously submerged organisms high and dry. Taking turns to inspect the interior of a small cave will lessen the chances of damaging contact.
- Do not collect or buy shells or other remains of marine organisms. The same goes for marine archaeological sites (mainly shipwrecks). Respect their integrity; some sites are protected from looting by law.
- Plastics in particular are a serious threat to marine life. Ensure that you take home all your rubbish and any litter you may find as well.

Diving at the Tugboat Rozi wreck, off Ċirkewwa (p30)

dive centre, and must be at least an advanced open-water diver, with certification.

Safety

Speedboat and ferry traffic can be heavy, especially in peak summer months and in the Gozo Channel area. For their own protection, divers are required to fly the code-A flag and always use a surface-marker buoy. Boats are required to keep a distance of over 100m from divers' buoys, but it's wise to remain vigilant.

Ensure that your travel insurance policy covers you for diving. Some policies specifically exclude 'dangerous activities', which can include scuba diving.

Malta's public general hospital is Mater Dei Hospital (p173), southwest of Sliema; there is a decompression chamber here. Staff at the hospital can be contacted for any diving incidents requiring medical attention on ☎2545 5269. There is another decompression chamber at Gozo's General Hospital (p173).

Snorkelling

You can sample the delights of a shallower underwater world by donning mask, snorkel and fins and exploring the rocks and bays around Malta's coastline. You can usually rent or buy the necessary equipment from hotels, lidos (recreational facilities with a swimming pool) and water-sports centres in all the tourist areas. Some dive centres offer snorkelling trips, and you can also take an organised trip at Park tal-Majjistral (p91).

Top snorkelling spots are off Comino and Gozo. On Comino they include the Blue Lagoon (p182), where you can rent equipment from the kiosk, and the crags and caves east of Santa Marija Bay. On Gozo, head for the cave-riddled coastline at Dwejra, the long, narrow inlet at Wied il-Għasri and San Dimitri Point, and along the salt-pan rocks west of Xwieni Bay near Marsalforn. Good spots off Malta include the natural rocky St Peter's Pool (p120) near Marsaxlokk and Għar Lapsi.

MACIEJ NICGORSKI/SHUTTERSTOCK ©

Snorkelling at Wied il-Għasri, Gozo (p144)

Top Diving & Snorkelling Spots

Northern Malta

Aħrax Point (average depth 7m, maximum depth 18m) Caverns and a tunnel opening up to a small inland grotto with good coral growth. Suitable for all levels. Shore dive; snorkellers can also view it.

Anchor Bay (average depth 6m, maximum depth 12m) Not much to see in the bay itself, but around the corner are good caves. Suitable for all levels. Shore dive.

Ċirkewwa Arch (average depth 10m, maximum depth 36m) Underwater walls and a magnificent arch, where divers can encounter a variety of fish and sometimes seahorses. Suitable for all levels.

Marfa Point (average depth 12m, maximum depth 18m) Large dive site with caves, reefs, promontories and tunnels. Can be accessed from the shore. Decent snorkelling opportunities.

P29 (average depth 30m, maximum depth 37m) Former minesweeper deliberately sunk in Paradise Bay in 2007, close to Tugboat Rozi. Can be accessed from the shore.

St Paul's Islands (multiple sites, average depths 6m to 12m, maximum depth 25m) Popular dive sites with a wreck between the shore and inner island, a reef on the eastern side of the northernmost island, and a valley between the two islands. Suitable for all levels. The wreck can be accessed from the shore.

Tugboat Rozi (average depth 30m, maximum depth 36m) A boat deliberately sunk in 1991 as an underwater diving attraction and now colonised by thousands of fish. Can be accessed from the shore.

Valletta & St Julian's Area

Bristol Beaufighter (average depth 33m, maximum depth 36m) A WWII aeroplane that crashed in 1941, near St Julian's; only the body, wings and undercarriage remain intact.

Carolita Barge (average depth 12m, maximum depth 22m) Possibly mistaken for a submarine, this barge was hit by a torpedo in 1942 and sank immediately. Well preserved and home to grouper and octopus. Popular training site for divers and, therefore, busy. Suitable for all levels. Shore dive.

Fortizza Reef & Coral Gardens (average depth 14m to 16m, maximum depth 18m) Close to Sliema, this reef is fantastic for beginners; profuse sea life including octopus, moray eels, damsel fish, lobsters and crabs.

Hellespont (average depth 35m, maximum depth 41m) A paddle steamer and former supply boat sunk in 1942, close to the Grand Harbour. An exposed site.

HMS Maori (average depth 13m, maximum depth 18m) Below Fort St Elmo is the wreck of the HMS *Maori*, sunk in 1942. Silted up, but home to fish and octopus. Suitable for all levels. Shore dive.

Tug no 2 (average depth 17m to 19m, maximum depth 21m) Scuttled at St Julian's, just off Exiles Reef, in 2013, this is the only wreck in this area, and great for beginners. Dentex and stingrays to spot. Shore dive.

Southern Malta

Blenheim Bomber (maximum depth 42m) Exploring the well-preserved wreck of this WWII bomber, with engine and wings intact, is an exciting dive. For experienced divers only.

Delimara Point (average depth 12m, maximum depth 25m) Usually excellent visibility for divers, with vertical cliffs and many caverns. Varied and colourful flora and fauna. Suitable for all levels of experience. Shore dive.

Għar Lapsi (average depth 6m, maximum depth 15m) Popular training site for divers; a safe, shallow cave that winds through the headland.

Shore dive, reasonable snorkelling and suitable for all levels.

Wied iż-Żurrieq (average depth 9m, maximum depth 30m) Close to the Blue Grotto. Underwater valley and labyrinth of caves. Shore dive, reasonable snorkelling and suitable for all levels. Nearby, the 1995 wreck of the *Um El Faroud,* a Libyan freighter, can be accessed from the shore.

Western Gozo

Blue Hole & Chimney (average depth 20m, maximum depth 45m) The Blue Hole is a natural rock formation and includes a large cave plus a fissure in the near-vertical wall. Popular, busy site. Shore dive, excellent snorkelling and suitable for all levels. Nearby it's possible to see the underwater remains of the Azure Window.

Coral Cave (average depth 25m, maximum depth 30m) Huge semicircular opening with a sandy bottom, where divers can view varied and colourful flora and fauna. Shore dive.

Crocodile Rock (average depth 35m, maximum depth 45m) Rocky reef between the shore and crocodile-shaped rock off the west coast. Natural amphitheatre and deep fissures. Shore dive, decent snorkelling and suitable for all levels.

Fungus Rock (average depth 30m, maximum depth beyond 60m) Dramatic underwater scenery with vertical walls, fissures, caverns and gullies. Good site for underwater photography and suitable for all levels.

San Dimitri Point (average depth 25m, maximum depth beyond 60m) Lots of marine life and exceptional visibility (sometimes exceeding 50m). Good snorkelling and suitable for all levels.

Xlendi Cave & Reef (average depth 6m, maximum depth 25m) Easy cave dive in shallow water and popular with beginners. Brightly coloured cave walls. Rocky headland dips steeply to the sea. An abundance of flora and fauna. Shore dive; OK snorkelling.

Northern Gozo

Billinghurst Cave (average depth 20m, maximum depth 35m) Long tunnel leading to a cave deep inside the rock, with a multitude of coloured sea sponges. There's very little natural light (torch required). Experienced divers only.

Double Arch Reef (average depth 30m, maximum depth 45m) Site characterised by a strange formation, with an arch dividing two large openings in the rock. Prolific marine life. For experienced divers.

Reqqa Point (average depth 25m, maximum depth beyond 70m) Near-vertical wall cut by fissures, caves and crevices. Large numbers of small fish, plus groups of amberfish and grouper if conditions are favourable. Shore dive and good snorkelling.

Wied il-Għasri (average depth in cave 12m, maximum depth 30m) A deep, winding cut in the headland makes for a long, gentle dive. Possible to view seahorses in the shallows. Cathedral Cave has a huge domed vault and walls covered in corals. Can be done as a shore dive; very good snorkelling; suitable for all levels.

Southern Gozo

Fessej Rock (average depth 30m, maximum depth 50m) A prominent column of rock. Vertical wall dive descending to 50m amid large shoals of fish. A popular deep-water dive.

Ta'Ċenċ (average depth 25m, maximum depth 35m) Sheltered bay – access is by 103 steps from the car park of a nearby hotel. Canyon with large boulders, plus cave. Good marine life, but visibility can occasionally be poor. Good spot for night dives. Shore dive; suitable for all levels.

BEST BEACHES FOR...

Swimming

- Blue Lagoon (p148)
- St Peter's Pool (p120)
- Għar Lapsi (p125)

Soft Sand

- Golden Bay (p90)
- Għajn Tuffieħa Bay (p90)
- Ramla Bay (p144)

Water Sports

- Mellieħa Bay (p90)
- Buġibba Beach (p97)
- Golden Bay (p90)

Peace & Quiet

- Fomm ir-Riħ (p115)
- Selmun (Imgiebah) Bay (p92)
- Wied il-Għasri (p144)

Scenery

- Paradise Bay (p95)
- San Blas Bay (p146)
- Mġarr ix-Xini (p136)

ALTERNATIVE ACTIVITIES

Look beyond Malta's stellar dive sites, golden beaches and heritage architecture for a few days, and explore a few different sides to the Med's most surprising island nation.

Good options include the following:

Offbeat Malta Food Trails (p60) Guided walking tours taking in the best of Valletta's eating and drinking scene.

Merill Eco Tours (p101) Rural tours meeting farmers and small-scale producers of cheese, wine, olives.

Rolling Geeks (p68) Negotiate the Three Cities area on a self-drive electric buggy.

Malta Film Tours (p60) Visiting locations from *Game of Thrones*, *Gladiator* and *Troy*.

Gozo Segway Tours (p130) Itineraries include the famous Marsalforn salt pans.

Eco Bikes Malta (p100) Mountain bike and e-bike tours including Mdina, Valletta or the Three Cities.

Sea Adventure (p99) Optimum family fun with underwater viewing windows and a water slide.

Xatt l'Aħmar (average depth 9m, maximum depth 30m) Small bay, excellent for observing a large variety of fish including mullet, grouper, sea bream, octopus and cuttlefish. Shore dive; OK snorkelling; suitable for all levels. Two vessels were scuttled here in August 2006 to create an artificial dive site.

Comino

Blue Lagoon (average depth 6m, maximum depth 12m) Easy site to the north of the sheltered lagoon, very popular with divers and snorkellers. Plenty of boat traffic. Shore dive. Suitable for all levels.

Lantern Point (average depth 30m, maximum depth 45m) Popular dive site. Dramatic dive down a vertical wall. Rich fauna and an abundance of colour. OK snorkelling.

Santa Marija Cave (average depth 7m, maximum depth 10m) Large cave and cavern system; one of the most popular sites for cave dives. An abundance of fish in the area. Very good snorkelling and suitable for all levels.

MARATHONS

Several major running events are held each year in Malta, including triathlons and half-marathons, culminating in the Malta Marathon (www.maltamarathon.com) and half-marathon, held in late February/early March.

Beaches & Swimming

Malta and Gozo's coastlines combine rocks and natural pools with sandy stretches.

Malta's best sandy beaches are to the northwest, including Golden Bay (p88), Għajn Tuffieħa Bay (p90), Mellieħa Bay (p92) and the small, white-sand Paradise Bay (p95). Elsewhere there are great rocky swimming spots along the Sliema waterfront, and rocky coves along the southeastern coast.

Gozo's best sandy beaches – Ramla Bay (p144) and San Blas Bay (p146) – are to the northeast, and there are rocky swimming coves and bays both north and south.

The wondrous Blue Lagoon (p182) on Comino gets extremely busy in summer, but if you head here in the late afternoon you'll find it less so and it's also better when the sun is lower in the sky as there's no shade nearby.

All beaches get busy in summer, when the weather's baking hot, though you'll often find hidden rocky coves less crowded. Wherever you swim, keep an eye on the weather.

Don't swim when the sea is rough, as undercurrents can be powerful.

Diving & Snorkelling Malta & Gozo

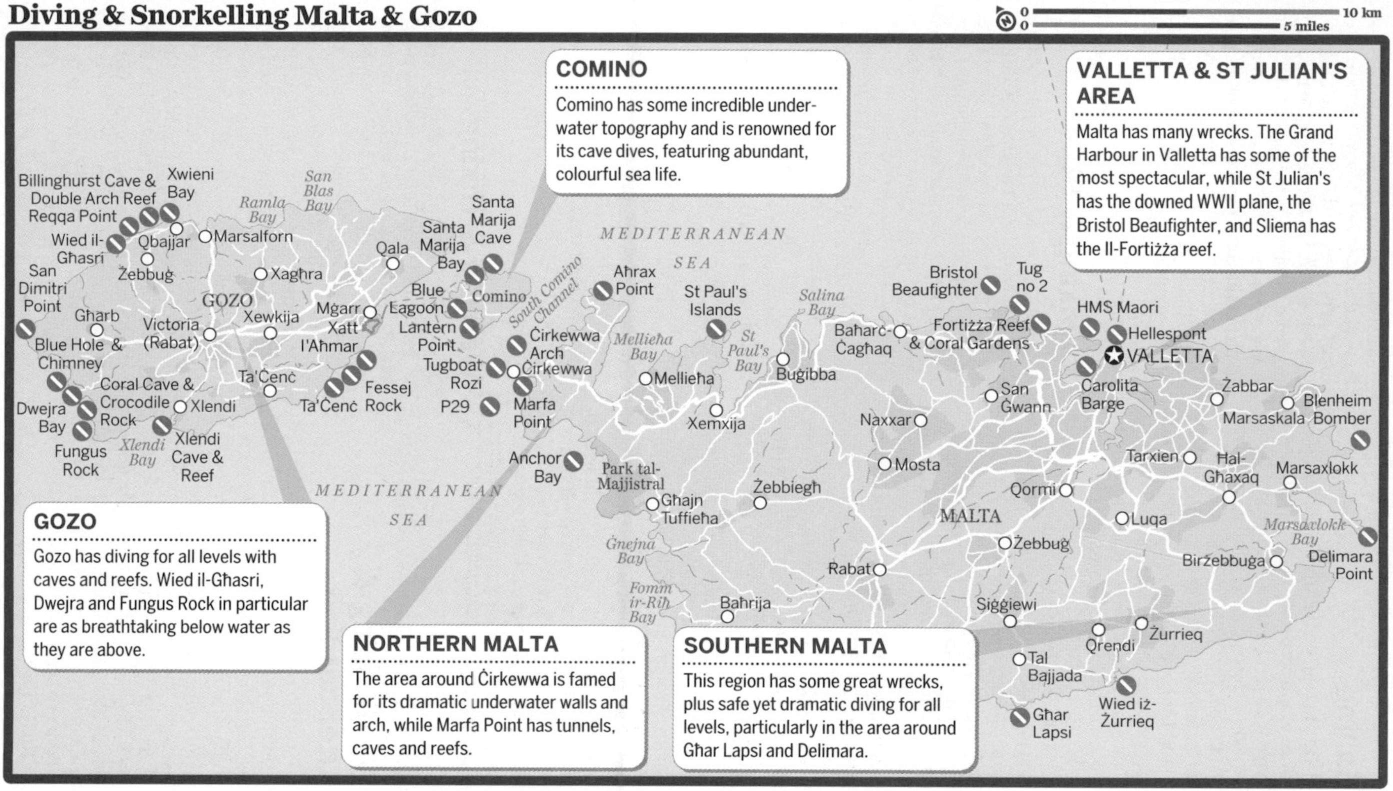

COMINO

Comino has some incredible underwater topography and is renowned for its cave dives, featuring abundant, colourful sea life.

VALLETTA & ST JULIAN'S AREA

Malta has many wrecks. The Grand Harbour in Valletta has some of the most spectacular, while St Julian's has the downed WWII plane, the Bristol Beaufighter, and Sliema has the Il-Fortizza reef.

GOZO

Gozo has diving for all levels with caves and reefs. Wied il-Għasri, Dwejra and Fungus Rock in particular are as breathtaking below water as they are above.

NORTHERN MALTA

The area around Ċirkewwa is famed for its dramatic underwater walls and arch, while Marfa Point has tunnels, caves and reefs.

SOUTHERN MALTA

This region has some great wrecks, plus safe yet dramatic diving for all levels, particularly in the area around Għar Lapsi and Delimara.

Sailing

Malta's magnificent harbours, sheltered coves, island scenery and great facilities make it an ideal sailing destination. It's a major yachting centre, with marinas at Msida and X'biex, Gozo's Mġarr harbour, Portomaso development in St Julian's, Grand Harbour Marina, at Vittoriosa, and the boutique Laguna Marina at Valletta Waterfront. Many yacht owners cruise the Med in summer, and winter their vessels in Malta.

A full program of races and regattas is held between April and November (great for participants and spectators). The popular **Rolex Middle Sea Race** (www.rolexmiddlesearace.com; Oct) is a highly rated offshore classic staged annually in October. For details of events and opportunities for crewing, contact the **Royal Malta Yacht Club** (2133 3109; www.rmyc.org; Ta'Xbiex Seafront).

Boatlink (9988 2615; www.boatlinkmalta.com) and **Fairwind** (7955 2222; www.fairwindsailing.com.mt) offer sailing courses for children and adults.

Sailing dinghies can be rented at most tourist resorts for around €15 an hour. Qualified sailors are able to hire a yacht by the day or the week from one of several charter companies. If you don't have a RYA Coastal Skipper qualification you'll need to pay extra for a skipper (around €100/180 per day/night). Try **S & D Yachts** (2133 1515; www.sdyachts.com; low/high season for a 6-berth Bavaria 31 sailing yacht per week from €2100/3000, per day €400/450).

Windsurfing & Kiteboarding

You can windsurf year-round in Malta, in beautiful settings and with excellent facilities. Equipment hire and instruction are available at all the main tourist resorts. Mellieħa Bay is most popular, offering flat and gusty surfing in a large sheltered bay. Experienced surfers also head to Ghallis Rock (close to St Julian's). Other locations include Armier, St Thomas Bay and the channel between Gozo and Malta (for experienced surfers). Fairwind offers windsurfing courses.

Kiteboarders are not permitted between June and September, when there are too many people on the beaches and in the sea, but the rest of the year there is plenty of choice. Mellieħa is an excellent location for kiteboarders when the wind is blowing from the east. Torri, near Armier, is a tiny bay but popular for its northeasterly winds. Golden Bay and Gnejna Bay offer prime conditions and waves.

Kayaking & SUP

Kayaking is a great way to see the islands' coast from a different angle, to paddle through sea caves and explore hidden inlets. You can hire kayaks by the hour from resorts such as Xlendi (Gozo) and Mellieħa (Malta), but usually this means you have to stay within the bay. To explore for longer, it's best to arrange a guided kayak excursion. Gozo Adventures (p130) has a half-/full-day excursion to Comino and Gozo (€45/65); Sea Kayak Malta (p130) does day trips to Comino or St Paul's Island, with a stop at Selmun (Imgiebah) Bay, as well as longer kayaking holidays.

The re-emerging sport of SUP (stand-up paddleboarding) uses a long surfboard and a paddle and is ideally suited to Malta's flat water. Hire equipment at Mellieħa, Xlendi and Golden Bay. On Gozo and Comino, check out Gozo Fun (p130).

Walking & Hiking

The winding backroads and clifftop paths of Malta and Gozo offer some fantastic walks. Distances are small and you can easily cover much of the islands on foot. A circuit of Gozo is a good objective for a multiday hike. Tourist offices have lots of walking leaflets and pamphlets that detail trails all over the islands, and you can download walking routes from www.visitmalta.com/en/walks. If you'd like a guided long walk, Gozo Adventures (p130) does half-/full-day walks (€45/65) and **Malta Activities** (9942 5439; www.maltaoutdoors.com; per person €30-100) has 2½-hour treks on Malta.

A great source of information is the Ramblers' Association of Malta (www.ramblersmalta.org), which organises infor-

WALKING ON GOZO

With moderate terrain, stellar clifftop vistas and many historic and natural attractions a short distance apart, Gozo is an excellent walking and hiking destination. Comprehensive bus services mean it's also easy to schedule return transport after a day's walking.

One of the most popular routes is the **Xlendi Walk**, a 12km journey from Gozo's harbour at Mġarr west to the sheltered cove at Xlendi. En route, the walk takes in the beautiful bay at Mġarr ix-Xini and the cliffs along Ta'Ċenċ. Other walks on Gozo include around the spectacular marine-scapes of Dwejra, the salt pans of Marsalforn, and on the island of Comino.

Detailed route maps and track instructions can be downloaded for eight different walks at www.visitgozo.com. Search 'Country Walks/Rambling' on the website.

mal guided country walks for like-minded folk from October to early June (the best time for walking). This organisation is dedicated to safeguarding public access to the Maltese countryside; read about its campaigns on its comprehensive website.

Birdwatching

A stop-off point for migrating birds and with many local species, Malta has some fascinating bird life. *Where to Watch Birds & Other Wildlife in the Maltese Islands,* written by Alex Casha and published by BirdLife Malta, is a comprehensive guide.

Birdlife Malta (☎2134 7646; www.birdlifemalta.org) is the best contact for birders visiting Malta. The organisation manages the Għadira Nature Reserve (p90) at Mellieħa Bay, the Is-Simar Nature Reserve (p96) at Xemxija and the Salina Nature Reserve (p99) at Buġibba. It also monitors activity that threatens wild birds. Its website details recent sightings and documents the campaign against illegal hunting.

Rock Climbing

The Maltese Islands are a thrilling destination for climbers, though you're advised to avoid high summer when temperatures can hit 40°C. There are more than 1500 established rock-climbing routes (all on limestone), with some of the most popular sites for climbers below the Dingli Cliffs in the west, at Għar Lapsi and near the Victoria Lines below Naxxar.

Gozo alone has more than 300 sport climbs, with many concentrated in the Munxar-Xlendi Valley (for all abilities) and Mgarr ix-Xini, and others at spectacular coastal locations such as the Wied il-Mielah Sea Arch. There's an incredible variety of climbs for such a small area, all within a short drive of each other. You can learn to climb here and there's plenty for experienced climbers too, with multiple climbs at grades 7 and 8.

The Malta Rock Climbing Club (www.climbmalta.com) and Gozo Climbing (www.gozo-climbing.com) can provide information for visiting climbers, and you can organise climbing, bouldering and abseiling trips through Gozo Adventures (p130).

Malta Activities facilitates 2½-hour climbing or abseiling trips for all levels. Trips include opportunities to traverse sea cliffs, and all equipment is provided.

Horseriding

Horses have long played an important part in Maltese life, and you can often see owners out exercising their favourite steeds. Horseriding is a fun way to explore the islands' rugged countryside, with routes along the northwest coast and in Gozo, and it's possible to arrange sunset tours. Recommended stables, offering rides for adults and children, include Golden Bay Horse Riding (p90), and Bidnija Horse Riding School (p112) outside Mosta. On Gozo, contact Lino's Stables (p144) to arrange rides for all levels.

Plan Your Trip

Eat & Drink Like a Local

Like the Malti language, Maltese cuisine is an exotic mix of flavours. Different occupiers introduced their foodstuffs and dishes, with Italian, French, British and Arabic all strong influences. Locals usually feast on home-cooked Maltese food on special occasions, and eat anything from gourmet burgers to fusion when dining out.

The Year in Food

Spring (March–May)

Broad beans, zucchini, chickpeas, olives, apricots, cherries, loquats, medlars. Lent specialities include *warezimal* (almond cakes without fat or eggs), and for Easter there's the almond-studded *qagħqa tal-appostli* ('apostle's bagel').

Summer (June–August)

Aubergines, peppers, capers, wild fennel, melons, white-skinned peaches and bambinella (miniature pear). The first fig crop is the 'tin ta San Gwann' (of St John), which starts on St John's day (24 June). Drinkers head for July's Marsovin Wine Festival and Farsons Great Beer Festival.

Autumn (September–November)

Artichokes, fennel, grapes, olives, pomegranates, strawberries. St Martin's Day (11 November) calls for recipes involving walnuts, almonds, hazelnuts and dried figs. *Lampuki* (dolphin fish) is at its most plentiful.

Winter (December–February)

Christmas dishes include *qaghaq tal-ghasel* (pastry honey rings) and *imbuljuta* (sweet chestnut soup). It's the time for famously luscious and fragrant blood oranges. Carnival sweets include *prinjolata* (pastry, candied fruit, cream, pine nuts, chocolate and meringue).

Food Experiences

Meals of a Lifetime

Noni (p62) Modern Med cuisine with an innovative and lighter touch.

Osteria Scottadito (p146) Italian excellence emblematic of new arrivals to Gozo.

Terrone (p121) Beautifully prepared seafood in the harbour town of Marsaxlokk.

Diar il-Bniet (p112) Farm-to-table dining with supremely local produce.

Cheap Treats

Crystal Palace (p111) Malta's best *pastizzi*, fresh from the oven.

Ta' Doni (p111) Try a *ftira* (sandwich in traditional Maltese bread) before shopping for local jams, honey and preserves.

Mekrens Bakery (p146) and **Maxokk Bakery** (p146) Famous across Gozo for their freshly baked *ftira* and pizza.

Dare to Try

Fenek (rabbit) The islands' national dish, usually served fried or in a tasty stew.

Bebbux (snail salad) Local snails are boiled then dipped in olive oil, herbs, garlic and chilli, and served with salad.

Local Specialities

Bread, Cheese & Pastizzi

Malta's national gap-filler is the *pastizzi,* a small parcel of flaky pastry, Arabic in origin, which is filled with either ricotta cheese and parsley or mushy peas and onions. It's served warm, and is around €0.35 apiece. A couple of *pastizzi* make for a tasty and substantial breakfast or afternoon filler. They're available in most bars or from *pastizzerijas* (hole-in-the-wall takeaway *pastizzi* shops).

For bread-and-cheese picnics, bakeries sell the famously delicious traditional bread *ħobż,* made in a similar manner to sourdough bread, using a scrap of yesterday's dough to leaven today's loaves. You'll see it on menus as *ħobż biż-żejt,* slices of bread rubbed with ripe tomatoes and olive oil until they are pink and delicious, then topped with a mix of tuna, onion, capers, olives, garlic, black pepper and salt.

Ftira is traditional Maltese bread baked in a flat disc. It makes for delicious sandwiches when stuffed with a substantial, punchy mixture of olives, capers and anchovies, together with the tangy local tomato paste made from sun-dried tomatoes ground with rosemary, sugar and other secret ingredients.

Gozo is famous for its cheeses, especially *ġbejna,* a small, hard, white cheese traditionally made from unpasteurised sheep's or goat's milk. It's often steeped in olive oil and flavoured with salt and crushed black peppercorns. The best is said to come from Żebbuġ.

Another delicious snack is stuffed olives *(Żebbuġ mimili)* filled with tuna, breadcrumbs, capers, garlic and herbs.

Soup & Pasta Dishes

Soups are popular in traditional local cooking, with several recipes cooking meat in the broth, so the soup is served as a followed by the meat as a main cou was a practical measure; many ho don't have traditional ovens.

Aljotta, a delicious fish broth made with tomato, rice and lots of garlic, is most commonly served in restaurants. In spring, you may encounter *kusksu,* a soup made from broad beans and small pasta shapes, often served with fresh *ġbejniet* (Gozo cheese), ricotta and an egg floating in the middle.

Soppa tal-armla means 'widow's soup' (probably named because of its inexpensive ingredients). It's traditionally made only with components that are either green or white: a tasty mix of cauliflower, spinach, endive and peas, with protein provided by a poached egg, *ġbejniet* and a lump of ricotta.

Minestra is a thick soup of tomatoes, beans, pasta and vegetables, similar to some variations of Italian minestrone, but thicker and more golden in colour, as it includes pumpkin.

Two other Italian-influenced dishes are *ravjul/ravjuletti* (pasta pouches filled with ricotta, Parmesan and parsley, a Maltese variety of ravioli) and *timpana,* a rich pie filled with macaroni, cheese, egg, minced beef, tomato, garlic and onion (a Sicilian dish similar to the Greek *pastitsio*). *Timpana* is usually cooked for special occasions but appears on menus.

Meat Dishes

Maltese main courses are hearty. Meat pies and roast beef, lamb, pork, quail and duck feature heavily.

Most typical of all is *fenek* (rabbit). Introduced by the Normans, the bunny became a symbol of feudal repression when the Knights, to save enough game for the hunt, banned the peasantry from eating it. Adding insult to injury, rabbits persistently attacked the farmers' crops. The Maltese have certainly got their own back: it's now the island's favourite national dish, whether fried in olive oil, roasted, stewed, served with spaghetti or baked in a pie. *Fenek bittewm u l-inbid* is rabbit cooked in garlic and wine, *fenek moqli* is fried rabbit and *stuffat tal-fenek* is stewed rabbit.

A *fenkata* is a rabbit feast – usually spaghetti with rabbit sauce, followed by fried rabbit. This is for special occasions, particularly L-Mnarja on 29 June, the Feast of St Peter and Paul, when locals celebrate

EATING PRICE RANGES

The following price ranges refer to a standard main course.

€ less than €10

€€ €10–20

€€€ more than €20

Pastizzi (p3

through the night at Buskett Gardens with *fenkata* and lots of wine. (It used to be written in to the marriage contract that a husband had to take his wife to L-Mnarja.) On non-special occasions you can find it at places such as Ta'Marija (p112) in Mosta.

Braġioli (beef olives) are prepared by wrapping thin slices of beef around a stuffing of breadcrumbs, chopped bacon, hard-boiled egg and parsley, then braising them in a red wine and tomato sauce. *Tigieja* is roast chicken stuffed with beef, pork, ham, eggs, parsley and basil. *Stuffat tal-Laham* (beef stew) is cooked with mushrooms, onions, carrots and potatoes.

Maltese sausages *(zalzetta tal-malti)* are notably good, showing English and Portuguese influences and made in either fresh (which have more garlic) or cured versions.

Seafood

Unsurprisingly in these Mediterranean islands, fresh seafood is a staple. The most favoured of fishes is the *lampuka* (dolphin fish), and *torta tal-lampuki* (also known as *lampuki* pie) is the classic dish. It's typically baked with tomatoes, onions, black olives, spinach, sultanas and walnuts – although there are lots of other recipes too. *Ċerna* (grouper), *pagru* (sea bream), *dentiċi* (dentex), *spnotta* (sea bass) and John Dory are other versatile and popular fish that you'll find on lots of menus. Cod is not found in the Mediterranean, so Maltese recipes sometimes make use of *bakkaljaw* (salt cod). Octopus and cuttlefish are also excellent menu additions.

Sweets

Kannoli are Sicilian but are widely found in Malta. These tubes of crispy, fried pastry are best eaten when they've been freshly filled with ricotta (to avoid the tubes going soggy); sometimes they're also sweetened with chocolate chips or candied fruit. *Mqaret* are almond-shaped pastries stuffed with chopped, spiced dates and deep fried – they're particularly good accompanied by vanilla ice cream.

Deliciously chewy Maltese nougat, flavoured with almonds or hazelnuts and traditionally sold on festa (feast) days, is known as *qubbajt. Gagħħ tal-għasel,* honey or treacle rings made from a light pastry, are served in small pieces as an after-dinner accompaniment to coffee.

Fresh prawns and mussels from Marsaxlokk Bay (p120)

Drinks

Alcoholic Drinks

Maltese bars serve every kind of drink you could ask for, from pints of British beer to shots of Galliano liqueur. Malta has a long tradition of beer making, brought over by the British. The most popular locally made (from imported hops) beers, Cisk Lager and Hopleaf Ale, are cheaper than imported brews.

Lord Chambray (p137) is a craft brewery on Gozo producing various beers including San Blas IPA, Blue Lagoon wheat beer and Fungus Rock stout. Its products are now widely available across Malta. Other local craft breweries to look for include Stretta, named after the Italian name for Strait St, and Huskie Brewing. Valletta bars including 67 Kapitali, Wild Honey and Cafe Society are all good venues for travelling beer fans, and regularly feature local craft brews.

The main players on the local wine scene are Camilleri Wines, Emmanuel Delicata, Marsovin (www.marsovin.com), Meridiana (http://meridiana.com.mt) and Maria Rosa Winery (p115). These companies make wine from local grapes and also produce more expensive 'special reserve' wines – merlot, cabernet sauvignon, chardonnay and sauvignon blanc – using imported grapes from Italy. There are

COOKING CLASSES

The Mediterranean Culinary Academy (p58) in Valletta offers an excellent three-hour cooking workshop focused on how surrounding food cultures have impacted Maltese cuisine. Much of the produce is sourced sustainably from its own network of local suppliers. In Dingli, cookery classes can be arranged at Diar il-Bniet (p112) using the freshest of ingredients from its own nearby farm.

To learn more about Maltese cooking, read the *Food & Cookery of Malta*, by Anne and Helen Caruana Galizia, which includes recipes.

some excellent results and the quality is improving all the time. The vineyards offer worthwhile tours and tastings; check their websites for details. Across on Gozo, Ta' Mena (p144) is also recommended.

Maltese liqueurs pack a punch and make good souvenirs. Look out for Zeppi's potent liqueurs concocted from local honey, aniseed or prickly pear. Gozo-produced *limunċell* (a variant on the Italian lemon liqueur *limoncello*) is delicious; there are orange and mandarin variants too.

Non-Alcoholic Drinks

Good Italian coffee and a strong British-style cup of tea are widely available in cafes and bars. Local cafes and simple bars also serve milky tea in a squat glass, often to accompany a few freshly baked *pastizzi*. For a more contemporary take on coffee, including good Australian- and New Zealand–style flat whites, head to Lot Sixty One (p64) or No 43 (p60) in Valletta.

Malta's tap water is safe to drink, if a little unpalatable because of its high chloride and sodium levels.

Cold soft drinks are available everywhere. Kinnie (its advertising signs are all over the place in Malta) is the brand name of a local soft drink flavoured with bitter oranges and aromatic herbs, drunk on its own or as a mixer.

How to Eat & Drink

When to Eat

Breakfast is usually a coffee or tea with a biscuit, croissant or cereal, but some Maltese will skip an early breakfast and grab a sweet tea and a *pastizzi*. Older people like a breakfast of good Maltese *hobz* (bread).

Lunch was once the largest meal of the day, eaten between around 1pm and 3pm, but few people get home for lunch these days, and so will eat a sandwich, wrap or *pastizzi* (though people are getting increasingly health conscious). Nowadays dinner tends to be the main meal, with people dining out from around 8pm.

The time for a big lunch is on Sunday. In summer, locals will spend all day at the beach and graze on picnics, wrapping it up with a beach barbecue in the evening.

Many restaurants are not open on Sunday and Monday nights, so check opening hours accordingly.

Where to Eat

Restaurants

Restaurants range from laid-back to quite formal. It's common for fine-dining restaurants to open only in the evening, and many don't accept young children, so the atmosphere is restrained and peaceful. For an excellent guide to Malta's restaurants, buy the *Definitive(ly) Good Guide to Restaurants in Malta & Gozo* (€8) online or at local bookshops. portions in Malta are typically huge.

Kiosks

Kiosks are a common sight in Malta: small roadside or waterside restaurants in huts with outdoor tables and chairs.

Cafes

Cafes in Malta are relaxed and are usually open all day. Many morph from daytime cafe to night-time cafe-bar, staying open until midnight or later and serving cocktails, wine and snacks. More contemporary cafes serving a wider range of coffees are now more common.

Pastizzerijas

Look out for small hole-in-the-wall *pastizzerijas* selling authentic *pastizzi* and other pastries. Most larger towns have at least a couple. Cricket-ball-sized *arancini* (deep-fried savoury balls) are also good for a filling on-the-go snack.

VEGETARIANS & VEGANS

Until relatively recently, meat was a rare luxury on many Maltese tables, so there are plenty of traditional Maltese vegetable dishes, using ingredients such as artichokes, broad beans, cauliflower and cabbage, depending on the season. However, these often use meat stock or tuna, so check before you order. Some restaurants offer meat-free dishes as main courses, and most have vegetarian pizza and pasta options.

While vegetarians are reasonably well catered for, vegans are less so, though there are a few places offering vegan options including Mint (p79) in Sliema.

Plan Your Trip

Family Travel

Sun and sea, boat trips and snorkelling, countryside and caves, forts and castles: there's lots for kids to see and do in Malta and Gozo. Add pedestrianised town centres, friendly locals, lots of laid-back, open-air restaurants, and short distances between places, and you have an ideal family holiday destination.

Malta for Kids

As in most Mediterranean countries, families will receive a warm welcome, and the sunny weather and easygoing lifestyle makes it easy to entertain children without too much effort. There's a good health care system here and most people speak English; a smaller proportion also speak Italian and sometimes French. The **Malta Baby & Kids Directory** (www.maltababyandkids.com; €6.50) lists lots of useful information, including days out, activities and general advice. You can buy the directory online or register to obtain its listings.

Open Spaces

Malta's sandy beaches tend to be the best for younger children, as they have gentle approaches and shallow areas for swimming. The more popular ones have water-sports and boating facilities, which makes them especially good for older children too. The rocky bays that dot the coast are better for older children and adults only, because these natural sea pools do not always have shallow areas for less-confident swimmers.

Although Malta's main roads are busy, the main square of each town is almost always closed to traffic, and village promenades are often pedestrianised, which

Best Regions for Kids

Valletta

Pedestrianised lanes, piazzas, forts, fountains, boat trips and museums. Look forward to Malta's best ice-cream shops too.

Sliema, St Julian's & Paceville

Rocky beaches, one small sandy bay, and child-friendly cafes and restaurants. Waterfront playgrounds are also a feature.

Northern Malta

Malta's best beaches, with lots of water-sports facilities, boat-trip opportunities and the various marine species of the Malta National Aquarium.

Southern Malta

Marsaxlokk's fun Sunday market, natural swimming pools, caves and hilltop temples. Perfect for adventurous children.

Gozo & Comino

Malta's neighbours are fun to get to (by boat) and once there you can slow your pace, swim, explore, snorkel, boat and dive.

means there's space to run about even in a town centre. Valletta's pedestrianised centre has fountains, on Pjazza San Gorg.

By the coast, long, wide promenades often have playgrounds (there's one at Sliema and a great one at Qawra as part of the Malta National Aquarium (p97) complex) and kiosks for snacks. Marsaskala, in the southeast, has the large, free St Antnin Park, which includes a climbing wall. Mdina has a large playground just outside the city walls, and the city's Ditch Garden (p106) is a good place to run around in. There's a small playground next to the ferry stop in Cospicua (Three Cities) and a recommended playground in Paola (close to the Hypogeum and Tarxien Temples).

As for parks, some of the best include San Anton Gardens (p115) in Attard and the Argotti Botanical Gardens in Floriana, and Valletta has the Upper Barrakka Gardens (p53), Lower Barrakka Gardens (p58) and the Hastings Garden. The wooded Buskett Gardens (p113) near Dingli on Malta are somewhat wilder and a great place to explore.

On Gozo there are lots of walking trails, beaches and open areas to run around in, but Dwejra, with its rocky moonscape coast, inland sea and boat trips, is one of the most spectacular areas for kids.

Dining Out

Children are welcome at most restaurants, though many of the smarter places don't permit very young children. In child-friendly restaurants, high chairs are usually available, there's normally a children's menu, and sometimes changing facilities. Children's menus tend to offer a similar roll call of chicken nuggets, pizza and so on; if you want to provide more variety, ask for a half-portion of an adult dish instead. As in Italy, people won't blink an eye at children staying up late, particularly in summer when many children will have had a siesta in the heat of the afternoon.

BABYSITTING

Large hotels will usually offer a babysitting service, or you can enquire at your guesthouse or apartment complex whether they provide babysitting. Otherwise, try Stepping Stones Early Learning Centre (www.steppingstonesmalta.com) on Malta, which offers trustworthy services.

Children's Highlights

Theme Parks & Aquariums

- **Buġibba Water Park** (p97) A free water-play park, with colour-coded areas for different ages (up to age 12).
- **Malta National Aquarium, Qawra** (p97) Qawra's state-of-the-art glimpse into the world of the sea.
- **Splash & Fun Park, Baħar Iċ-Ċagħaq** (p101) Waterslides and playground.
- **Popeye Village, Mellieħa** (p92) Film set from the 1980 film *Popeye* turned into a fun theme park; take boat trips and make a movie.

Forts, Castles & Cannons

- **Fort St Elmo, Valletta** (p52) Parade ground, missiles and the Malta National War Museum.
- **In Guardia, Valletta** (p65) Costumed re-enactments in Fort St Elmo and Fort St Angelo.
- **Fort St Angelo, Vittoriosa** (p68) Restored by Heritage Malta, with magnificent views.
- **Fort Rinella, Vittoriosa** (p69) Historic fort, enthusiastic volunteers and cannon- and rifle-firing.
- **Upper Barrakka Gardens, Valletta** (p53) Get up close when they fire the cannon.
- **Inquisitor's Palace, Vittoriosa** (p69) Prison cells and cesspits.
- **Red (St Agatha's) Tower, Marfa Peninsula** (p94) Mini-fortress with a chance to try on armour.

Caves & Tunnels

- **St Agatha's Crypt & Catacombs, Rabat** (p110) and St Paul's Catacombs, Rabat (p110) Older children will enjoy these mysterious caverns.
- **Ninu's Cave, Xagħra** (p144) and Xerri's Grotto, Xagħra (p143) Gozo caves under ordinary houses, full of stalagmites and stalactites.
- **Għar Dalam Cave, Birżebbuġa** (p121) Malta's largest cave, full of fossilised remains.

Child-Friendly Museums

- **National War Museum, Valletta** (p52) In Fort St Elmo, a fascinating museum with lots of imaginative audiovisual exhibits.

➡ **Armoury, Valletta** (p51) Older children will get a kick out of the audio guides and weaponry.

➡ **Pomskizillious Museum of Toys, Xagħra** (p144) Houses historic toys in glass cases.

➡ **Toy Museum, Valletta** (p58) Also home to historic toys.

➡ **Maritime Museum, Vittoriosa** (p69) Lots of model boats and the chance to role-play in the mock sailors' bar.

➡ **Malta Aviation Museum, Rabat** (p110) Impressive array of engines and aircraft.

➡ **Esplora, Three Cities** (p68) Views aplenty, playgrounds and more than 200 interactive science displays.

Beaches & Coves

➡ **Golden Bay** (p90) Gentle sandy beach with lots of facilities.

➡ **Għajn Tuffieħa Bay** (p90) A bit hard to reach (186 steps) but gentle and sandy.

➡ **Mellieħa Bay** (p92) Sandy, with safe paddling and swimming, and lots of facilities.

➡ **St Peter's Pool, Marsaxlokk** (p120) Limpid sea pool; confident swimmers only.

➡ **Għar Lapsi** (p125) Natural sea-swimming pool.

➡ **Ramla Bay, Xagħra** (p144) A lovely red-sand beach with cafe.

➡ **San Blas Bay, Nadur** (p146) Another great beach, less crowded than Ramla; steep approach but you can hop on a jeep.

➡ **Wied il-Għasri, Marsalforn** (p144) Great cove with azure sea and adventurous steep approach.

➡ **Blue Lagoon, Comino** (p148) The ultimate sea-swimming pool.

Outdoor Activities

➡ **Boat trips** Round the islands in a glass-bottomed boat; speed boats to see coves or to Comino and Gozo.

➡ **Diving** Great beginners' diving (p27) and centres dotted all over the islands (over 10s only).

➡ **Horse riding, Golden Bay, Mosta and Gozo** All have good horse riding (p35) centres.

➡ **Water sports** All the major resorts offer sailing, dinghies for hire, pedalos etc.

➡ **Rock climbing** Beginners' climbing (p35) or abseiling offered by local organisations.

➡ **Kayaking** Take an organised sea-kayaking (p35) trip to explore the coast.

Exhibitions

➡ **Audiovisual exhibitions** Cinematic presentations such as the Malta Experience (p58) and the Mdina Experience (p107) will entertain kids aged around seven to 12 years.

➡ **Waxworks** Vivid evocations of the past are found at the Sacra Infermeria (p58) in Valletta.

Planning

For all-round information and advice, check out Lonely Planet's *Travel with Children*.

When to Go

If you're travelling in July and August, when the weather is at its hottest, easy access to the sea or a pool is recommended. Plan for an afternoon siesta to avoid the heat of the early afternoon; there's usually a lull in general activity from around 1pm to 4pm, which is the hottest time of day.

In late spring, early summer and autumn the sea is warm, the weather milder, prices lower and places less crowded. Children will enjoy the colourful parades at Carnival (February) and Easter (March/April), and the living nativity on Gozo at Christmas, but swimming will be chilly in these months; in March/April pack wetsuits to enjoy a dip.

Accommodation

As Malta and Gozo are such family-centred destinations, there are lots of suitable, reasonably priced options, including self-catering accommodation. The farmhouses for rent on Gozo are ideal; they offer plenty of space and often a pool. Most boutique hotels in Valletta only accept older children.

What to Pack

You'll find everything you need available for sale in Malta, so don't panic about forgetting something: formula, nappies (diapers), wipes, clothes, toys and English-language children's books are all easy to find. Mosquitoes are an issue – pack some child-friendly repellent or there's a chance kids will get badly bitten on their first night.

GIANNIS PAPANIKOS/SHUTTERSTOCK ©

Top: Travelling with children, Maltese coast.

Bottom: Malta National Aquarium, Qawra (p97)

Regions at a Glance

Valletta, Malta's beautiful little capital, is rich in history and culture, and has some of Malta's best restaurants and bars. Nearby lie Sliema, St Julian's and Paceville, seafront settlements that together form Malta's dining and nightlife capital. To the northwest are Malta's best beaches and the island's major resorts. Central Malta is the most traditional-feeling area of the main island, home to the historically fascinating towns of Mdina and Rabat. The southeast has more gorgeous coast, a vibrant fish market and some of Malta's finest prehistoric temples. To slow down, head to Gozo and Comino for epic scenery, walks, outdoor activities and relaxation.

Valletta

History
Food
Prehistory

Knights & Fortresses

Valletta was built after the triumph of the Knights of St John at the Siege of Malta in 1565, and the city's narrow grid of baroque streets and fortifications remain intact.

Creative Dining

Dine spectacularly in Malta's capital, showcasing some of the islands' best restaurants and an emerging and exciting gourmet scene.

Mysterious Temples

Close to Valletta are two of Malta's most amazing prehistoric sites: the Hal Saflieni Hypogeum and Tarxien Temples, a 5000-year-old necropolis and a temple complex.

p49

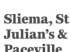

Sliema, St Julian's & Paceville

Food
Nightlife
Boat Trips

Buzzing Culinary Scene

Chic Sliema and St Julian's are packed full of restaurants – encompassing Maltese, Italian and creative fusion cuisine – and sleek bars. There's an after-dark sparkle.

Bars & Clubs

If you're under 25 and looking for a party, Paceville could be heaven, with a fiesta-style atmosphere on summer nights, as swarms of international students, tourists and young locals descend.

Yachting & Cruising

Sliema's promenade has one of the best views in Malta, looking across to Valletta's grand fortifications. From here you can explore the harbours by boat or take a trip to Gozo and Comino.

p77

Northern Malta

Beaches
Views
Food

Golden Sands

Malta's finest sandy fringes lie on the northwestern coast. The beaches here may not be huge but they are beautiful, backed by hills and with soft sand underfoot.

Remote Clifftops

You may think it's hard to get away from it all on Malta, but a short drive or walk along the headland to Ras il-Qammieħ will leave you feeling like you've reached the end of the world.

Farm-to-Table Dining

Join a day trip with Merill Eco Tours to meet local farmers working to organic and sustainable principles and producing excellent wine, cheese and olive oil.

p87

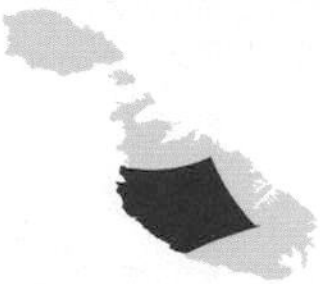

Central Malta

History
Architecture
Scenery

Romans, Knights & Catacombs

In central Malta you'll feel as though you have travelled back in time. Here is the silent city of Mdina, the Roman villa excavated at Rabat, and Rabat's intriguing catacombs.

Medieval Meets Baroque

Whether it's the jumble of medieval and baroque architecture in Mdina and Rabat, or the great dome at Mosta, central Malta yields some illustrious architectural splendours.

Dizzying Cliffs

The Dingli Cliffs feature some of the islands' most sumptuous scenery. The 60m cliffs drop into the royal-blue sea, and new walking trails offer endless views over the Mediterranean.

p103

Southern Malta

Food
Prehistory
Coastline

Seaside Food

Southeast Malta is the place to go for fresh-off-the-boat seafood. The seafront at Marsaxlokk is lined with restaurants while Marsaskala, off the tourist path, is a favourite of foodie locals.

Clifftop Temples

Ħagar Qim and Mnajdra temples have the most thrilling location of any of Malta's prehistoric sites. The great ruins, with their massive slabs of limestone pitched precisely to catch the sun's rays, are perched on sea cliffs.

Natural Pools

There are some lovely spots along the southern coast to have a dip: take a trip to the Blue Grotto, swim in the natural pool of Għar Lapsi or seek out St Peter's Pool or Il-Kalanka Bay.

p117

Gozo & Comino

Swimming
Scenery
Activities

Red Sand & Rocky Bays

As well as its distinctive red-sand beaches on the northeast coast, Gozo has some glorious rocky bays to swim in, including the coves of Mġarr-ix-Xini and Wied il-Għasri. Comino's Blue Lagoon is unmissable.

Hills & Cliffs

Nineteenth-century nonsense artist and poet Edward Lear invented new words to describe the beautifully strange landscape of Gozo, calling it 'pomskizillious and gromphiberous'.

Diving, Horse-riding & Boating

Gozo is a particularly beguiling destination for underwater exploration and other water-sports, and also yields fantastic horse-riding and boat trips.

p127

On the Road

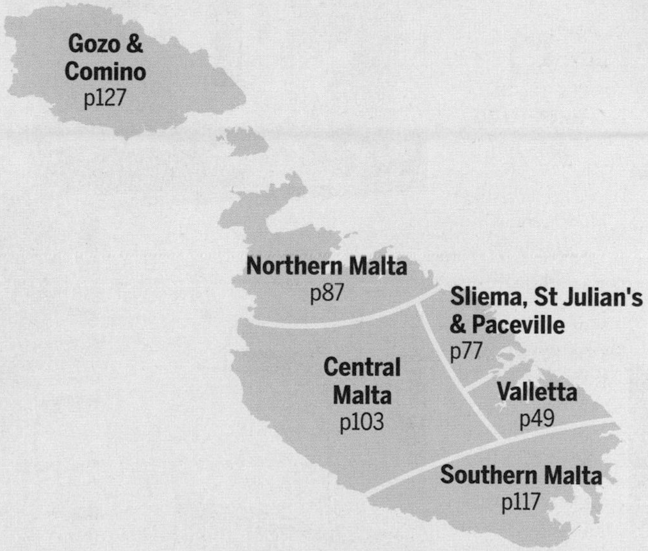
Gozo &
Comino
p127
Northern Malta
p87
Sliema, St Julian's
& Paceville
p77
Central
Malta
p103
Valletta
p49
Southern Malta
p117

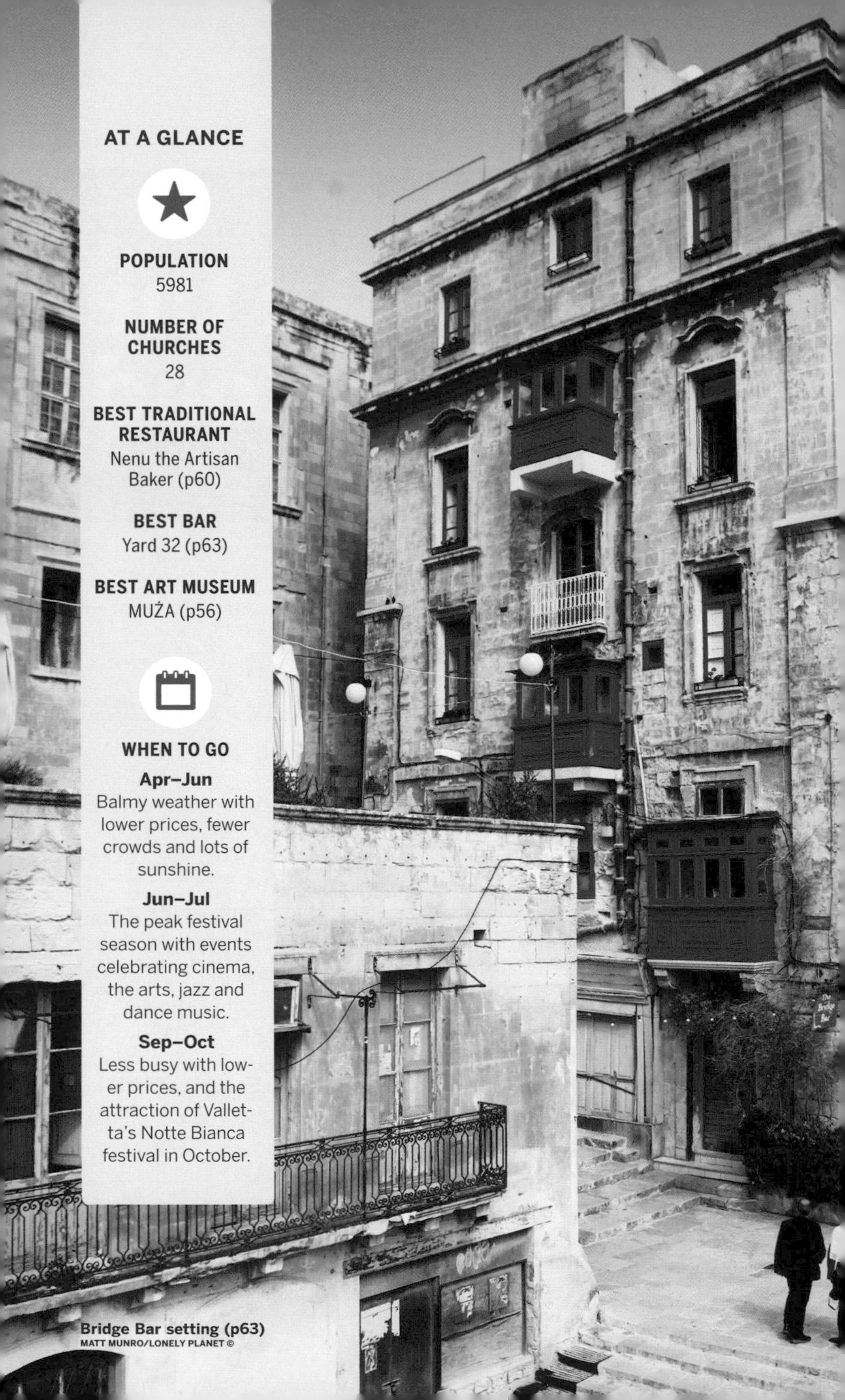

AT A GLANCE

POPULATION
5981

NUMBER OF CHURCHES
28

BEST TRADITIONAL RESTAURANT
Nenu the Artisan Baker (p60)

BEST BAR
Yard 32 (p63)

BEST ART MUSEUM
MUŻA (p56)

WHEN TO GO

Apr–Jun
Balmy weather with lower prices, fewer crowds and lots of sunshine.

Jun–Jul
The peak festival season with events celebrating cinema, the arts, jazz and dance music.

Sep–Oct
Less busy with lower prices, and the attraction of Valletta's Notte Bianca festival in October.

Bridge Bar setting (p63)
MATT MUNRO/LONELY PLANET ©

Valletta

Valletta is Malta's Lilliputian capital, built by the Knights of St John on a peninsula that's only 1km by 600m. Its founder decreed that it should be 'a city built by gentlemen for gentlemen', and it retains its 16th-century elegance. It may be small but it's packed full of sights; when Unesco named Valletta a World Heritage site, it described it as 'one of the most concentrated historic areas in the world'.

The Renzo Piano–designed City Gate, Parliament Building and Opera House have galvanised the cityscape, while Valletta's status as European Capital of Culture for 2018 brought new museums, restored golden-stone fortresses, and new hotels, bars and restaurants.

Valletta's outskirts are also worth a visit. Take the beautiful ferry trip to the Three Cities or visit the astounding prehistoric Hal Saflieni Hypogeum.

INCLUDES

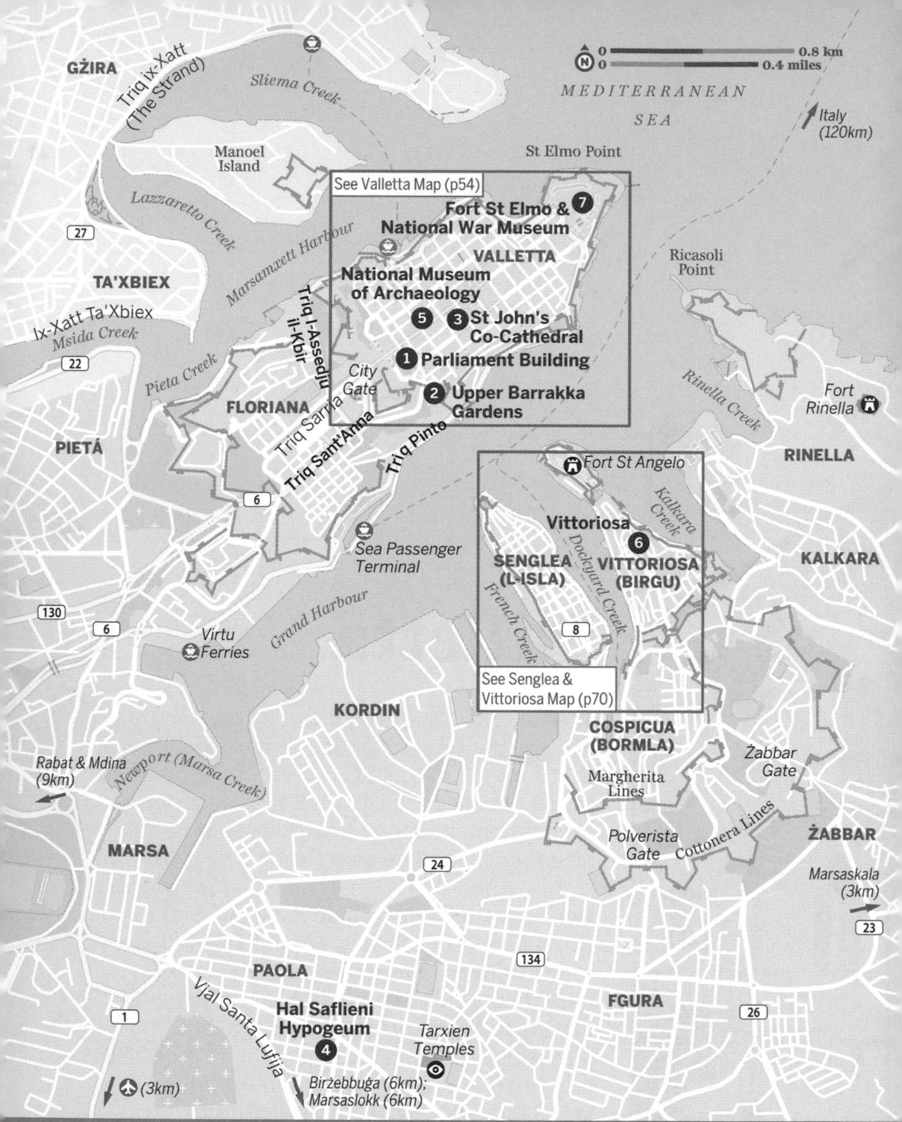

Valletta Highlights

❶ **Parliament Building** (p57) Enjoying the angles of Renzo Piano's spectacular architectural statement.

❷ **Upper Barrakka Gardens** (p53) Checking out the stunning view that puts the 'grand' in Grand Harbour.

❸ **St John's Co-Cathedral** (p51) Discovering the glories of the magnificent church of the Knights.

❹ **Hal Saflieni Hypogeum** (p67) Visiting this extraordinary underworld from millennia past.

❺ **National Museum of Archaeology** (p52) Admiring the modelling of the 'fat ladies' statues.

❻ **Vittoriosa** (p68) Getting lost in charming backstreets followed by a cruise of the Grand Harbour.

❼ **Fort St Elmo & National War Museum** (p52) Discovering Valletta's fascinating war heritage amid the centuries-old ramparts of this historic fort.

History

Before the Great Siege of 1565, the Sceberras Peninsula was uninhabited and unfortified, except for Fort St Elmo at its furthest point. Fearing another attack by the Turks, Grand Master Jean Parisot de la Valette (of the Knights of St John) began the task of building a new city on a barren limestone ridge. Valletta was the first planned city in Europe, with buildings tall enough to shade the streets from the hot sun, and straight streets to allow cooling sea breezes to circulate. A great ditch – 18m deep, 20m wide and nearly 1km long – was cut across the peninsula to protect the landward approach, and massive curtain walls were raised around the perimeter of the city. Spurred on by the fear of a Turkish assault, the Knights completed the job in a mere five years.

Sights

★St John's Co-Cathedral CHURCH
(2122 0536; www.stjohnscocathedral.com; Triq ir-Repubblika; adult/child €10/free; 9.30am-4.30pm Mon-Fri, to 12.30pm Sat) St John's Co-Cathedral, Malta's most impressive church, was designed by the architect Gerolamo Cassar. It was built between 1573 and 1578, taking over from the Church of St Lawrence in Vittoriosa as the place where the Knights would gather for communal worship. The interior was revamped in the 17th century in exuberant Maltese baroque style, and it's an astounding surprise after the plain facade. One of its greatest treasures is a huge painting of John the Baptist by Caravaggio.

The nave is long and low and every wall, pillar and rib is encrusted with rich ornamentation, giving the effect of a dusty gold brocade. The floor is an iridescent patchwork quilt of marble tomb slabs, and the vault dances with paintings by Mattia Preti that illustrate events from the life of St John the Baptist. Beyond here, the Oratory contains two paintings by Caravaggio.

Currently undergoing an extensive remodelling, the **Cathedral Museum** houses the beautiful 16th-century Graduals of L-Isle Adam, illuminated choral books and a magnificent collection of 17th-century Flemish tapestries based on drawings by Rubens. A new feature is an excellent exhibition on the life and times of Caravaggio.

By a papal decree of 1816, St John's was raised to a status equal to that of St Paul's Cathedral in Mdina – the official seat of the Archbishop of Malta – hence the term 'co-cathedral'. Visitors should dress appropriately. To protect the marble floor, stiletto heels are not allowed.

★Grand Master's Palace HISTORIC BUILDING
(www.heritagemalta.org; Pjazza San Ġorġ; adult/child incl Palace State Apartments, Armoury & audio guide €10/5; Armoury 9am-5pm, State Apartments 10am-4pm Fri-Wed) The stern exterior of the 16th-century Grand Master's Palace conceals a sumptuous interior. This was once the residence of the Grand Masters of the Knights of St John. From Malta's independence until 2015 the building was the seat of Malta's parliament, before it moved into the new Parliament Building (p57). The **Armoury** is housed in what was once the Grand Master's stables.

Originally, the armour and weapons belonging to the Knights were stored at the Palace Armoury (the Great Hall), and when a Knight died these became the property of the Order. The collection of more than 5000 suits of 16th- to 18th-century armour is all that remains of an original 25,000. general neglect, Napoleon's light-fingered activities and over-enthusiastic housekeeping by the British put paid to the rest.

Some of the most interesting pieces are the breastplate worn by la Valette, the beautifully damascened (steel inlaid with gold) suit made for Alof de Wignacourt, the captured Turkish Sipahi (cavalry) armour, and reinforced armour with bullet marks (the development of guns marked the beginning of the end for armour). There are also displays of some beautiful weapons, including crossbows, muskets, swords and pistols.

In the **State Apartments**, five rooms are usually open to the public, although special one-off exhibitions mean some rooms may be closed. The Grand Master's Palace remains the official residence of the Maltese president, so rooms are occasionally closed. The long **Armoury Corridor**, decorated with trompe l'œil painting, scenes of naval battles and the portraits and escutcheons of Grand Masters, leads to the **Council Chamber** on the left. It is hung with 17th-century Gobelins tapestries gifted to the Order in 1710 by Grand Master Ramon de Perellos. They feature exotic scenes of Africa, India, the Caribbean and Brazil, including an elephant beneath a cashew-nut tree; an ostrich, cassowary and flamingo; a rhino and a zebra being attacked by a leopard; and a tableau with palm trees, a tapir, a jaguar and an iguana.

Beyond lie the **State Dining Room** and the **Supreme Council Hall**, where the Supreme Council of Order met. It is decorated with a frieze depicting events from the Great Siege of 1565, while the minstrels' gallery bears paintings showing scenes from the Book of Genesis. At the far end of the hall a door opens into the **Hall of the Ambassadors**, or Red State Room, where the Grand Master would receive important visitors, and where the Maltese president still receives foreign envoys. It has portraits of the French kings Louis XIV, Louis XV and Louis XVI, the Russian Empress Catherine the Great and several Grand Masters. The neighbouring **Pages' Room**, or Yellow State Room (despite the abundance of greenish tones), was used by the Grand Master's 16 attendants.

★National Museum of Archaeology — MUSEUM

(☎2122 1623; www.http://heritagemalta.org; Triq ir-Repubblika; adult/child €5/2.50; ⌚9am-6pm Mar-Dec, to 5pm Jan & Feb) The National Museum of Archaeology is housed in the impressive Auberge de Provence. Exhibits include delicate stone tools dating from 5200 BC, Phoenician amulets and an amazing temple model from Ta' Haġrat: a prehistoric architectural maquette.

More impressive still are the beautifully modelled prehistoric figurines found locally. Best is the **Sleeping Lady**, found at the Hypogeum (p67), which is around 5000 years old. It shows a recumbent woman with her head propped on one arm, apparently deep in slumber.

The **'fat ladies'** sculptures, found at Ħaġar Qim, have massive rounded thighs and arms, but tiny, doll-like hands and feet. They wear pleated skirts and sit with their legs tucked neatly to one side. The so-called **Venus de Malta**, also from Ħaġar Qim, is about 10cm tall and displays remarkably realistic modelling. There are also beautiful stone friezes from the Tarxien Temples (p67).

Upstairs displays showcase the coarser pottery from the Bronze Age, animal figurines and jewellery, as well as information on the island's mysterious cart ruts.

★Fort St Elmo & National War Museum — FORTRESS, MUSEUM

(☎2123 3088; www.heritagemalta.org; adult/child €10/5.50; ⌚9am-6pm Mon-Sat, noon-6pm Sun Apr-Sep, 9am-5pm Oct-Mar) Guarding Marsamxett and Grand Harbours is Fort St Elmo, named after the patron saint of mariners. The fort was built by the Knights in 1552 in just four months to guard the harbours on either side of the Sceberras Peninsula, and bore the brunt of Turkish arms during 1565's Great Siege. After restoration, the fort reopened in 2015, and now contains the National War Museum, which covers Malta's wartime history, includfing its WWII ordeal.

The museum showcases absorbing audiovisual displays, bringing history to life and illustrating aspects of war such as the struggle to get supplies through to the islands under German bombardment. Artefacts include the Gloster Gladiator biplane called Faith (minus wings), the sole survivor of the three planes that so valiantly defended the island when Italy declared war in 1940. Pride of place goes to the George Cross medal that was awarded to the entire population of Malta in 1942.

The courtyard outside the entrance to the fort is studded with the lids of underground

VALLETTA IN TWO DAYS

Start the day with coffee at **Lot Sixty One** (p64) or **No 43** (p60) before wandering Valletta's history-loaded streets. Be sure to visit major attractions evoking the island's illustrious history; **St John's Co-Cathedral** (p51), the **Grand Master's Palace** (p51) and the **National Museum of Archaeology**. Admire Valletta's recent contemporary additions at **MUŻA** (p56) and Renzo Piano's **Parliament Building** (p57) and **City Gate**, before taking in astounding Grand Harbour views from **Upper Barrakka Gardens**.

On day two, visit the **National War Museum** at Fort St Elmo, then take a tour of the **Hal Saflieni Hypogeum** (p67) (having prebooked online a few months' ahead). Afterwards enjoy a boat trip around the harbour and spend the afternoon exploring the beguiling Three Cities area. Take in an evening show in Valletta at **Manoel Theatre** (p64) or **St James' Cavalier Centre for Creativity** (p65), or dine at **Noni** (p62) or **59 Republic** (p63) before a nightcap at **Cafe Society** (p64) or **Yard 32** (p63).

VALLETTA'S NEW CONTEMPORARY EDGE

Inspired by Valletta's tenure as a European Capital of Culture in 2018, the city is now becoming known as an emerging European centre for art and design. An outstanding new museum and several modern and innovative galleries are all worth seeking out if you have an interest in the arts.

Housed in the 16th-century Auberge d'Italie, the original home of the Italian Knights of St John, MUŻA (p56) combines many original works from Malta's Museum of Fine Arts (which closed in 2016) with a more modern focus on promoting community-based exhibitions illuminating Malta's heritage and culture.

Private galleries worth visiting include **Valletta Contemporary** (www.facebook.com/vallettacontemporary; 15-17 Triq il-Levant; ⏲10.30am-2.30pm & 3-7pm Tue-Fri) opened in 2018 and inspiring the urban renewal of Triq il-Levant ('East St'), and **Malta Contemporary Art** (☎2711 0298; www.maltacontemporaryart.com; Triq Felix; ⏲1-6pm Tue-Fri), now in its own central space after several years operating from ad hoc venues around Malta. There's also regular, short-term pop-up exhibitions, often from resident artists, at **Blitz** (☎2122 4992; www.thisisblitz.com/programme; Triq Santa Lucija; ⏲hours vary).

granaries. You can visit the parade ground and the 1559 chapel where Knights fought to the death during the siege trying to protect the altar, as well as the later 1729 church.

The military pageant In Guardia (p65) takes place here between October and June.

★Upper Barrakka Gardens — PARK

(👪) These colonnaded gardens perched high above Grand Harbour were created in the late 16th century as a relaxing haven for the Knights from the nearby Auberge d'Italie. They provide a shady retreat from the bustle of the city, and the balcony has one of the best views in Malta.

The terrace below is occupied by the Saluting Battery, where a cannon once fired salutes to visiting naval vessels.

Upper Barrakka Lift — LIFT

There was a lift between the Grand Harbour and the Upper Barrakka Gardens from 1905 to 1973. In 2012, this was finally replaced by the marvellous panoramic lift that connects Upper Barrakka Gardens with the Lascaris Ditch, just a short walk from Valletta Waterfront and ferries and water taxis to the Three Cities. It's 58m high and can carry 21 passengers. Pay on the way up (€1), but not on the way down; if you have a ferry ticket, it's free.

Saluting Battery — HISTORIC SITE

(☎2180 0992; www.salutingbattery.com; adult/child incl audio guide €3/1; ⏲10am-5pm, guided tours 11am, 12.15pm & 3pm) The Saluting Battery is where a cannon once fired salutes to visiting naval vessels. The battery has been restored, and a cannon is fired every day at noon and 4pm with great ceremony – it's well worth making time to see this, and children will enjoy it. Try to time your visit for a tour – the enthusiastic, costumed guides explain how the cannon is loaded and fired.

War HQ Tunnels — HISTORIC SITE

(☎21225277; www.warhqmalta.com; Triq il-Batterija, access from the Saluting Battery; adult/child €15/5; ⏲10.30am & 1pm) Twice-daily one-hour tours negotiate the wartime tunnels under Valletta and focus on Maltese history from WWII to the Cold War. Good walking shoes are necessary and it's a good idea to bring a torch (flashlight).

Lascaris War Rooms — MUSEUM

(☎2123 4717; www.lascariswarrooms.com; Lascaris Ditch; adult/child/family €12/5/25; ⏲10am-5pm) A mechanically ventilated underground tunnel complex that lies 40m beneath the Upper Barrakka Gardens, this housed Britain's top-secret command in Malta during WWII and remained in use until 1977. Lovingly restored in 2009, the rooms are laid out as they would have been, staffed by waxwork figures, and provide a fascinating behind-the-scenes glimpse. Get here by going to the Saluting Battery in the Upper Barrakka Gardens – the staff there will direct you.

There are plans to restore the adjacent Combined Operations Centre, Malta's WWII nerve centre where the unified offensive response for all naval, air force and military action was coordinated.

City Gate — MONUMENT

The Renzo Piano–designed City Gate forms part of the architect's dramatic and harmonious development. It echoes the dimensions of the original 1633 entrance, rather

Valletta

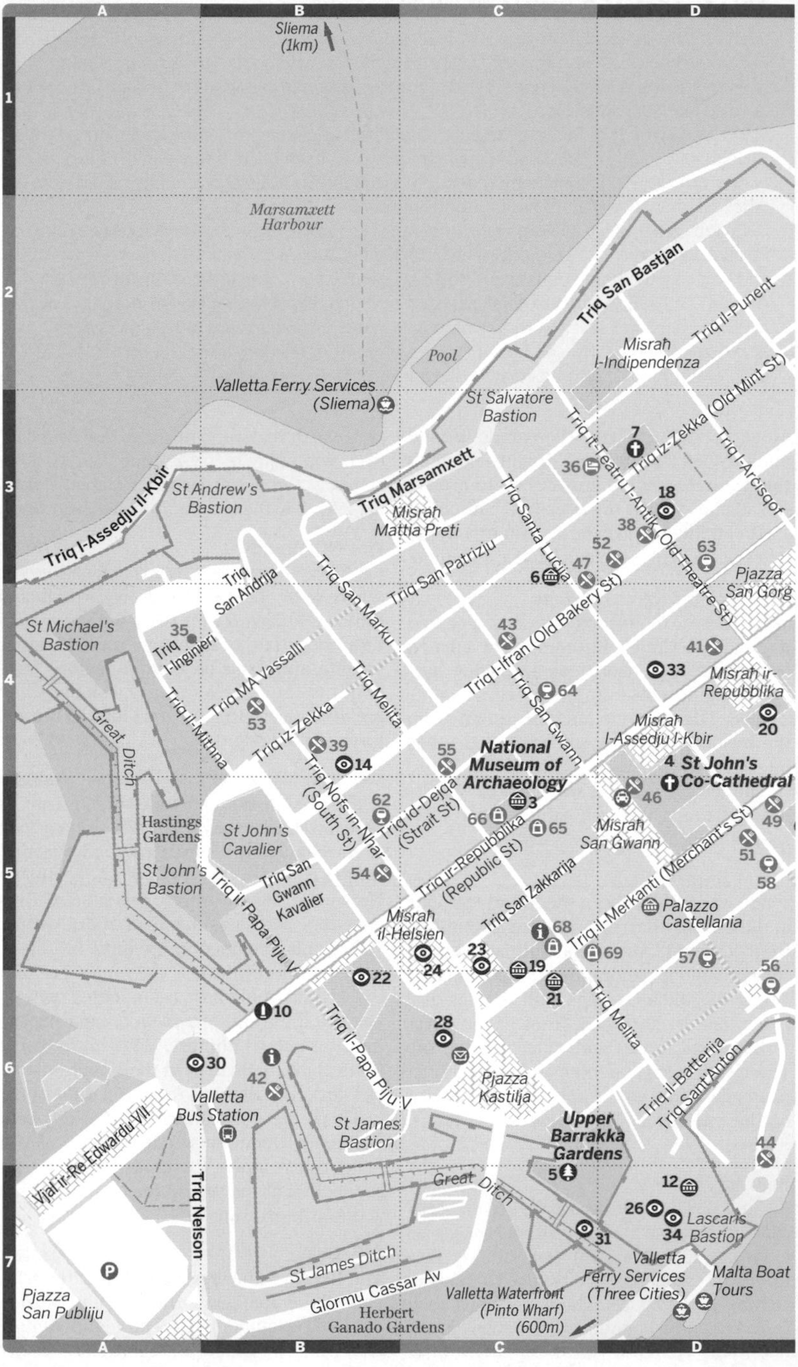

A
B
C
D
1
2
3
4
5
6
7
Sliema (1km)
Marsamxett Harbour
Pool
Valletta Ferry Services (Sliema)
St Salvatore Bastion
Triq San Bastjan
Triq il-Punent
Misraħ l-Indipendenza
Triq iz-Zekka (Old Mint St)
Triq l-Arċisqof
Triq it-Teatru l-Antik (Old Theatre St)
Triq Marsamxett
Triq l-Assedju il-Kbir
St Andrew's Bastion
Misraħ Mattia Preti
Triq Santa Luċija
Triq San Patrizju
Triq San Andrija
Triq San Marku
Pjazza San Ġorġ
St Michael's Bastion
Triq l-Inginieri
Triq MA Vassalli
Triq l-Ifran (Old Bakery St)
Triq Melita
Triq San Ġwann
Misraħ ir-Repubblika
Triq il-Mithna
Triq iz-Zekka
Great Ditch
Misraħ l-Assedju l-Kbir
National Museum of Archaeology
St John's Co-Cathedral
Triq Nofs in-Nhar (South St)
Triq id-Dejqa (Strait St)
Hastings Gardens
St John's Cavalier
Misraħ San Ġwann
Triq ir-Repubblika (Republic St)
Triq il-Merkanti (Merchant's St)
St John's Bastion
Triq il-Papa Piju V
Triq San Ġwann Kavalier
Triq San Zakkarija
Palazzo Castellania
Misraħ il-Helsien
Triq Melita
Triq il-Papa Piju V
Pjazza Kastilja
Triq il-Batterija
Triq Sant'Anton
Valletta Bus Station
Vjal ir-Re Edwardu VII
St James Bastion
Upper Barrakka Gardens
Great Ditch
Triq Nelson
Lascaris Bastion
St James Ditch
Valletta Ferry Services (Three Cities)
Malta Boat Tours
Ġlormu Cassar Av
Valletta Waterfront (Pinto Wharf) (600m)
Pjazza San Publiju
Herbert Ganado Gardens
1
3
4
5
6
7
10
12
14
18
19
20
21
22
23
24
26
28
30
31
33
34
35
36
38
39
41
42
43
44
46
47
49
51
52
53
54
55
56
57
58
62
63
64
65
66
68
69

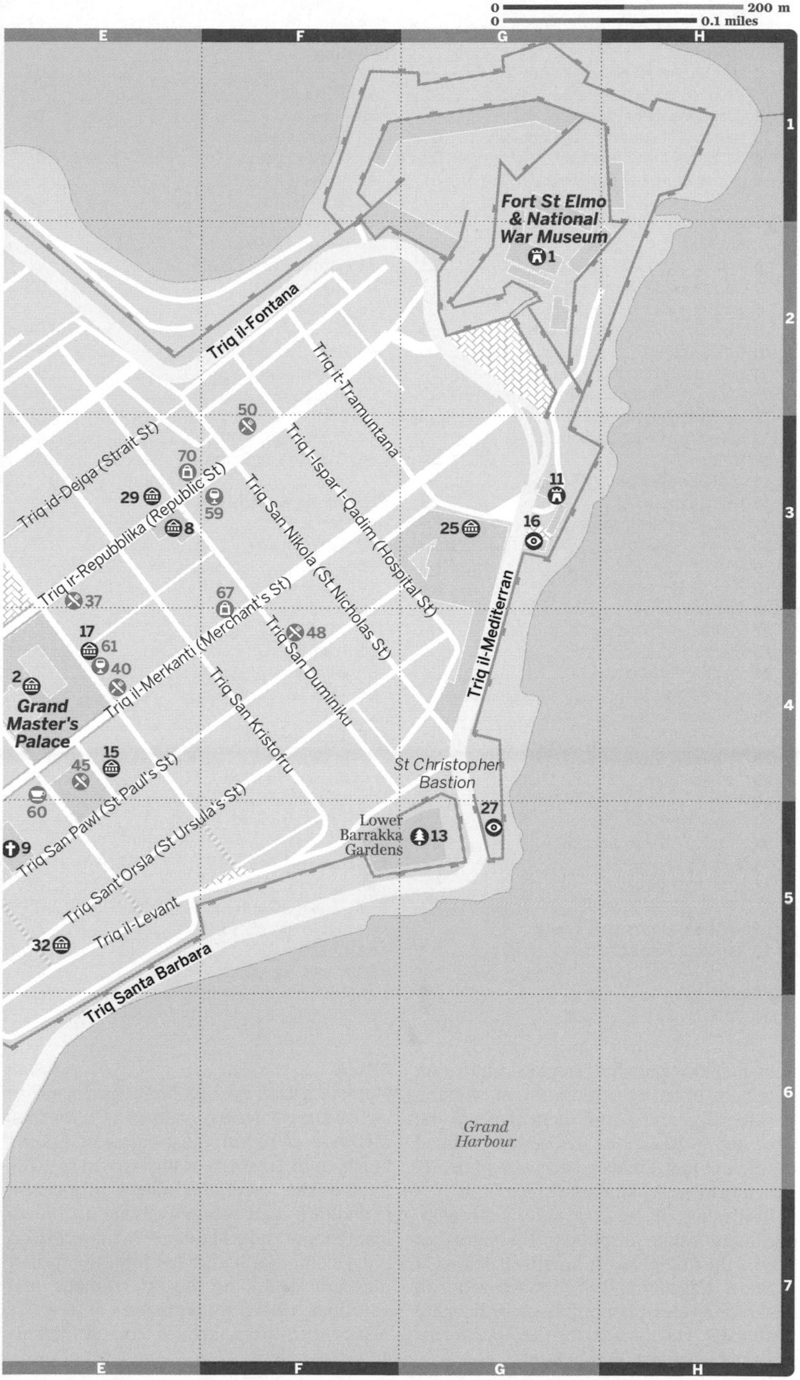
0 200 m
0 0.1 miles
E
F
G
H
1
2
3
4
5
6
7
Fort St Elmo & National War Museum
1
Triq il-Fontana
Triq it-Tramuntana
50
Triq l-Ispar l-Qadim (Hospital St)
Triq id-Dejqa (Strait St)
70
29
Triq ir-Repubblika (Republic St)
59
8
Triq San Nikola (St Nicholas St)
11
16
25
Triq il-Mediterran
37
67
Triq il-Merkanti (Merchant's St)
Triq San Duminku
48
17
61
40
2
Grand Master's Palace
Triq San Kristofru
15
45
60
St Christopher Bastion
Triq San Pawl (St Paul's St)
Triq Sant'Orsla (St Ursula's St)
27
Lower Barrakka Gardens
13
9
Triq il-Levant
32
Triq Santa Barbara
Grand Harbour

Valletta

Top Sights

1	Fort St Elmo & National War Museum	G2
2	Grand Master's Palace	E4
3	National Museum of Archaeology	C5
4	St John's Co-Cathedral	D5
5	Upper Barrakka Gardens	C7

Sights

	Armoury	(see 2)
6	Blitz	C3
7	Carmelite Basilica	D3
8	Casa Rocca Piccola	E3
9	Church of St Paul's Shipwreck	E5
10	City Gate	B6
11	Entrance to Fort St Elmo & National War Museum	G3
12	Lascaris War Rooms	D7
13	Lower Barrakka Gardens	G5
14	Malta 5D	B4
15	Malta Contemporary Art	E4
16	Malta Experience	G3
17	Malta Postal Museum	E4
18	Manoel Theatre	D3
19	MUŻA	C5
20	National Library	D4
21	Palazzo Parisio	C6
22	Parliament Building	B6
23	Pjazza de Valette	C5
24	Royal Opera House	C5
25	Sacra Infermeria	G3
26	Saluting Battery	D7
27	Siege Bell Memorial	G5
28	St James' Cavalier	C6
29	Toy Museum	E3
30	Triton Fountain	A6
31	Upper Barrakka Lift	C7
32	Valletta Contemporary	E5
33	Valletta Living History	D4
34	War HQ Tunnels	D7

Activities, Courses & Tours

35	Mediterranean Culinary Academy	A4

Sleeping

36	Casa Ellul	C3

Eating

37	59 Republic	E3
38	67 Kapitali	D3
39	Adesso	B4
40	Ambrosia	E4
41	Caffe Cordina	D4
42	Dates Kiosk	B6
43	Guze Bistro	C4
44	Harbour Club	D6
45	Is-Suq Tal-Belt	E4
46	Kantina Cafe & Wine	D5
47	Legliglin	C3
48	Nenu the Artisan Baker	F4
49	No 43	D5
50	Noni	F3
51	Piadina Caffe	D5
52	Rubino	D3
53	Sotto	B4
54	Trabuxu Bistro	B5
55	Trattoria da Pippo	C4

Drinking & Nightlife

56	Bridge Bar	D6
57	Cafe Society	D5
58	Cru	D5
59	Ġugar Hangout & Bar	F3
60	Lot Sixty One	E4
61	The Pub	E4
62	Trabuxu	B5
63	Wild Honey	D3
64	Yard 32	C4

Entertainment

	In Guardia	(see 1)
	Manoel Theatre	(see 18)
	St James' Cavalier Centre for Creativity	(see 28)

Shopping

65	Agenda	C5
66	Artisans Centre	C5
67	C Camilleri & Sons	F4
68	Ċekċik	C5
69	Mdina Glass	C5
70	Silversmith's Shop	E3

than the 1960s gate that it replaced, allowing passers-by to have the sensation of crossing a real bridge, and giving them views of the ditch and fortifications. The gate is framed by a pair of metal blades, each 25m high, designed to look like knights' sabres.

Inside the gate, a pair of wide, gently sloping flights of steps, inspired by the stairs that framed the original gate, link the bastions of St James' Cavalier and St John's Cavalier to the lower-level Republic St. Looking back up Republic St, you'll notice the City Gate forms a distinct 'V' shape (for Valletta).

MUŻA MUSEUM

(Auberge d'Italie; ☎2122 5769; www.muza.heritagemalta.org; Auberge d'Italie; ⊙9am-5pm) MUŻA is a recent incarnation of Malta's Museum of Fine Arts, which closed in 2016. Sited in the Auberge d'Italie, a 16th-century building that was once home to Italian members of the Knights of St John, MUŻA today combines highlights from the former museum, including historical maps and paintings, with a contemporary, interactive 21st-century approach to community art and storytelling.

St James' Cavalier ARTS CENTRE
(☎2122 3216; www.sjcav.org; Castille Pl) This 16th-century fortification has been transformed into a dazzling arts centre encompassing galleries, theatre and a cinema. Recent exhibitions have encompassed contemporary Libyan art.

Malta Postal Museum MUSEUM
(☎2596 1750; www.maltapostalmuseum.com; 135 Triq l-Arċisqof; adult/child €5/2; ⏰10am-4pm Mon-Fri, to 2pm Sat & Sun) Highlights of the permanent exhibition in this compact but interesting museum include the fascinating story of the postal system of the Knights of St John. The building is also often used for both heritage and contemporary photographic exhibitions.

Parliament Building NOTABLE BUILDING
Renzo Piano's breathtaking Parliament Building was completed in 2014. Its design includes two massive volumes of stone that look suspended in air, but are supported by stilts. The blocks have been machine-cut to lighten their appearance, while reducing solar radiation and letting in daylight. Covering the rooftop are 600 sq metres of photovoltaic panels, which generate most of the energy required to heat the building in winter and cool it in summer.

The northern block contains the parliament chamber, while the south block accommodates MPs' offices. As little has changed architecturally in Valletta since it was established in the 16th and 17th centuries, it's unsurprising that Renzo Piano's modern and dramatic additions, including the Parliament Building, City Gate and Opera House, have proved controversial in Malta. Everyone definitely has an opinion!

Manoel Theatre THEATRE
(☎2559 5523; www.teatrumanoel.com.mt; 115 Triq it-Teatru l-Antik; tours €5; ⏰guided tours half-hourly 9.30am-noon Mon-Fri) Malta's national theatre was built in 1731 and is one of the oldest in Europe. The building is being slowly restored, but is still in use for events, and can be visited on interesting guided tours. Booking ahead a few days prior is recommended. Highlights of the theatre include a baroque, gilt-twinkling auditorium with a huge chandelier.

Church of St Paul's Shipwreck CHURCH
(Triq San Pawl, enter from Triq Santa Luċija; donations welcome; ⏰9.30am-noon & 3.30-6pm Mon-Sat, 10.45-11.45am & 4-6pm Sun) FREE In AD 60 St Paul was shipwrecked on Malta and brought Christianity to the population. This church has a 19th-century facade, but the interior dates from the 16th century and houses many treasures, including a dazzling gilded statue of St Paul, carved in Rome in the 1650s and carried shoulder-high through the streets of Valletta on the saint's feast day (10 February). There's also a golden reliquary containing some bones from the saint's wrist, and part of the column on which he is said to have been beheaded in Rome.

Casa Rocca Piccola HISTORIC BUILDING
(☎2122 1499; www.casaroccapiccola.com; 74 Triq ir- Repubblika; adult/under 14yr €9/free; ⏰hourly tours 10am-4pm Mon-Sat) The 16th-century

VALLETTA FOR CHILDREN

Valletta is a great city to wander through with kids. Much of the centre is pedestrianised, there are plenty of child-friendly eateries (though some only accept older children) and some places have baby-change facilities. The Upper Barrakka Gardens (p53), with the entertaining Saluting Battery, and Lower Barrakka Gardens (p58) are good places for a run around, as is Pjazza San Ġorġ (St George's Sq), with its fountains.

Excellent museums include the state-of-the-art National War Museum (p52) and the Toy Museum (p58), and there's an impressive collection in the Armoury in the Grand Master's Palace (p51). Audiovisuals include Malta 5D (p58) and Malta Experience (p58). There are historical re-enactments at Fort St Elmo (p52) and cannon firing at Fort Rinella (p69), just outside Valletta. Nearby is the new Esplora (p68) science centre, with excellent children's playgrounds and interesting interactive displays. Finally, taking a boat across the harbour always makes for a fun trip.

Valletta has several public family restrooms; see www.facebook.com/freshtot for details of locations. Access around Valletta is relatively straightforward in the city's main squares and plazas, but note that negotiating a stroller down stairs and the steeper side lanes and streets is more challenging. Malta's public buses all have low floors and access ramps, and children's menus are routinely offered at many restaurants.

LOCAL KNOWLEDGE

CORNER MONUMENTS

You'll notice that on almost every corner of Valletta there is some kind of statue or monument. When the Knights of St John planned Valletta, they issued regulations, called *capitoli*, that all corners had to be embellished by statues or niches.

palazzo Casa Rocca Piccola is the family home of the 9th Marquis de Piro, who still lives here and has opened part of the palazzo to the public. Visits allow a unique insight into the privileged lifestyle of the aristocracy, and include the family's WWII air-raid shelters, which lie 100ft underground.

National Library LIBRARY
(8.15am-1pm Mon-Sat mid-Jun–Sep, to 5pm Mon-Fri Oct–mid-Jun) This grand classical edifice was the last building erected by the Knights. It's worth popping in to admire the book-lined stacks, and there are occasional temporary exhibitions.

Malta 5D THEATRE
(2735 5001; www.malta5d.com; Triq l-Ifran; adult/child €9/6; 9.30am-5pm Mon-Sat, 10am-2pm Sun) The most multisensory of Valletta's audiovisual evocations of the past, this 20-minute show enlivens Malta's history with 3D effects, aromas, gusts of air and moving seats.

Valletta Living History THEATRE
(2722 0071; Embassy Complex, Triq Santa Luċija; adult/child/family €7/4/25; 10am-3.15pm, shows every 45min) A glossy, entertaining 35-minute sweep through Malta's eventful history (available in eight languages).

Triton Fountain FOUNTAIN
Sculpted by Maltese sculptor Vincent Apap in 1959, this grand fountain has been restored to perfection and reopened in early 2018 in time for Valletta's inauguration as the 2018 European Capital of Culture.

Malta Experience THEATRE
(2124 3776; www.themaltaexperience.com; Triq il-Mediterran; adult/child incl Sacra Infermeria €16/6; hourly 11am-4pm Mon-Fri, 11am-2pm Sat & Sun) A whip through 7000 years of history, this 45-minute show also highlights Malta's scenic attractions. It's screened in the basement of the Mediterranean Conference Centre, which occupies the Sacra Infermeria, the 16th-century hospital of the Order of St John. The entrance fee includes a tour of the hospital, visiting the Grand Hall that once housed around 300 patients.

Royal Opera House NOTABLE BUILDING
(Triq ir-Repubblika) Built in the 1860s, the once imperious Opera House was destroyed during a German air raid in 1942. Its gutted shell was left as a reminder of the war, and now acts as a framework for the Renzo Piano–designed open-air performance space, where bottle-green seating is raised above the ruins. It's a wonderful place to catch a concert, which are most frequent during the Arts Festival.

Sacra Infermeria MUSEUM
(2124 3840; www.themaltaexperience.com; Triq it-Tramuntana; adult/child incl Malta Experience €16/6; hourly 11am-4pm Mon-Fri, to 2pm Sat & Sun) In the impressive former Sacra Infermeria, a 16th-century hospital of the Order of St John, this exhibition brings to life the sometimes alarming achievements of medieval medicine and allows a glance inside this fascinating building. Admission is included with entry to the Malta Experience.

Lower Barrakka Gardens PARK
This compact harbourfront park contains a Doric temple commemorating Sir Alexander Ball, the British captain who successfully captured Malta from the French in 1800.

Toy Museum MUSEUM
(2125 1652; 222 Triq ir-Repubblika; adult/child €3/free; 10am-3pm Mon-Fri, to 1pm Sat & Sun) This doll-sized museum houses an impressive private collection of model toys, such as tin cars from 1950s Japan, tin toys from 1912 Germany, as well as Matchbox cars, farmyard animals, train sets and dolls.

Courses

Mediterranean Culinary Academy COOKING
(9970 4909; www.mcamalta.com; Triq l-Inġinieri; per person €80) This excellent initiative runs 'Cooking & Culture in Valletta' workshops showcasing how the cuisine of the island nation has been impacted by the surrounding Mediterranean Sea. Hosted by a professional chef, the three-hour cooking courses are definitely hands-on, and much of the produce comes from sustainable farms and fisheries. Meals are shared over a bottle of wine at the conclusion. Check the website for the course schedule.

ST JOHN'S CO-CATHEDRAL

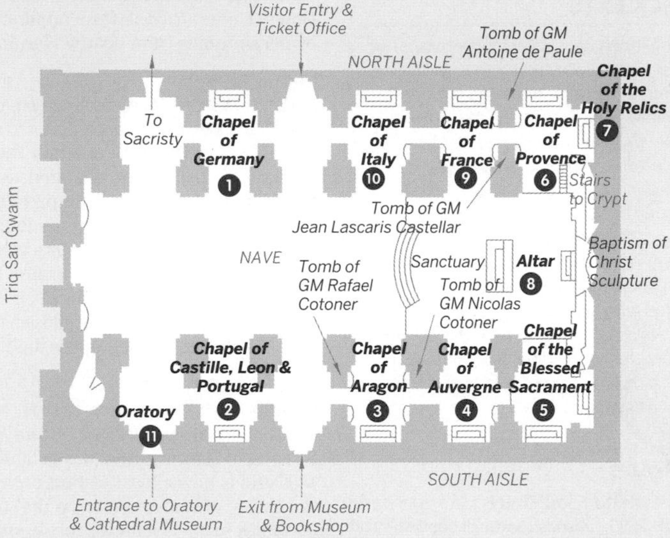

Walking Tour
St John's Co-Cathedral

START CHAPEL OF GERMANY
END ORATORY
LENGTH TWO HOURS

The cathedral has eight chapels allocated to the various langues (divisions, based on nationality). Enter and turn to your right. You'll see the **1 Chapel of Germany**; look out for the German Langue's emblem of a double-headed eagle.

Cross the nave to the **2 Chapel of Castille, Leon & Portugal**, with its Mattia Preti altarpiece and monuments to Grand Masters Antonio Manoel de Vilhena and Manuel Pinto de Fonseca. Next is the sumptuous **3 Chapel of Aragon**, with another Preti altarpiece and the extravagant tombs of the brothers (and consecutive Grand Masters) Rafael and Nicolas Cotoner.

Next is the **4 Chapel of Auvergne**, with the tomb of Grand Master Fra Annet de Clermont de Chattes Gessan. Beyond is the **5 Chapel of the Blessed Sacrament**, which once contained an icon of the Virgin brought from Rhodes, removed from here when Napoleon expelled the order. It contains a 15th-century crucifix from Rhodes and keys of captured Turkish fortresses.

Opposite is the dark **6 Chapel of Provence**, with the tombs of Grand Masters Antoine de Paule and Jean Lascaris Castellar. The crypt (usually closed) contains the first 12 Grand Masters, including Jean Parisot de la Valette.

The **7 Chapel of the Holy Relics** guards a wooden figure of St John, said to be from the galley in which the Knights departed from Rhodes in 1523. The **8 Altar** is dominated by the *Baptism of Christ* by Giuseppe Mazzuoli; Preti's paintings of St John decorate the vaulted ceiling.

The austere **9 Chapel of France**, with a Preti altarpiece of St Paul, houses lavish funerary monuments, including to Grand Masters Adrien de Wignacourt and Fra Emmanuel de Rohan. Preti's painting, *The Mystic Marriage of St Catherine,* hangs in the exquisite baroque **10 Chapel of Italy**, overlooking a bust of Grand Master Gregorio Carafa.

The **11 Oratory** was built in 1603 as an unadorned building for novices, and later redecorated by Preti. It contains Caravaggio's menacing *Beheading of St John the Baptist* (c 1608), the artist's largest painting, and his *St Jerome,* full of quiet power and pathos.

LOCAL KNOWLEDGE

QUICK EATS

Eating lunch only at restaurants can get expensive in Valletta, but there are a few convenient and better-value options.

Follow your nose to the many hole-in-the-wall places dotted around town, where you can pick up fresh hot *pastizzi* for around €0.40 from about 7.30am Monday to Saturday. Near the bus station, **Dates Kiosk** (mqaret €0.30; 9am-7pm Mon-Fri, to 1pm Sat) sells traditional *mqaret* (deep-fried pastries stuffed with spiced dates).

In Valletta itself, try the Italian-style sandwiches at Piadina Caffe or select from a daily variety of salads at the cool and compact No 43.

Tours

Offbeat Malta Food Trails FOOD & DRINK
(2180 2383; www.offbeatmaltafoodtrails.com; per person €65; 10am-1pm Sat) Informed local guides lead small group tours around the best of Valletta's eating and drinking scene. While there is plenty of focus on delicious local flavours including *fenek* (rabbit) and *pastizzi,* the tours also provide an excellent overview of the historical and cultural forces that have shaped Malta. Book ahead and schedule a tour when you arrive in Malta.

Malta Film Tours CULTURAL
(www.maltafilmtours.com; group/private tours €59/295) Runs *Game of Thrones* location tours every Saturday morning and also private tours from Sunday to Friday focusing on flicks filmed in Malta flicks such as *Gladiator, Troy* and *The Count of Monte Christo.*

Eating

Eating opportunities in Valletta have grown in recent years, now spanning fine dining, traditional cafes and more contemporary eateries. Note that many restaurants are closed either Sunday or Monday, so check each establishment's opening hours carefully.

No 43 CAFE €
(2703 2294; www.facebook.com/no43valletta; 43 Triq il-Merkanti; snacks & salads €3-6; 8am-5pm Mon-Sat;) Salad specials, plump sandwiches and chicken wraps all feature at this compact Australian-owned cafe. Fruit salad with Greek yoghurt and cold-pressed juices are both healthy options, and some of Valletta's best coffee is served with genuine Down Under friendliness. Apparently, the owner's mum is from nearby Floriana.

Is-Suq Tal-Belt FOOD HALL €
(2210 3500; www.facebook.com/pg/suqtalbelt; Triq il-Merkanti; mains €7-13; 7am-10pm Sun-Thu, to 1am Fri & Sat) Valletta's traditional fresh market has been restored as a food hall serving everything from pizza to Asian street food. Maltese offerings include a good bakery and seafood, and there's a convenient (if pricey) supermarket downstairs if you're renting an apartment and self-catering. Many Valletta eateries are closed on Sundays, but Is-Suq Tal-Belt opens daily.

Caffe Cordina CAFE €
(2123 4385; www.caffecordina.com; 244 Triq ir-Repubblika; mains €8.25-16; 8am-7pm Mon-Sat, to 3pm Sun) Cordina was established in 1837 and is now a local institution. You have the choice of waiter service at the sun-shaded tables in the square or inside, or joining the locals at the zinc counter inside for a quick caffeine hit.

Piadina Caffe ITALIAN €
(2122 5983; www.piadinacaffe.com; 24 Triq Santa Luċija; snacks €4-5; 7.30am-4pm) Piadina sandwiches – think a quesadilla with an Italian accent – are excellent at this hole-in-the-wall cafe. Order one with prosciutto, cheese and rocket, then grab an espresso, and either sit outside on bean bags or across the lane in the cafe's compact dining room. Salads and focaccia sandwiches are also available for a quick lunch.

Nenu the Artisan Baker MALTESE €€
(2258 1535; www.nenuthebaker.com; 143 Triq San Duminiku; mains €10-13; 11.45am-2.30pm Tue-Sun, 6-11.30pm Tue-Sat) Often the answer when you ask a local, 'What's the best place to try *ftira*?', Nenu's decades-old wood-fired oven turns out a dizzying selection of Malta's traditional pizza-like, baked flatbreads. Olives, capers, cheeses and meats all feature. The menu also strays deliciously into other Maltese classics. As weekends are busy with local families, try and visit on a weekday.

Sotto PIZZA €€
(2122 0077; www.sottopizzeria.com; 32 Triq Nofs in-Nhar; mains €10-14; noon-2.45pm & 7-11pm Tue-Sun) Just maybe Malta's best pizza is the star at this Italian-owned pizzeria. That means the pizzas are served in a square

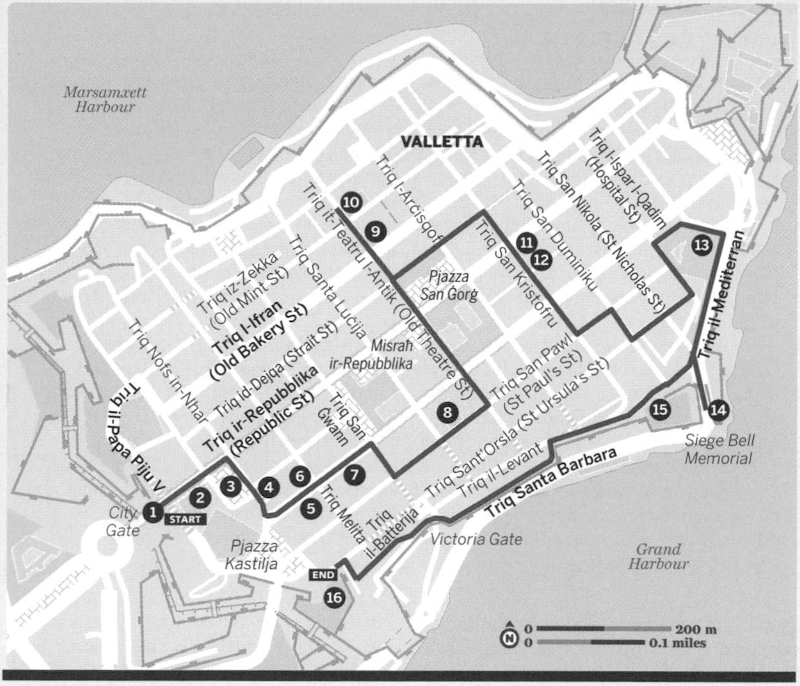

Walking Tour Valletta

START CITY GATE
END UPPER BARRAKKA GARDENS
LENGTH 2.25KM; ONE HOUR

Begin at **1 City Gate** (p53). Just beyond it is the Renzo Piano–designed **2 Parliament Building** (p57) and **3 Royal Opera House** (p58). Walk past the Opera House and turn right into Triq Nofs in-Nhar; you'll pass through the new **4 Pjazza de Valette**. Next turn left at Triq il-Merkanti. You'll see the **5 Palazzo Parisio** (Triq il-Merkanti) on your right, where Napoleon stayed during his six days on Malta, and the Auberge d'Italie (1574) on your left. The latter building now houses **6 MUŻA** (p56). Walk another few blocks and you'll see **7 Palazzo Castellania** (15 Triq il-Merkanti), which used to house Valletta's law courts. The figures above the 1st-floor balcony represent Justice and Truth.

Turn right into Triq San Ġwann, then left into Triq San Pawl, passing the 16th-century **8 Church of St Paul's Shipwreck** (p57). Turn left along Triq it-Teatru l-Antik, where you'll see the **9 Manoel Theatre** (p57) on the right, and the domed **10 Carmelite Basilica** (Triq l-Arċisqof) beyond. Double back and then turn left down Triq id-Dejqa (Strait St); note the faded bar signs from its years as a red light district. Turn right along Triq San Kristofru, passing the 16th-century **11 Palazzo Messina** and **12 Palazzo Marina**. Follow Triq San Kristofru, then turn left onto Triq San Pawl, right on Triq San Duminiku then left again down Triq Sant'Orsla. Walk around the Knights' 16th-century hospital, **13 Sacra Infermeria** (p58).

Heading south, you'll see the **14 Siege Bell Memorial** (St Christopher Bastion), commemorating the lives lost in the WWII convoys. Follow Triq il-Mediterran past the **15 Lower Barrakka Gardens** (p58), which contain a little Doric temple commemorating Sir Alexander Ball, the naval captain who took Malta from the French in 1800. Continue along Triq Santa Barbara, cross the bridge above Victoria Gate and turn left to climb steep Triq il-Batterija to the **16 Upper Barrakka Gardens** (p53).

LOCAL KNOWLEDGE

VALLETTA'S REBIRTH

Over the last few years, Valletta has been undergoing a renaissance. From its construction until WWII, the city was home to the nobility and businesspeople. However, WWII resulted in a lot of damage, and after the war, the city's empty houses were used for social housing, with around 3000 units spread across the empty mansions. The demographic changed – the rich all moved to their seaside homes in Sliema, and by the 1980s and '90s many of Valletta's beautiful houses were empty and falling apart.

People began to buy up Valletta's houses with views first, but now even inner-city ones are selling and increasingly being repurposed as boutique hotels or short-term apartment accommodation. Prices have gone up, real estate agents are sprouting, and like other heritage cities around the world, some long-term residents are being priced out of where they have spent the majority of their lives.

Renzo Piano's 2015 designs, including the Parliament Building (p57) and the City Gate (p53), have also given Valletta a different feel. As renowned local architect Chris Briffa says, 'The last time we had something of that scale and detail and that technically advanced were the 18th-century bastions... It's a statement that Valletta is not just a museum city, but it's vibrant and a city of the 21st century'.

Looking ahead, there are plans to redevelop and restore Valletta's City Gate ditch garden, including opening the former Farson's Brewery as a museum and dining precinct. A €24-million framework to regenerate lower Valletta in the proximity of Fort St Elmo is also on the cards. The plan includes social housing, accommodation for retired locals – both vital to offset the area's gentrification – and green spaces and access to the water.

shape Roman-style. Service is uniformly excellent, and antipasto and pasta dishes are also available. Booking ahead is recommended, but the Sotto team can often fit in casual diners on a couple of shared tables.

67 Kapitali CAFE €€

(☎2738 0010; www.67kapitali.com; 67 Triq l-Ifran; mains €6-10, shared platters €8-20; ⊙noon-11pm Mon-Wed, 9.30am-midnight Thu-Sat, 9.30am-4pm Sun) Robust *ftira* sandwiches, fresh salads and hearty soups are the standouts at this friendly cafe. It's one of the only places in Valletta with the full range of Gozo's Lord Chambray craft beers on tap. Brews from the UK and Germany are also poured, and a fridge full of other brews makes it a good spot for an evening session.

Trabuxu Bistro BISTRO €€

(☎2122 0357; www.trabuxu.com.mt; 8 Triq Nofs in-Nhar; mains €12-24; ⊙noon-3pm & 7-11pm Mon-Sat) This place feels vaguely Parisian, and with dark red walls punctuated with paintings the setting entices you to linger. The Mediterranean menu is up to scratch too, and there's a fine range of wines. Over-12s only.

Harbour Club MEDITERRANEAN €€

(☎2122 2332; www.theharbourclubmalta.com; 4 Barrierra; mains €16-24; ⊙noon-2.30pm Tue-Sun, 7-10.30pm Tue-Sat) In converted 17th-century boathouses, the Harbour Club has a superb terrace and wonderful harbour views. With excellent vistas across to the Three Cities, it's one of Valletta's best spots for a leisurely meal. Asian influences underpin a largely Mediterranean menu and service is excellent. Booking ahead is recommended; seating will be inside if it is a windy day.

Kantina Cafe & Wine CAFE €€

(☎2723 0096; www.facebook.com/KantinaCafeWine; Triq San Ġwann; mains €12-23; ⊙8am-11.30pm Mon-Sat, 9am-11.30pm Sun) This friendly cafe has a great location – its outdoor tables are scattered under the trees in the pedestrianised area outside St John's Co-Cathedral (p51). The menu stretches from bagels, *ftira*, sandwiches and salads to cocktails and local wines.

★Noni MEDITERRANEAN €€€

(☎2122 1441; www.noni.com.mt; 211 Triq ir-Repubblika; mains €19-26; ⊙6-10pm Mon-Sat, noon-2.30pm Thu-Sat) Descend into Noni's stylish stone-lined basement space and be surprised by modern spins on traditional Maltese and Mediterranean flavours. Dishes are prepared with a light touch and could include a silky smooth parfait of rabbit liver, or wonderfully tender slow-cooked octopus with Israeli couscous. An excellent wine list and craft beers from Malta and Belgium are other tasty diversions.

Adesso MEDITERRANEAN €€€
(☎7974 0460; www.adesso.com.mt; Triq Nofs in-Nhar; mains €18-29; ⊙noon-2.30pm Mon-Sat, 6-10.30pm Mon & Wed-Sat) Translating from Italian to 'now' in English – the giveaway is clocks with no hands throughout the space – Adesso is a thoroughly modern bistro adding contemporary spins to culinary classics amid a cosy, stylish interior. Try truffle-laced *lasagna nera* with veal and mushrooms, or the simply named but delicious 'steak and chips' with Black Angus beef.

Rubino MEDITERRANEAN €€€
(☎2122 4656; www.rubinomalta.com; 53 Triq l-Ifran; mains €17-24; ⊙noon-2.30pm Mon-Fri, 7.30-10.30pm Tue-Sat) White-tableclothed Rubino is a classy place that earns rave reviews for its seasonal dishes such as spaghetti with sea urchins or sea-bass *involtini* (rolls) stuffed with pine nuts and mint. The velvety risotto is particularly renowned. Leave room for dessert – the house speciality is *cassata siciliana* (sponge cake soaked in liqueur, layered with ricotta cheese). Over-fives only.

59 Republic INTERNATIONAL €€€
(☎2123 8014; www.fiftyninerepublic.com; 59 Triq ir-Repubblika; mains €21-32; ⊙12.30-4pm daily, 6.30pm-late Mon-Sat) The menu changes every couple of months and fresh and seasonal produce is proudly showcased in 59 Republic's compact and stylish space. Bookings are recommended, especially for weekend evenings, for the opportunity to partner one of Valletta's best wine lists with dishes such as a tartare of local prawns with Asian flavours, or black meagre (a meaty fish) with shellfish.

Guze Bistro BISTRO €€€
(☎2123 9686; www.guzevalletta.com; 22 Triq l-Ifran; mains €17-28; ⊙12.30-2.30pm Thu-Sat, 5.45-10pm Mon-Sat) In the flagstone interior of a 16th-century house, hung with chandeliers and decked with wooden tables, Guze offers a short menu of spectacular dishes, such as rabbit wrapped in *guanciale* (pig's cheek) and stuffed with leek and cabbage.

Trattoria da Pippo MEDITERRANEAN €€€
(☎2124 8029; Triq Melita; mains around €22; ⊙11.30am-3pm Mon-Sat) This hidden-away, informal Valletta hub, all green woodwork and gingham tablecloths, is a local favourite, with something of an old boys' club feel, and is the place for those in the know. The food is a delightful mix of Maltese, Sicilian and Italian. Book ahead.

Ambrosia MEDITERRANEAN €€€
(☎2122 5923; www.ambrosia.com.mt; 137 Triq l-Arċisqof; mains €23-26; ⊙12.30-2.30pm Mon-Fri, 7-9.30pm Mon-Sat) With a relaxed and intimate feel, this is one of Valletta's loveliest restaurants. Locals love this place and the welcome is warm (the chef might just pop by to see how you enjoyed your meal). It uses mainly local produce, farmed and cooked according to the Slow Food philosophy, and creates Maltese dishes that play with traditions. Older children only.

Legligin MALTESE €€€
(☎7993 2985; Triq l-Ifran; lunch/dinner tasting menu €17.50/27.50; ⊙1pm-midnight Sat-Thu, from 1.30pm Mon, from 12.30pm Sun) With tiled floors and brick arches, this is an intimate cellar wine bar, serving Maltese tapas alongside a fine list of tipples. The name means 'glug' in Maltese. Dinner includes up to nine small dishes, while there is a cheaper three-dish option for lunch. Bookings recommended.

Drinking & Nightlife

Valletta has awoken from a long sleep to become a great place to hang out at night. There's a cluster of bars centred on narrow Strait St, and other excellent options tucked away down side thoroughfares. Closing times vary depending on how busy individual venues are.

★**Yard 32** COCKTAIL BAR
(☎9993 6734; www.yard32.com; 32 Strait St; ⊙noon-late Tue-Sat) Almost 250 gins from around the world partner with traditional Spanish-style *pinchos* tapas at this stylish bar at the quieter southern end of Strait St. There's regular live music too, usually kicking off around 8.30pm. Entertainment with your botanicals-infused beverage of choice could include jazz, acoustic guitar or a violin soloist.

★**Bridge Bar** BAR
(⊙8pm-4am Fri May-Oct) The Bridge Bar is a weekly event, with brightly coloured cushions all over a junction of steps in the eastern part of Valletta. There are views, live jazz from 8.30pm to midnight and the feel of an impromptu party.

Cru WINE BAR
(☎7946 1576; www.facebook.com/crumalta; 16 Triq Santa Luċija; ⊙noon-10pm Mon-Fri, to 11.30pm Sat) Set amid the shimmering shopfronts of Valletta's traditional jewellery street, Cru is an excellent place to try wines from around

LOCAL KNOWLEDGE

STRAIT STREET

Strait St was once the notorious haunt of sailors on shore leave. In *Strait Street: Malta's 'Red Light District' Revealed* (2013), an interesting book about the street, the authors John Schofield and Emily Morrissey describe hole-in-the-wall bars, where the toilet was a bucket behind a curtain. But there was also bohemian theatricality amid the squalor, and the street has come alive once again to celebrate this.

The street's artistic director, Giuseppe Schembri Bonaci, who's from the area, says, 'It developed into a cultural hub from its initiation. It used to house artists that were working at the Grand Master's (Manoel) Theatre. It developed into "the Gut", in a sense like a microscopic version of Montmartre (in Paris). You had a mix of bohemian characters'.

As local people moved out of Valletta post-WWII and the British Navy left in 1979, Strait St became a shadow of its former self, with faded vintage bar signs the only clue to its past. But this is now changing fast, as people realised the appeal of Valletta's fine architecture and the city was renovated to assume the mantle of European Capital of Culture for 2018. See local listings for upcoming events, or just wander past and see what's going on. Barely 4m wide for its 660m length, Strait St is at its best on weekend evenings. It's no nostalgic trip, but a rebirth, with occasional concerts, gigs and art exhibitions.

Malta and the Mediterranean. The owner is very knowledgable, and the regular lunch special of two small dishes for €14 is a great way to while away an afternoon. Tastings of new wines are held at 7pm on Wednesdays.

Cafe Society BAR
(☎2713 7491; www.facebook.com/cafesocietyuptown; 13 Triq San Ġwann; ⏰5.30pm-1am) Customers spill out onto tables set on Valletta's limestone steps at this cool and compact bar. Often there's a DJ dispensing beats inside, and a considered approach to mixology is partnered by international and local craft beers. Views across to the Three Cities are excellent. Look for the vintage 'Ladies Hair Stylist' sign and you're in the right place.

Ġugar Hangout & Bar BAR
(www.facebook.com/gugarmalta; 89 Triq ir-Repubblika; ⏰10am-1am Wed-Sat, 3pm-1am Tue & Sun) Easily the most laid-back bar in Valletta, Ġugar's slightly hippy vibe extends to local students downing bottles of frosty Cisk lager at tiny tables out front, and a compact food menu of mainly vegan and vegetarian dishes.

Wild Honey CRAFT BEER
(☎7761 3772; www.facebook.com/WildHoneyValletta; 127 Triq Santa Luċija; ⏰noon-1am Mon-Fri, 5.30pm-midnight Sat) Eight taps and a fridge full of international brews make Wild Honey Valletta's best bar for craft beer. Classic rock usually partners the retro album covers on the walls, and there's platters and pizza if you're peckish. Sit outside on the sloping street, but just watch for cars making the incredibly tight turn down the hill.

Lot Sixty One CAFE
(☎7984 1561; www.lotsixtyonecoffee.com.mt; Triq it-Teatru l-Antik; ⏰8am-5pm Mon-Thu, 8am-8pm Fri, 9am-5pm Sat & Sun) Lot Sixty One's modern take on a Valletta coffee house includes organic and fair-trade beans roasted locally, and a selection of snacks including muffins, brownies and bliss balls. It's very popular for takeout coffee with locals, but it's worth securing a table on wildly sloping Old Theatre St for a more leisurely experience.

Trabuxu WINE BAR
(☎2122 3036; www.trabuxu.com.mt; 1 Triq id-Dejqa; ⏰7pm-late Tue-Sat) Trabuxu ('corkscrew') is housed in a cool 350-year-old cellar – an atmospheric place to munch on perfect platters and quaff wine.

The Pub PUB
(☎7980 7042; www.facebook.com/thepubmalta; 136 Triq l-Arċisqof; ⏰11am-late) Fans of the late British actor Oliver Reed might want to raise a glass to their hero in this succinctly named watering hole. This is the homely little hostelry where the wild man of British cinema enjoyed his final drinking session before last orders were called forever in 1999.

☆ Entertainment

Manoel Theatre THEATRE
(☎2124 6389; www.teatrumanoel.com.mt; 115 Triq it-Teatru l-Antik; ⏰booking office 10am-1pm & 5-7pm Mon-Fri, 10am-1pm Sat) This beautiful place is Malta's national theatre, and the islands' principal venue for drama, concerts, opera and ballet, with a season running from October to May (tickets €10 to €40). It

also organises performances at other Valletta venues like Fort St Elmo or the Biblioteca for events such as the Baroque Festival.

St James' Cavalier Centre for Creativity THEATRE, CINEMA
(☎2122 3200; www.sjcav.org; Triq Nofs in-Nhar) Has a cinema that regularly shows National Theatre, Royal Shakespeare Company and Met Opera Live broadcasts. Also has regular classic and creative theatre, and shows international and arthouse films.

In Guardia LIVE PERFORMANCE
(☎2123 7747; www.visitmalta.com; adult/child €10/5; ⏲11-11.45am most Sun Oct-Jun) In Guardia is a colourful, military pageant in 16th-century costume that includes a cannon-firing demonstration that'll clear the wax from your ears. Most performances are held at Fort St Elmo (p52), but a few take place across Grand Harbour at Fort St Angelo (p68), Vittoriosa. Check upcoming dates and locations at the tourist office (p66) or at Visit Malta's online events calendar.

Shopping

Triq Santa Luċija, behind Misraħ ir-Repubblika (Republic Sq), is home to a number of jewellery stores offering silver filigree – the most popular souvenir here is a silver eight-pointed Maltese Cross on a chain. Also popular in stores around town is traditional Maltese lace, and glass and ceramic items.

Ċekċik CLOTHING
(☎7940 2108; www.cekcik.com.mt; 15 Triq Melita; ⏲10am-6pm Mon-Fri, to 3pm Sat) Named after the Malti word for 'knick-knack', Ċekċik features contemporary Maltese T-shirts, tote bags and screen prints amid its otherwise global selection of ethnically inspired items.

Silversmith's Shop JEWELLERY
(218 Triq ir-Repubblika; ⏲9am-5pm Mon-Fri, to 3pm Sat, to 1pm Sun) Fine filigree work is the speciality at this traditional workshop. Current artisan Matthew Borg is the son of the original owner.

Artisans Centre ARTS & CRAFTS
(☎2122 1563; 288 Triq ir-Repubblika; ⏲9am-7pm Mon-Fri, to 6pm Sat) Good selection of ceramics, silver and glass from both Malta and Gozo. Especially popular are traditional brass door knockers. Designs include lions (for protection) and dolphins (for prosperity).

Mdina Glass ARTS & CRAFTS
(☎2141 5786; www.mdinaglass.com.mt; 14 Triq il-Merkanti; ⏲10am-7pm Mon-Fri, to 4pm Sat) Mdina Glass features hand-blown glass produced by craft workshops near Mdina, in a range of styles and colours from traditional to decidedly modern – vases, bowls, paperweights, collectables and more.

Agenda BOOKS
(☎2123 3621; www.facebook.com/AgendaBookshop; 26 Triq ir-Repubblika; ⏲8.30am-7pm Mon-Sat, 9am-1pm Sun) A cramped shop with an excellent selection of travel guides and fiction, history and reference books.

C Camilleri & Sons FOOD & DRINKS
(☎2124 1642; www.ccamilleriandsonsltd.com.mt; Triq il-Merkanti; ⏲9am-7pm Mon-Sat, to 1pm Sun) Historic dessert and sweets shop, open since 1843, selling 'pick-and-mix' and beautifully decorated, delectable cakes as well as homemade biscuits.

Cafe meals are also served outside on pavement tables.

Information

EMERGENCY

Malta Police Headquarters (p174) is at Pjazza San Kalcidonju a short walk away in Floriana. Valletta's main **Police Station** (☎2294 3101) is at 111 Triq l-Arċisqof.

INTERNET ACCESS

Many bars and cafes offer wi-fi access, and there are also free public hot spots in Valletta's main plazas.

For a list of these, see www.mca.org.mt/wifi-hotspots.

MONEY

There are plenty of ATMs, plus places to change money on and near Triq ir-Repubblika.

Bank of Valletta (cnr Triq ir-Repubblika & Triq San Ġwann; ⏲8.30am-2pm Mon-Thu, to 3.30pm Fri, to 12.30pm Sat) ATMs are available.

HSBC Bank (32 Triq il-Merkanti; ⏲8.30am-1.30pm Mon-Thu, to 4.30pm Fri, to 12.30pm Sat) ATMs.

POST

Main Post Office (www.maltapost.com; Pjazza Kastilja; ⏲8.15am-3.45pm Mon-Fri, to 12.30pm Sat) Found under the St James' Cavalier, opposite the Auberge de Castille.

TOURIST INFORMATION

Tourist Information Branch (☎2369 6073; www.visitmalta.com; Malta International

Airport; ⌚10am-9pm) Helpful tourist office in the airport arrivals hall, where you can access the internet and print documents (useful for boarding passes).

Tourist Information Office (☎2122 0193; www.visitmalta.com; 28 Triq Melita; ⌚9am-5pm Mon-Sat, to 1pm Sun & public holidays) Helpful tourist office with plenty of maps, walking trail pamphlets and brochures. There's also a smaller **kiosk** (Valletta bus station) near the bus station and the entrance to the City Gate; its opening hours are flexible (based on availability of staff), but it's usually open during July and August.

Getting There & Away

BOAT

Valletta Ferry Services operates from Valletta Waterfront to the Three Cities (p68) and from Marsamxett Harbour to Sliema (p179).

A *dgħajsa* (traditional rowing boat or water taxi; pronounced 'die-sa') can be hailed to cross from Valletta to the Three Cities. The cost is €2 per person, and for €8 the friendly boatmen will take you on a 30-minute cruise around Grand Harbour. Get in contact with **Malta Boat Tours** (☎2780 5278; www.maltaboattours.com; Valletta–Three Cities €2, harbour cruises €8).

BUS

The Valletta **bus station** (Vjal Nelson) has buses for all over the island. A two-hour ticket in winter/summer/at night costs €1.50/2/3. You can also buy a block of 12 tickets for €15 or a one-week Explorer pass for €21.

DESTINATION	ROUTE NO.
Airport	72, 73
Birgu	2
Buġibba	31, 45, 48
Ċirkewwa	41, 42
Marsaxlokk	81, 85
Mdina & Rabat	51, 52, 53
Mellieħa	41, 42
Mosta	31, 41, 42, 44
Paceville	13, 16
St Julian's	13, 16
Sliema	13, 15
Żurrieq	71

You can also take a hop-on, hop-off tour with either CitySightseeing Malta (p180) or **Malta Sightseeing** (☎2169 4967; www.maltasightseeing.com; per day adult/child €20/13), whose tours make a circuit of Valletta before heading off around the island.

> **MUSEUM PASS**
>
> If you're going to visit more than a few historical sites and museums in Valletta, it's well worth investing in a multisite pass (adult/child €50/25) from Heritage Malta (www.heritagemalta.org), which offers a total discount of over €200. This covers you for admission to all 23 Heritage Malta sites (except the Hypogeum), as well as the Malta National Aquarium (p97). The pass is valid for 30 days from its first use.

Getting Around

TO/FROM THE AIRPORT

Express bus X4 connects Malta International Airport (p177) with Valletta (25 minutes; every 15 minutes). As for everywhere in Malta, buses cost €1.50/2 (winter/summer). You can arrange for a direct transfer from the airport to most hotels in Malta using **MaltaTransfer** (☎2133 2016; www.maltatransfer.com; per person from €5), which has a desk in the airport baggage claim hall.

You'll find a taxi information desk in the airport arrivals hall and you can organise and pay for your taxi there. The set fare from the airport to Valletta or Floriana is €20.

TO/FROM THE SEA PASSENGER TERMINAL

The Upper Barrakka Lift (p53) connects Valletta to the Sea Passenger Terminal at the Valletta Waterfront. There are also regular buses, as well as stops for the hop-on, hop-off services. As at the airport, there's a taxi information kiosk on Valletta Waterfront where you organise and pay the set rate for your taxi journey upfront. The cheapest fare (to a Valletta or Floriana address) is €12.

BUS

Bus 133 is a circular bus route that zips half-hourly around Valletta's city walls, calling at Castille, Marsamxett and Floriana. As well as being a good way to get around, it offers great views.

CAR & MOTORCYCLE

If you're driving, parking is limited within the city walls, but not impossible – look for a space not demarcated by green lines. Otherwise there's an underground **car park** (www.mcpcarparks.com.mt/mcp-floriana) just outside the City Gate in Floriana. Valletta is easily walkable so you don't need a car to get around.

TAXI

There's a taxi rank just outside City Gate (p53), and, within the city walls, **Smart Cabs** (☎7741 4177; 3 people within city perimeter/

to cruise-ship terminal €5/8) electric taxis can be picked up outside St John's Co-Cathedral (p51). Taxis also wait near the Castille Hotel outside the pedestrian entrance to the Upper Barrakka Gardens (p53).

AROUND VALLETTA

Centuries of history overlap in these compact areas easily reached by bus and ferry from Valletta. Set on two narrow peninsulas, the Three Cities area, comprising Vittoriosa, Senglea and Cospicua, was the original home of the Knights of St John in Malta. The district's narrow laneways are now mainly residential, while at Vittoriosa's northern end, the recently restored Fort St Angelo offers superb views across Grand Harbour to Valletta.

To the southwest of Malta's capital, the Hal Saflieni Hypogeum is one of the country's essential sights. Around 5000 years old, the mysterious subterranean burial chambers inspire awe and provide a unique insight into life and death across the millennia.

Hal Saflieni Hypogeum & Tarxien Temples

The suburb of Paola, 2km southwest of Cospicua, conceals two of Malta's most important prehistoric sites. The Hal Saflieni Hypogeum is an ancient subterranean necropolis, while the nearby Tarxien Temples include massive stone blocks dating from around five millennia ago.

Sights

★ Hal Saflieni
Hypogeum ARCHAEOLOGICAL SITE
(☑ 2180 5019; www.heritagemalta.org; Triq iċ-Ċimiterju; adult/child €35/15, audiovisual only adult/child €5/3.50; ⊘ 9am-5pm, 50min tours on the hour, last tour 4pm) The Hypogeum (from the Greek, meaning 'underground') is a subterranean necropolis, discovered in 1902. To visit is to step into a mysterious and silent world. Its halls, chambers and passages, immaculately hewn out of the rock, cover some 500 sq metres; it is thought to date from around 3600 to 3000 BC, and an estimated 7000 bodies may have been interred here. Note that prebooking online is essential; try to book three months in advance.

The ancient workers mimicked built masonry in carving out these underground chambers, and exploited the rock's natural weaknesses and strengths to carve out the spaces by hand and create a safe underground structure. Carbon dioxide exhaled by visiting tourists did serious damage to the delicate limestone walls of the burial chambers, and it was closed to the public for 10 years up to mid-2000. It has been restored with Unesco funding; the microclimate is now strictly controlled and visitor numbers to the site are limited (10 per tour and eight tours per day).

A few last-minute tickets for the noon and 4pm tours are available the day prior from Fort St Elmo in Valletta or the Gozo Museum of Archaeology. A 20-minute audiovisual presentation is also available at the Hypogeum. This does not need to be booked in advance but does not include access to the Hypogeum itself. For health and safety reasons, children under the age of six cannot visit the Hypogeum.

Tarxien Temples TEMPLE
(☑ 2169 5578; www.heritagemalta.org; Triq it-Templi Neolitiċi; adult/child €6/3; ⊘ 9am-5pm) The Tarxien Temples (Tarxien is pronounced 'tar-sheen') are hidden up a backstreet several blocks east of the Hypogeum. These megalithic structures were excavated in 1914 and are thought to date from between 3600 and 2500 BC. There are four linked structures, built with massive stone blocks up to 3m by 1m by 1m in size, decorated with spiral patterns, pitting and animal reliefs.

The large statue of a broad-hipped female figure was found in the right-hand niche of the first temple, and a copy remains in situ. In 2015 works took place to add a visitor centre and erect a cover to protect the temples.

Getting There & Away

Myriad buses pass through Paola, including buses 1, 2 and 3 from Valletta (15 to 20 minutes, frequent). They stop at various points around the main square, Pjazza Paola. From the main square, the Hypogeum is a five-minute walk; the Tarxien Temples are 10 minutes away.

The Three Cities

Despite their picturesque narrow streets and stunning views, the village-like 'Three Cities', Vittoriosa, Senglea and Cospicua, are largely off the tourist radar and are lovely places to absorb some local atmosphere.

Vittoriosa and Senglea occupy two narrow peninsulas, and are now connected by a pedestrian bridge linking visitors to recent Senglea developments, including a luxury hotel and the privately run American University of Malta (AUM). Cospicua merges into Vittoriosa and lies just south of it. Regular ferries from Valletta make the area a pleasure to visit. Other attractions nearby include the recently opened Esplora science centre, which is an excellent destination for families.

After the Great Siege, Birgu was renamed Vittoriosa (Victorious), L'Isla became Senglea (after Grand Master Claude de la Sengle) and Bormla turned into Cospicua (as in conspicuous courage). Local people and signs often still use the old names.

Sights

Esplora SCIENCE CENTRE

(☎2540 1900; www.esplora.org.mt; Villa Bighi, Triq Marina; adult/child €6/3; ⏲9am-3pm Tue-Fri, 10am-6pm Sat & Sun; 👪) Cosmology, plate tectonics, wave action and other aspects of the natural world are explored at this new science centre housed in and around the historic Villa Bighi. With more than 200 interactive exhibits and outside playgrounds, it's an excellent destination for children. There are superb views from the manicured gardens and rooftop decks, especially towards Valletta and Fort St Angelo.

On occasional weekends and public holidays there are shows at Esplora's planetarium. Check the website for details.

Xghajra Smart City AREA

This Dubai-style development has been created along the coast east of Ricasoli Point to serve the burgeoning local interactive gaming (iGaming) industry, and combines restaurants, apartment blocks and office space. The restaurant-lined centrepiece is **Laguna Walk**, which has a musical fountain that's spectacular at night.

Tours

Rolling Geeks DRIVING

(☎2180 5339; www.rolling-geeks.com; Vittoriosa Waterfront; 2 people €75, additional 2 people each €10) Explore the Three Cities area in one of Rolling Geek's self-drive electric buggies. Pre-programmed directions are given via GPS throughout the route so it's impossible to get lost as the compact vehicles negotiate charming backstreets, the area's main historic points of interest, and museums, churches, gardens and piazzas. An audio commentary available in eight languages provides information en route. Booking ahead is recommended.

Getting There & Away

BOAT

Valletta Ferry Services (☎2346 3862; www.vallettaferryservices.com; single/return daytime adult €1.50/2.80, child €0.50/0.90, after 7.30pm adult €1.75/3.30; ⏲half-hourly 7am-7pm Oct-May, to midnight Jun-Sep) operates from Cospicua/Vittoriosa to Valletta Waterfront.

To get from Valletta to the Three Cities, another option is on a traditional wooden *dgħajsa*. A one-way journey is €2 per person, and for €8 you can do a short harbour cruise.

BUS

Bus 2 (25 minutes, hourly) runs between Valletta and Vittoriosa (Birgu). From the airport (40 minutes), change from buses X2 or X3 at Paola to bus 2. To get to Fort Rinella, Esplora or Xghajra Smart City, take bus 3 from Valletta (35 minutes, half-hourly Monday to Saturday, hourly Sunday). It stops outside the fort and at Smart City. For Esplora alight at the Esplora bus stop.

Vittoriosa

POP 2630

Vittoriosa is only 800m long and 400m at its widest, so it's hard to get lost – it's a sheer pleasure to wander aimlessly through its flower-bedecked alleys. There are several interesting sights, and stunning views across to Valletta. Fort St Angelo, on the tip of Vittoriosa's peninsula, has been restored and is now open to the public. Packed with super-yachts and good harbourside restaurants, the promenade stretching down from Vittoriosa's Cottonera Waterfront makes for a gorgeous amble.

Sights

★**Fort St Angelo** FORTRESS

(☎2540 1800; www.heritagemalta.org; adult/child €8/5; ⏲9am-5pm Oct-Mar, to 6pm Apr-Sep) The Knights took over this medieval fort in 1530 and strengthened it, and Fort St Angelo served as the residence of the Grand Master of the Order until 1571 and was the headquarters of la Valette during the Great Siege. In the 17th century the talented engineer Don Carlos Grunenberg added more defences. Heritage Malta has recently opened restored sections of the fort providing public access to amazing harbour views. Multi-

OFF THE BEATEN TRACK

FORT RINELLA

Built by the British in the late 19th century, **Fort Rinella** (☎2180 9713; www.fortrinella.com; Triq Santu Rokku; adult/child/family €12/5/29; ⏲10am-5pm Mon-Sat, guided tours on the hour) has been restored and converted into an interesting military museum with hands-on displays of fighting skills and signalling (from noon to 1.30pm). At 2pm there is an impressive military re-enactment outside the fort, plus the thrilling chance for visitors to fire a cannon or rifle (for a donation).

The fort, 1.5km northeast of Vittoriosa, was one of two coastal batteries designed to counter the threat of Italy's ironclad battleships.

The batteries (the second one was on Tigné Point in Sliema) were equipped with the latest Armstrong 100-tonne guns – the biggest muzzle-loading guns ever made. Their 100-tonne shells had a range of 6.4km and could penetrate 38cm of armour plating. The guns were never fired in anger, and were retired in 1906.

From Monday to Saturday a free bus service to Fort Rinella leaves the Saluting Battery (p53) in Valletta at 12.20pm and the Malta at War Museum in Vittoriosa at 12.45pm. This is one way only and public transport must be used to get back to Valletta.

media exhibitions bring Valletta and the fort's exciting history alive.

The British occupied the fort from the 19th century, and from 1912 until 1979 it served as the headquarters of the Mediterranean Fleet, first as HMS *Egmont* and from 1933 as HMS *St Angelo*. The upper part of the fort, including the **Grand Master's Palace** and the 15th-century **Chapel of St Anne**, is now occupied by the modern Order of St John. The tip of the Vittoriosa peninsula has been fortified since at least the 9th century; before that it was the site of Roman and Phoenician temples. Tours of Upper Fort St Angelo, including the Chapel of St Anne, are sometimes offered from April to October. Check Heritage Malta's website for details.

Malta at War Museum MUSEUM
(☎2189 6617; www.maltaatwarmuseum.com; Couvre Port; adult/under 16yr incl audio guide €12/5; ⏲10am-5pm) This museum, housed in a wartime police station, and the labyrinth of tunnels that lies beneath it, pays testament to Malta's pivotal part in WWII, and brings vividly to life the suffering of the islanders. As well as displays in glass cases, there's a stirring film with lots of original footage, narrated by Sir Laurence Olivier. Plus there's the opportunity to descend into the former air-raid shelters, which bring to life the underground existence necessary during the islands' fierce bombardment.

Inquisitor's Palace HISTORIC BUILDING
(☎2182 7006; www.heritagemalta.org; Triq il-Mina l-Kbira; adult/child €6/3; ⏲9am-5pm) The Inquisitor's Palace was built in the 1530s and served as law courts until the 1570s, when it became the tribunal (and prison) of the Inquisition, whose task it was to find and suppress heresy. Today the palace houses a small ethnographic museum, but the most fascinating part of the building is the former prison cells, with elaborate carvings by prisoners on the walls. Particularly sinister is the torture chamber, with its rope contraptions for extracting confessions.

The building was strengthened in 1698, as before then a prisoner managed to dig his way out eight times in one year. Outside the prison warden's room there is a delicate sundial, carved by an 18th-century warden.

Maritime Museum MUSEUM
(☎2166 0052; www.heritagemalta.org; Vittoriosa Waterfront; adult/child €5/2.50; ⏲9am-5pm) The old naval bakery, built in the 1840s and operating until the 1950s, now houses a wealth of material on Malta's maritime past. The collection includes huge Roman anchors, traditional Maltese fishing boats and models of the Knights' galleys. The small details of naval life are among the most fascinating: bone-dye and hashish pipes used for whiling away hours at sea, plus local prostitutes' licences indicating the lifestyle back on land.

Misraħ ir-Rebħa SQUARE
(Victory Sq) This compact square features the **Victory Monument**, erected in 1705 in memory of the Great Siege, and an 1880 statue of St Lawrence, patron saint of Vittoriosa. On the eastern side of the square, the magnificent building dating from 1888 is home to the Band Club of St Lawrence. A few good cafes make it a fine morning and afternoon pit stop.

Senglea & Vittoriosa

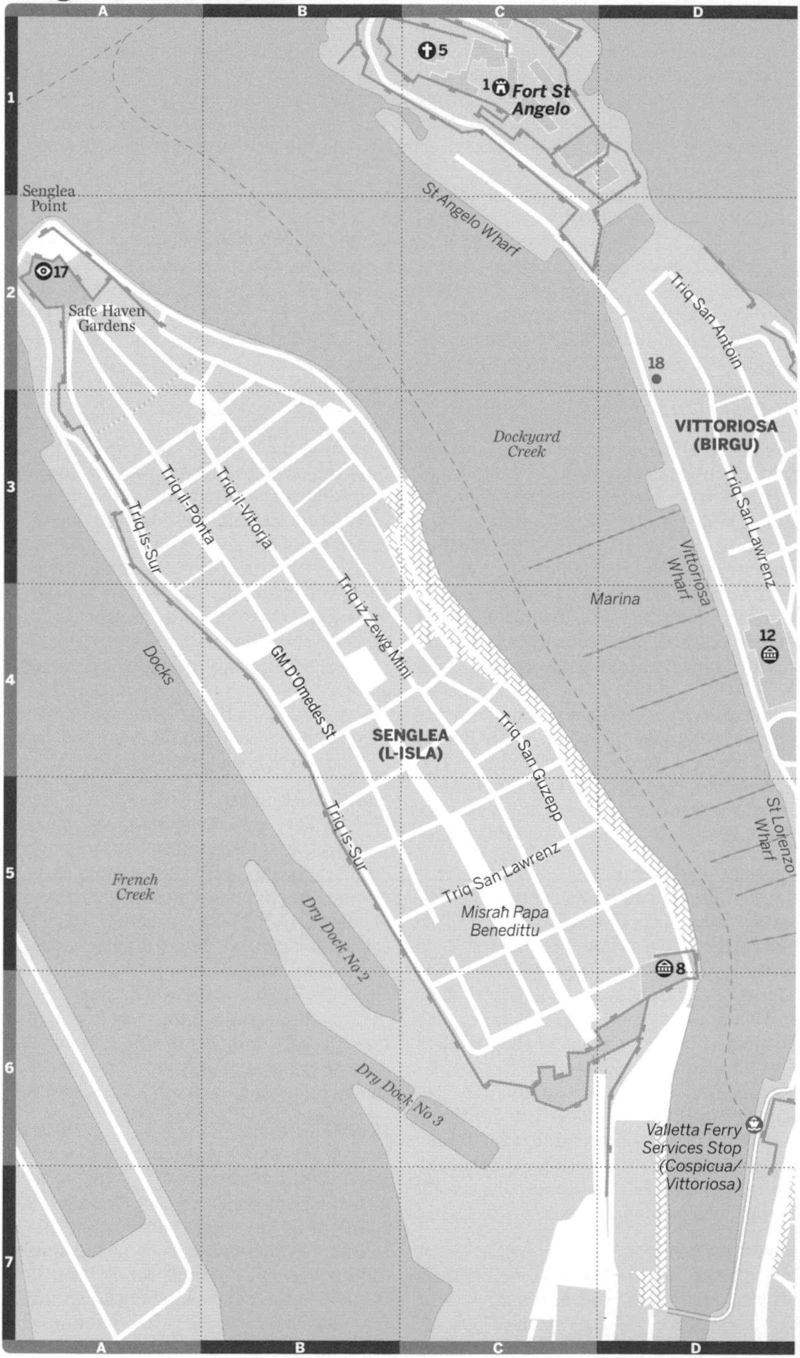

Senglea & Vittoriosa

Top Sights

1 Fort St Angelo C1

Sights

2 Armoury F4
3 Auberge d'Angleterre E4
4 Bighi Sally Port E3
5 Chapel of St Anne C1
6 Church of St Lawrence E4
7 Esplora F1
8 Gantry House D5
9 Il Collachio F4
10 Inquisitor's Palace E4
11 Malta at War Museum E6
12 Maritime Museum D4
13 Misraħ ir-Rebħa E4
14 Norman House F4
15 Oratory of St Joseph E4
16 Sacra Infermeria E3
17 Vedette (Watchtower) A2

Activities, Courses & Tours

18 Rolling Geeks D2

Sleeping

Cugó Gran Machina Grand Harbour .... (see 8)

Eating

Hammett's Macina .... (see 8)
19 Osteria VE F5
20 Tal-Petut F4

Drinking & Nightlife

21 Del Borgo E5

Armoury HISTORIC BUILDING

(Triq il-Kwartier) Built in the 16th century, this building was used by the Knights to store ammunition, and had a door on each of its four sides for ease of access. It was later used as a hospital during the Great Siege and the British converted it into a permanent hospital later.

At the time of research it was closed for restoration and will subsequently be occupied by the International Institute for Justice and the Rule of Law.

Festivals & Events

BirguFest CULTURAL

(www.facebook.com/birgufest; Oct) This festival features three days of cultural activities including music, dance and pageantry in Vittoriosa, culminating in 'Birgu by Candlelight' when the electric lights are switched off and the historic streets are lit by thousands of candles.

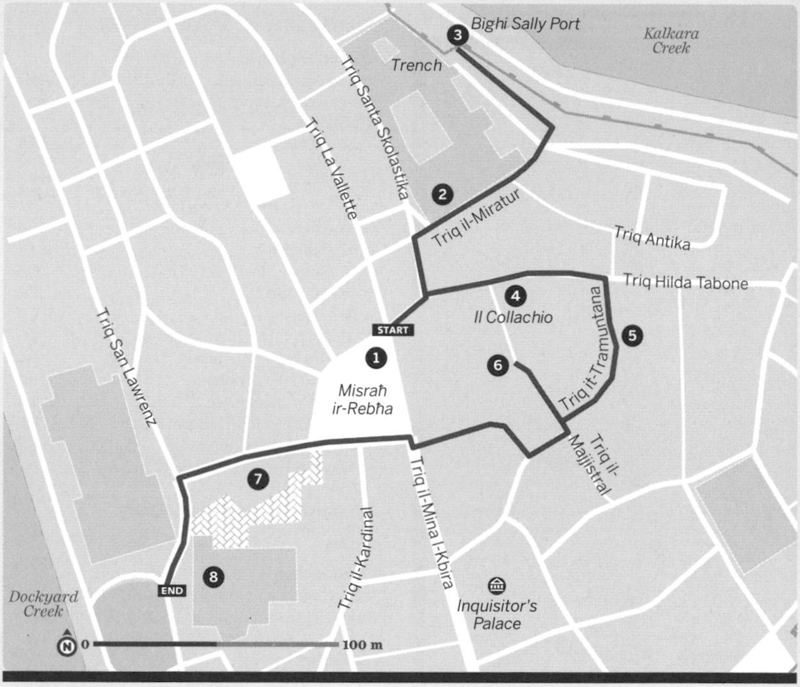

Walking Tour Vittoriosa

START MISRAĦ IR-REBĦA
END WATERFRONT
LENGTH 1KM; ONE HOUR

Start at **1 Misraħ ir-Rebħa** (p69) with its two monuments: the Victory Monument, erected in 1705 in memory of the Great Siege; and a statue of St Lawrence, patron saint of Vittoriosa, from 1880. You'll notice a magnificent building (from 1888) on the eastern side of the square; it's home to the Band Club of St Lawrence.

From the square head east on Triq Hilda Tabone, then take the first left (Triq Santa Skolastika) towards the massive blank walls of the **2 Sacra Infermeria** (Triq Santa Skolastika), the first hospital to be built by the Knights on their arrival in Malta. It's now a convent. Turn right down an alley (signposted Triq il-Miratur) and walk along the wall's perimeter. The stepped ramp descending into a trench in front of the *infermeria* leads to the **3 Bighi Sally Port**, where the wounded were brought by boat to the infirmary under the cover of darkness during the Great Siege.

Next, head back onto Triq Hilda Tabone. To your right lies a small maze of charming alleys, collectively known as **4 Il Collachio**, with some of the city's oldest surviving buildings. Wander up Triq it-Tramuntana to the so-called **5 Norman House** at No 11 (on the left) and look up at the 1st floor. The twin-arched window, with its slender central pillar and zigzag decoration, dates from the 13th century in a style described as Siculo-Norman. Also in this area are the first auberges built by the Knights in the 16th century – the **6 Auberge d'Angleterre** on Triq il-Majjistral, the auberge of the English Knights, is now occupied by Malta's health department.

Turn back to Misraħ ir-Rebħa, from where you can walk down to the waterfront. Turn left into the nearby chapel where the little **7 Oratory of St Joseph** contains relics of Grand Master la Valette, and continue down past the **8 Church of St Lawrence**. Built on the site of an 11th-century Norman church, St Lawrence's served as the conventual church of the Knights of St John from 1530 until the move to St John's Co-Cathedral.

Eating & Drinking

There are several restaurants lining the scenic, sun-splashed Cottonera Waterfront development facing the marina in Vittoriosa. Booking ahead is recommended for the evening dining options. For lunch or a light snack consider the daytime cafes on Misraħ ir-Rebħa, Vittoriosa's compact main square.

★Osteria VE ITALIAN €€

(☎7734 7136; www.osteriave.com; Triq Il-Papa Alessandru VII; mains €11-18; ⏲5pm-midnight Mon & Wed-Fri, noon-3pm & 6pm-midnight Sat & Sun) This lovely restaurant is tucked away down a backstreet in a 17th-century townhouse, and is run by a convivial Venetian pair, doing what Italians do best – simple food made with the best ingredients, with dishes such as beef with rosemary or tagliatelle with sausage and tomato.

Tal-Petut MALTESE €€

(☎7942 1169; www.talpetut.com; 20 Triq Pacifiku Scicluna; 5-course menu €28; ⏲6.30-10pm Tue-Sat) Intimate, characterful restaurant Tal-Petut occupies a former grocery but feels like a home away from home. It's presided over by host-with-the-most Donald, who's passionate about the restaurant's emphasis on seasonal local dishes and produce, including *lampuki* (fish) in white wine or slow-cooked pork.

Del Borgo WINE BAR

(☎2180 3710; www.delborgomalta.com; Triq San Duminku; ⏲5pm-late Mon-Sat) Settle into comfortable sofas in what used to be the cellar of the Prince of Wales' Own Band Club, with high stonework arches. This is an atmospheric wine bar with bottle-lined walls and a fine selection of local and international wines. Platters and tapas make it a great place to celebrate the end of the day.

Information

There's good information on Vittoriosa at www.birgu.gov.mt.

Tourist Information Branch (☎2180 0145; Inquisitor's Palace, Triq il-Mina l-Kbira; ⏲9am-5pm Mon-Sat, to 1pm Sun) is a useful tourist office.

Getting There & Away

Bus 2 **to Valletta** (Triq San Dwardu) and **from Valletta** (Triq San Lawrenz) leaves from near the waterfront, or catch a harbour ferry (p68) from Valletta Waterfront to **Cospicua/Vittoriosa**.

Another option is to catch a *dgħajsa* (traditional water taxi) with Malta Boat Tours (p66).

Senglea

POP 5395

Senglea is even more difficult to get lost in than Vittoriosa, as the streets form a grid pattern. The town was pretty much razed during WWII, so little of historic interest remains, but there are great views of Valletta and Vittoriosa, and the little vedette (watchtower) at the tip of the peninsula is one of the classic sights of Malta. In recent years a new boutique hotel has opened on the Senglea waterfront, and the former Auberge de Castille has been redeveloped as the private American University of Malta (AUM).

Sights

Vedette (Watchtower) LANDMARK

The vedette is decorated with carvings of eyes and ears, symbolising watchfulness, and commands a view to the west over the length of the Grand Harbour and southern flanks of Valletta. At noon and 4pm, the surrounding **Gardjola Gardens** are a wonderful location to watch the cannon firing at the Saluting Battery (p53) across the harbour.

Gantry House HISTORIC BUILDING

The galleys of the Knights of St John were moored here while their masts were removed, using machinery mounted on the wall above the walkway. In early 2018, the site reopened as a luxury hotel. Also known as the Sheer Bastion.

Eating

Hammett's Macina MEDITERRANEAN €€

(☎2779 4171; www.hammettsmacina.com; Triq il-31 ta' Marzu L-Isla; mains €15-28, shared plates €9-12; ⏲6-11pm daily & 11am-4pm Sun; ✎) Bringing a cosmopolitan sense of style to heritage Senglea, the signature restaurant at the new **Cugó Gran Machina Grand Harbour** (☎2711 2711; www.cugogranmalta.com; d low/high season from €190/270; ❄📶🏊) blends Mediterranean, Middle Eastern, Asian and North African flavours. Lunch offerings are more substantial dishes for one, while dinner is focused more on shared plates. The late afternoon/early evening cocktail list is one of Malta's best.

Getting There & Away

It's a 15-minute walk from the main gate at Vittoriosa around to the main gate at Senglea. Near the Cospicua ferry stop, a footbridge crosses the harbour to the location of the new American University of Malta.

TRABANTOS/SHUTTERSTOCK ©

1. Parliament Building (p57)
Renzo Piano's slick Parliament building in Valletta was completed in 2014.

2. Armoury, Grand Master's Palace (p51)
The collection comprises more than 5000 suits of 16th- to 18th-century armour.

3. Vedette (watchtower), Gardjola Gardens (p73)
The eyes and ears carved on the vedette overlooking the harbour symbolise watchfulness.

4. Upper Barrakka Gardens (p53)
These gardens were created as a relaxing haven for the Knights from the nearby Auberge d'Italie.

THELIFTCREATIVESERVICES/SHUTTERSTOCK©

AT A GLANCE

POPULATION
39,297

CAPITAL
Valletta

BEST LOCAL BAR
Hole in the Wall (p81)

BEST CASUAL DINING
Ali Baba (p81)

BEST VIEWS OF VALLETTA
Tigné Point (p79)

WHEN TO GO

Apr–May
Smaller crowds and tour discounts from the boat operators along Sliema's harbourfront.

Jul–Aug
Summer brings a party atmosphere, with big-name DJs playing Paceville's clubs and St Julian's beach bars.

Sep–Oct
Lower prices, guaranteed sunshine and few crowds make autumn a good time to visit.

Tigné Fort (p79)
CARON BADKIN/SHUTTERSTOCK ©

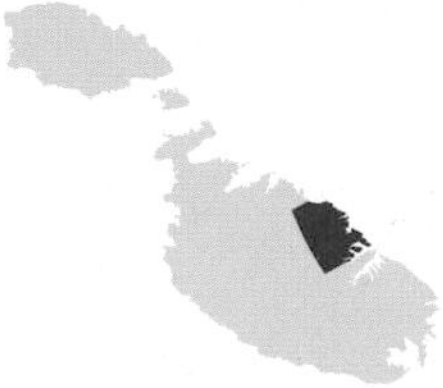

Sliema, St Julian's & Paceville

Malta's cool crowd flocks here to eat, drink, shop and party, and if you're looking for a base that mingles cosmopolitan sparkle with quiet backstreets, this is the perfect choice. Connected by a lovely seafront promenade, with shimmering Mediterranean views, this collection of districts merge into one another, and are packed with shops, restaurants and bars.

St Julian's was once a pretty fishing village, but now hotels and apartments dominate its pretty bays. It adjoins the small nightlife enclave of Paceville, which springs to life at night.

More exclusive-feeling Sliema has long been associated with the Maltese upper classes, and makes an enticingly peaceful base, just far enough from the action. Gracious townhouses sit along backstreets, while burgeoning apartment blocks line the seafront, which is blessed by rocky beaches and swimming spots.

INCLUDES

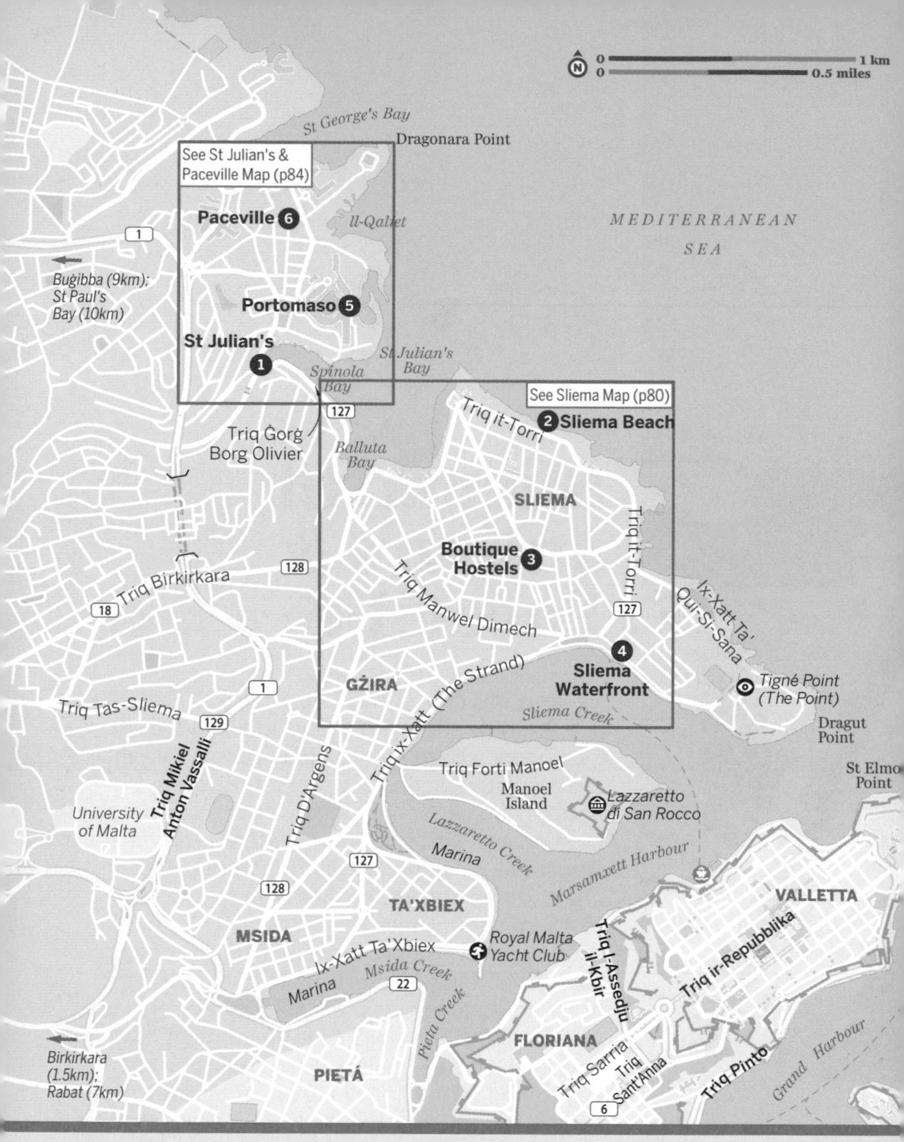

Sliema, St Julian's & Paceville Highlights

❶ **St Julian's** (p82) Wining and dining alfresco at the cafes and restaurants lining the compact coves at Spinola Bay and Balluta Bay.

❷ **Sliema Beach** (p79) Swimming off this flat, rocky and easily accessible beach, then relaxing with a *gelato* or *aperitivo* cocktail at oceanfront cafes.

❸ **Boutique hostels** Staying at one of the area's good-value hostels, offering either a party atmosphere or a quieter vibe.

❹ **Sliema Waterfront** (p79) Joining a boat trip and cruising right around Malta or spending a day exploring Comino and the Blue Lagoon.

❺ **Portomaso** (p82) Pushing the boat out with a flash cocktail amid the super-yachts lining this marina.

❻ **Paceville** (p85) Partying in the pubs and clubs around Malta's most popular and liveliest nightlife area.

Sliema & Around

Once a summer bolt-hole for Valletta's movers and shakers, Sliema is one of the island's most sought-after neighbourhoods, a melange of golden-stone townhouses and swish apartment blocks. Covering its own peninsula, it merges into the district of St Julian's to the northwest, and Gżira and Ta'Xbiex to the south, and is separated from Valletta by narrow Marsamxett Harbour. The main seafront drag is Triq it-Torri (which turns into Qui-si-Sana further south) and is marked by two towers: St Julian's Tower is one of the network of coastal watchtowers built by Grand Master de Redin in the 17th century, and Il-Fortiżża was built by the British in Gothic style. Most of the seafront is public, so you can swim off the rocks. The district has some very good restaurants and a couple of welcoming pubs. More raucous nightlife continues round the bays northwest to Paceville.

Sights

Sliema Beach BEACH
(Triq it-Torri) The Sliema waterfront is edged by flattish rocks, with stepped access at various points. It's a good place to swim from, though the water tends to be deep. There are also facilities for hire (sunbeds, water sports) at the private lidos scattered along the coast; admission costs around €10 per day.

In places along Triq it-Torri and at Qui-si-Sana, square pools have been cut into the soft limestone. These were made for the convenience of leisure-loving upper-class Maltese ladies, and are good for little kids.

Tigné Point (The Point) AREA
(www.thepointmalta.com; ⌚9.30am-7.30pm) Tigné Point, a promontory east of Sliema, was one of the sites where the Turkish commander Dragut Reis ranged his cannons to pound Fort St Elmo during the Great Siege in 1565. The tip of the peninsula is still known as Dragut Point, and now has some of the area's swankiest residential apartments, and Malta's largest shopping mall, the Point. **Tigné Fort**, built in 1793 by the Knights of St John, is being restored as a cultural, heritage and commercial venue.

Manoel Island HISTORIC SITE
Manoel Island, which can be accessed via a short bridge from Gżira, is largely taken up by boat-building yards and the partly restored Fort Manoel. The island was used as a quarantine zone by the Knights of St John; the shell of their 17th-century plague hospital, the **Lazzaretto di San Rocco**, can still be seen on the south side. There's a summer fun-fair on the island.

Fort Manoel was built in the early 18th century under Grand Master Manoel de Vilhena, and was bombed heavily during WWII, when nearby Lazzaretto Creek was used as a submarine base. At the time of writing, controversial plans to redevelop the area with apartment complexes were again progressing, albeit against a background of protest to protect the island's green spaces.

Activities & Tours

Dive Systems DIVING
(☎2131 9123; www.divesystemsmalta.com; Exiles, Triq it-Torri; courses from €65; ⌚8.30am-6.30pm Jun-Sep, to 5pm Mon-Sat Oct-May) Excellent dive school with fantast facilities and helpful staff.

Diveshack DIVING
(☎2133 8558; www.divemalta.com; Ix-Xatt Ta'Qui-si-Sana; courses from €60; ⌚8.15am-5pm) A PADI five-star diving centre.

Hera Cruises BOATING
(☎2133 0583; www.heracruises.com; Sliema Waterfront) Boat tours in a Turkish *gulet* (old-style sailing boat) leave from Sliema waterfront. Options include an all-day cruise right around Malta (adult/child €50/25) and the three-bay trip to Comino and Gozo (€45/25). Prices include lunch.

Eating

Mint CAFE €
(☎2133 7177; www.mintmalta.com; Triq Stella Maris; snacks €4-8; ⌚8am-4pm Mon-Fri; 📶👪) This chic New Zealand–owned cafe provides laid-back Kiwi-style and home cooking. Its food is smashing, with some really sumptuous snacks – quesadilla, vegan stew, savoury muffins, and delicious homemade cakes and cookies. Fresh juices and smoothies are a touch of antipodean healthy eating, and the lamb sausage roll with harissa provides tasty balance. There's outdoor seating.

L-Ahwa Bakery BAKERY €
(bread loaves from €0.60; ⌚11pm-6.30pm Mon-Sat, 11pm-1pm Sun) This bakery opened over 125 years ago and has been run by Carmelo Micallef since 1968. It uses traditional wood-fired ovens rather than electric ones, and has delicious jam tarts. At Christmas, lots of locals bring in their meat to be roasted here,

Sliema

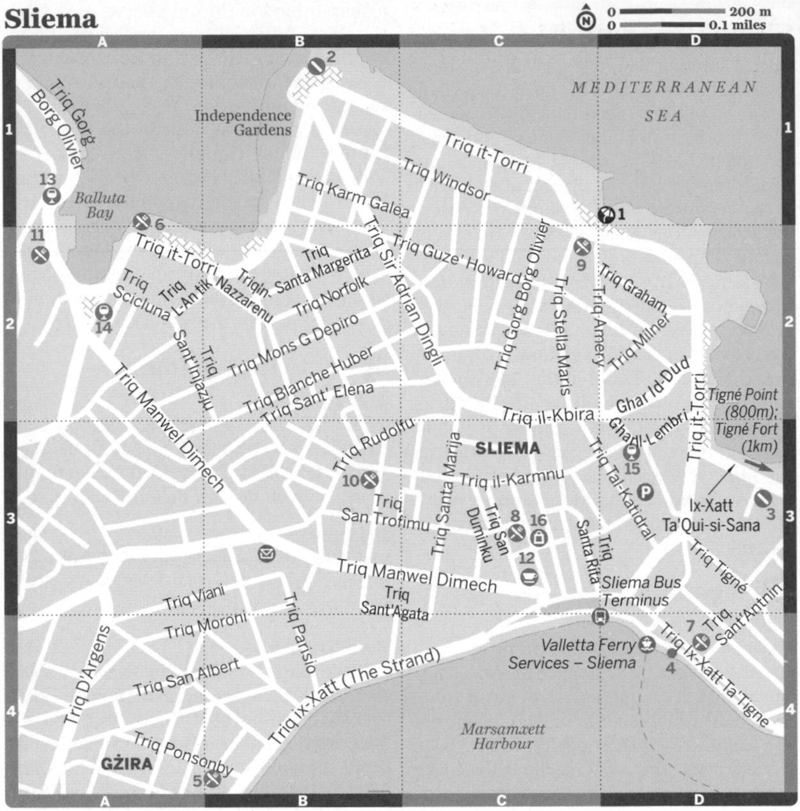

Sliema

Sights
1 Sliema Beach D1

Activities, Courses & Tours
2 Dive Systems B1
3 Diveshack D3
4 Hera Cruises D4

Eating
5 Ali Baba B4
6 Barracuda A1
7 Hammett's Gastro Bar D4
8 L-Ahwa Bakery C3
9 Mint C2
Piccolo Padre .... (see 6)
10 Simler's B3
11 Wigi's Kitchen A2

Drinking & Nightlife
12 Caffe Berry C3
13 City of London A1
14 Electro Lobster Project A2
15 Hole in the Wall D3

Shopping
16 Sunset Records C3

as many homes don't have ovens. There's no sign, so look for the adjacent White Store.

Simler's BAKERY €
(☎2133 2710; www.facebook.com/simlersconfectionery; Triq San Ġwann Battista; pastizzi €0.40; ⏱7.30am-6pm Tue-Sat, to noon Sun) This bakery was established in 1945, and unlike most *pastizzerijas,* it bakes everything on-site, rather than baking pre-prepared *pastizzi*. You can see the machinery in the back of the diminutive shop. It also sells chicken pies, tuna wraps and panini sandwiches.

Piccolo Padre ITALIAN €€

(☎2134 4875; www.piccolopadre.com; Triq il-Kbira; mains €10.50-24; ⏰6.15-11pm daily, noon-3pm Sat & Sun) This casual, family-friendly pizzeria has fabulous sea views; try to snare a coveted table on the enclosed balcony. Pizzas are crunchy and tasty – the house speciality is decorated with tomato, mozzarella, Maltese sausage and Gozo cheese. Also available are good pasta options, salads and burgers.

★**Hammett's Gastro Bar** TAPAS €€

(☎2134 1116; www.hammettsgastrobar.com; 33/34 Triq ix-Xatt Ta'Tigne; shared plates €8-14; ⏰11am-1am) OK, the view through a nearby car park to the Med may not be Sliema's best, but the menu at this modern bistro makes up for any shortcomings. Shared plates with global influences include Korean-style smoked duck with a crispy poached egg or dashi octopus. And the cocktail list is equally interesting.

Barracuda MEDITERRANEAN €€€

(☎2133 1817; www.barracudarestaurant.com; 195 Triq il-Kbira; mains €16-29; ⏰7-11pm) This is a traditional, elegant restaurant set in the drawing room of an early-18th-century seaside villa on the edge of the water. There are brilliant blue sea views framed by the windows, a sunshaded terrace and a menu of carefully prepared Italian and Mediterranean dishes. The degustation menu (€70) is a fine way to while away the hours.

Wigi's Kitchen ITALIAN €€€

(☎2137 7504; www.wigiskitchen.com; Triq Ġorġ Borg Olivier; mains €20-26; ⏰12.30-2.45pm Tue-Fri, 7-10.45pm Mon-Sat & 12.30-2.45pm Sat Sep-Jun only) Wigi's is the Malti pronunciation of 'Luigi's'. This much appreciated, family-run Italian restaurant offers views over the bay through its large plate-glass windows. It proffers delicious steaks, calamari and pork, among other delights; desserts include pear and ricotta cheesecake or date pudding.

Drinking & Nightlife

★**Hole in the Wall** PUB

(☎9983 4378; www.holeinthewall.com.mt; 31 Triq il-Karmnu; ⏰8.30am-1am Mon-Fri, 5pm-1am Sat & Sun) Indie rock and craft beers combine at the latest incarnation of Sliema's oldest pub. Posters of gigs you really wish you'd been to, including Joy Division and Nirvana in their prime, paper the walls, while friendly locals play a retro video-game machine. Beers include many surprising brews, and gourmet toasties (€4 to €5) help to fill the gap.

OFF THE BEATEN TRACK

Multiple recommendations from foodie locals add up to Malta's best Lebanese flavours at **Ali Baba** (☎2134 0119; www.hanyharb.com; 9 Triq Ponsonby, Gżira; mezze €5-15; ⏰noon-3pm Tue-Sat, 6.30-10.30pm Mon-Sat; 🌶). This popular restaurant is located in the Gżira district, around 1km west of Sliema waterfront. Bookings are highly recommended. More than 50 different dishes, designed to be shared *mezze* style, include black sesame-seed *tahini*, chicken and pistachio sausages, and *brik* pastries filled with squab and quail.

Caffe Berry CAFE

(☎9992 3183; www.facebook.com/caffeberry; 69 Triq San Duminku; ⏰7.30am-7pm Mon-Sat) Around 350m walk from the Sliema ferry, Caffe Berry is a firm favourite with locals, who like to combine some of the island's best coffee – the pistachio latte is deservedly famous in Malta – with an intriguing array of snacks.

Electro Lobster Project BAR

(☎2735 7357; www.facebook.com/electrolobsterproject; mains €17-25; ⏰7pm-late Tue-Thu, from 5pm Fri-Sun) This bar-club-restaurant has outside seating in a lovely spot overlooking Balluta Bay. There's nowhere else like this on Malta, with a bar and restaurant upstairs, and a small club/venue downstairs with live gigs. Cuisine is Sicilian with a healthy modern twist, and there's a separate vegetarian menu. Drinks include cocktails and smoothies made with fresh fruit. Check Facebook for what's scheduled.

City of London PUB

(☎21331706; www.facebook.com/www.cityoflondonmalta.net; 193 Triq il-Kbira; ⏰11am-late Mon-Sat, from 10am Sun) This tiny pub, almost in St Julian's, has been open since 1914. It's packed at weekends, and there's a great party atmosphere, plus outside seating. It's popular in the gay scene but everyone is welcome; there's a nicely mixed crowd of expats, locals and students.

Shopping

Sliema's Triq ix-Xatt and Triq it-Torri comprise Malta's prime shopping area. There are some decent shoe shops and clothing labels, including mainstream fashion labels. The shopping mall at Tigné Point (p79), on the tip of the peninsula, dwarfs all competition, with big-name chains. The area around Sliema High St (Triq it-Torri) running uphill from the waterfront is also a worthwhile shopping destination.

Sunset Records MUSIC
(☎2133 8835; www.facebook.com/sunsetrecordsmalta; 57 Triq San Piju V; ⊙noon-7pm Tue-Fri, 10am-5pm Sat) A cool discovery in the backstreets of Sliema with a very surprising selection of modern and vintage vinyl. Well worth the short stroll uphill from the restaurant strip.

Information

Police Station (☎2133 2282; cnr Triq Manwel Dimech & Triq Rudolfu; ⊙24hr)

Post Office (118 Triq Manwel Dimech; ⊙7.30am-1pm Mon-Sat)

Getting There & Away

BUS

Buses to Valletta and around the island leave from the **bus terminus** on Sliema Strand. Buses 202 and 203 (10 minutes, half-hourly) run to St Julian's and Paceville. Catch X2 (50 minutes, every 45 minutes) from the airport. Other buses include: **12/13** (Valletta), **202** (Ta'Qali Crafts Village, Rabat and Mdina) and **222** Ċirkewwa (for Gozo ferries), via Buġibba.

Night buses, running between midnight and 3am or 4am on Friday and Saturday nights, include the **N11** (Buġibba, Mellieħa and Ċirkewwa (for Gozo ferries)) and **N13** (Valletta).

BOAT

Valletta Ferry Services – Sliema (☎2346 3862; www.vallettaferryservices.com; single/return adult €1.50/2.80, child €0.50/0.90; ⊙7am-7pm Nov-May, to 12.15am Jun-Oct) operates ferries to Valletta's Marsamxett Harbour, which take around five minutes.

St Julian's & Paceville

St Julian's, on a prong of peninsula just north of Sliema, is as frenetic as it gets in Malta, a hubbub of restaurants, bars and English-language schools. Glitzy developments, such as Portomaso Marina, are ideal settings for cocktails with a view.

More rough and ready is Paceville, a few streets to the west of St Julian's – it's full of pubs, clubs and 'gentlemen's clubs', where a young party-loving crowd see it out until dawn. Following the recent expansion of after-dark options in Valletta, Paceville has definitely lost some of its night-time appeal, though. If you're in Malta to learn English, you'll probably enjoy the area's student vibe, but for a more stylish and grown-up night out, head to Valletta.

Sights & Activities

Portomaso Apartment & Marina Complex AREA
(www.themarinarestaurants.com) The glitzy development of Portomaso is overlooked by the towering Hilton Hotel, and centres on a marina ringed by restaurants and bars. It's a popular place to hang out, drink and dine while watching the sun bounce off the yachts and the water. Dining options include Italian, Thai and Japanese, and it's the perfect place for a sunset cocktail.

St George's Bay BEACH
Most of the beaches around St Julian's are of the bare rock or private lido variety (the five-star hotels offer beach clubs and water sports), but at the head of St George's Bay there's a small, sandy beach.

Villa Dragonara HISTORIC BUILDING
Villa Dragonara, an aristocratic residence that became the Dragonara Casino in 1964, is dramatically set on the rocky southern headland of St George's Bay. It was built in 1870 as the summer residence of the Marquis Scicluna, a wealthy banker.

Divewise DIVING
(☎2135 6441; www.divewise.com.mt; Westin Dragonara Resort; courses from €60) Respected dive school with a great team of instructors.

Eating

★**Crust** CAFE €€
(☎2138 0976; www.facebook.com/crustdelibake; Triq il-Mensija; snacks & mains €8-11; ⊙8.30am-11pm Tue-Sun, to 4pm Mon;) Settle in for great views on Crust's rooftop terrace high above Spinola Bay and enjoy excellent baking, including homestyle pies and buttery croissants. Gourmet deli sandwiches join healthy options like quinoa and acai breakfast bowls, and the spicy Colombian eggs are a good way to start the day. In the afternoon, gin cocktails are an essential diversion.

★**Shoreditch** CAFE €€
(☎21386748; www.facebook.com/shoreditchmalta; 43 Triq il-Wilga; mains €8-18; ⊙10.30am-10pm Mon, Wed & Thu, to 10.30pm Fri & Sat, to 4pm & 6.30-10.30pm Sun;) With a name refer-

encing London's hip 'hood, Shoreditch has a lot to live up to, and it doesn't disappoint. Sit outside on the corner terrace and partner a Blue 'Shroom burger (bacon, mushrooms and blue cheese), with a Maltesers (naturally) shake. Breakfasts include possibly Malta's best eggs Benedict, and later in the day classic cocktails like mojitos take centre stage.

Gululu MALTESE €€
(☎2133 3431; www.gululu.com.mt; 133 Ix-Xatt ta'Spinola; mains €12-20; ⏱noon-11pm) Offering water's-edge dining, this place has balconies overlooking Spinola Bay, where you can enjoy homestyle favourites such as *aljotta* (fish soup) and *torta al-fenek* (rabbit pie). It's packed with Maltese families on Sundays.

Avenue MEDITERRANEAN €€
(☎2131 1753; https://theavenuemalta.com; Triq Gort; mains €8-30; ⏱12.30-2.30pm & 6-11.30pm) Enduringly popular Avenue now takes up a sizeable stretch of the street. Despite its size, it's always bustling – families, students and groups of friends keep coming for its lively atmosphere and huge portions of good-value meat and fish, pizza and pasta. The interior combines bright colours and stained glass; there are also tables outside along the stepped narrow street.

Cuba MEDITERRANEAN €€
(☎2010 2323; www.cafecuba.com.mt; Triq San Ġorġ; mains €12-20; ⏱10am-10pm Sun-Thu, to 11pm Fri & Sat; ✎) Always busy and lively, there's a wide-ranging, crowd-pleasing menu here, with breakfast eggs, pizza, pasta and more. the sunny terrace here is a prime people-watching spot, almost jutting over the water, with a fantastic view of Spinola Bay.

Badass Burgers BURGERS €€
(☎2138 4066; www.badassburgers.eu; 1 Triq San Ġorġ; burgers €10-16; ⏱6-11pm Mon-Thu, noon-midnight Fri-Sun) Besides 100% gourmet beef, the menu includes 'Off the Hook' burgers with prawn and haddock, and the 'Maltese' with rabbit and sausage. All are tasty and top quality, and the setting is in the shaded rear garden of a historic building. Look forward to a decent selection of craft beer too.

★**Waterbiscuit** MEDITERRANEAN €€€
(☎2376 2225; www.facebook.com/waterbiscuitmalta; Triq Santu Wistin, Intercontinental Hotel; mains €12-29; ⏱8am-11pm, dinner from 7pm) Part of the Intercontinental Hotel on the edge of Paceville, Waterbiscuit is one of Malta's best dining experiences. Outside is bustling and energetic, but the restaurant's cool interior is a soothing haven. Lunch is a more informal occasion with a brioche beef burger, while dinner's more refined dishes include seabream with a squid-ink purée, squid beignet and wild fennel.

The wine list is also one of Malta's best, and from 5.30pm to 8pm, it's 'Gin O'Clock' with happy-hour cocktails.

Zest FUSION €€€
(☎2138 7600; www.hoteljuliani.com/dining/zest; Hotel Juliani, 12 Triq San Ġorġ; mains €21-28; ⏱7-11pm Mon-Sat) In the boutique **Hotel Juliani** (☎2138 8000; d low/high season from €100/160; ❄📶🏊), this fusion restaurant loved by locals offers a mix of Japanese, Thai, Indonesian and European flavours. Book ahead and specify an outside table if you want a bay view. From Wednesday to Saturday evening during summer, Zest has a rooftop bar combining gin cocktails and Japanese-style *yakitori* skewers of grilled meat and seafood.

Sciacca Grill ITALIAN €€€
(☎2133 1310; www.sciaccamalta.com; Triq Santu Wistin; mains €19-30, set menu €45; ⏱noon-11pm Tue-Sun, 6.30-11pm Mon) On the edge of Paceville lies this restaurant offering hearty Sicilian-style grilled meat and seafood in sophisticated yet relaxed surroundings. Choose your protein – including fresh lobster – and have it wood-fired and served with a variety of side dishes. For the hungry diner, there's the option of a four-course set menu including a platter of delicious sausages.

Lulu MEDITERRANEAN €€€
(☎2137 7211; www.facebook.com/lulurestaurantmalta; 31 Triq il-Knisja; mains €22-28; ⏱7-11pm Tue-Sat) Lulu, set on a quiet side-street close to the Portomaso complex, is informal yet sophisticated. It is prettily decorated in ochre, white and green, with a small terrace. Expect friendly service and a mod Med menu of bistro classics, including escalopes of veal and pan-roasted salmon.

🍷 Drinking & Nightlife

Nordic BAR
(☎2138 2264; www.facebook.com/thenordicbarmalta; St Rita's Steps; ⏱6pm-late Mon-Sat, from 2pm Sun) This popular Scandinavian-style bar is in the thick of Paceville's party strip. It has wood-lined walls, and like most bars it has TV screens showing live sport.

St Julian's & Paceville

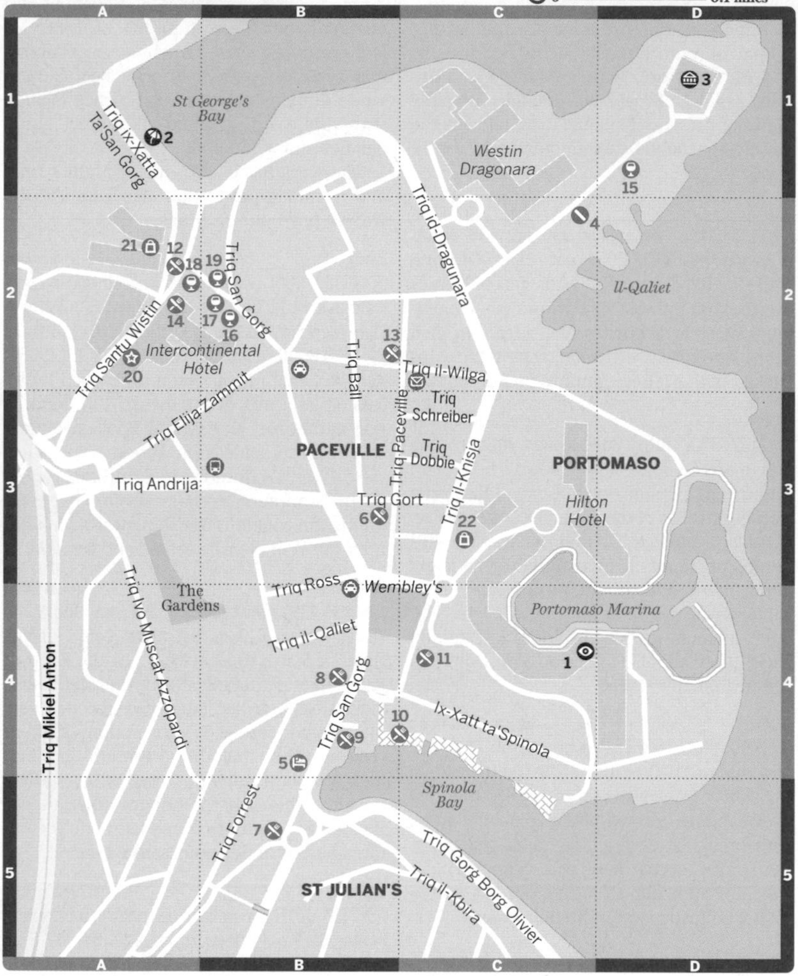

Hugo's Lounge

LOUNGE

(☎ 2138 2264; www.hugosloungemalta.com; Triq San Ġorġ; ⏲ noon-1am) Hugo's, on one of Paceville's main drags, is a lively alfresco, sleek-looking bar, and the nicest of the many 'Hugo' options in the area. It's a great place for cocktails and lounging on sofas, and you can soak up the booze with a menu of well-executed Asian food (mains from €14 to €21).

Bedouin Bar

BAR

(www.bedouinbarmalta.com; Triq Dragonara; ⏲ 10pm-4am Fri Jun-Sep) This waterside chill-out space, at the Westin Dragonara, is all white curtains and sofas, and has sparkling views over to St Julian's. It's popular with a mix of locals and tourists, and is a great place to hang out on a summer night over a cocktail listening to loungey DJ sounds.

Havana 808

CLUB

(☎ 2137 4500; www.facebook.com/havana808; 82 Triq San Ġorġ; ⏲ 8pm-4am) A mixed menu of R&B, soul, hip hop and commercial favourites keeps the crowds happy here.

Shadow Lounge

BAR

(☎ 7909 8181; www.shadowloungemalta.com; St Rita's Steps; ⏲ 8pm-late) On the 2nd floor above Hugo's Lounge, this place is more

St Julian's & Paceville

Sights
1 Portomaso Apartment & Marina Complex....C4
2 St George's Bay....A1
3 Villa Dragonara....D1

Activities, Courses & Tours
4 Divewise....C2

Sleeping
5 Hotel Juliani....B4

Eating
6 Avenue....B3
7 Badass Burgers....B5
8 Crust....B4
9 Cuba....B4
10 Gululu....C4
11 Lulu....C4
12 Sciacca Grill....A2
13 Shoreditch....B2
14 Waterbiscuit....A2
Zest....(see 5)

Drinking & Nightlife
15 Bedouin Bar....D1
16 Havana 808....B2
17 Hugo's Lounge....B2
18 Native Bar....A2
19 Nordic....B2
Shadow Lounge....(see 17)

Entertainment
20 Eden Century Cinemas....A2

Shopping
21 Bay Street Complex....A2
22 Portomaso Shopping Complex....C3

sophisticated than many of Paceville's other operations, and attracts an older crowd (in their 20s rather than their teens). The music policy is house and the vibe is laid-back.

Level 22 BAR
(☎2310 2222; www.22.com.mt; Level 22, Portomaso Tower; ⏰9.30pm-4am Wed-Sun) Sleek and glitzily chic, lounge-bar Level 22 is ideal if you're in the mood for cocktails with a touch of swank. Situated on the 22nd floor of Portomaso Tower, the bar has square-cornered sofas and an amazing view over the lights of Portomaso and St Julian's and out to sea. It turns into a club Friday and Saturday nights.

Native Bar BAR
(☎2138 0635; www.nativemalta.com; St Rita's Steps; ⏰11am-late, closed Wed Oct-May) This bar on Paceville's party street is always buzzing and has some of the longest hours on the strip. Its indoor and outdoor areas are generally packed with cocktail- and beer-slurping hedonists. If you tire of the flirtatious action there's live sport on TV.

Entertainment

Eden Century Cinemas CINEMA
(☎2371 0400; www.edencinemas.com.mt; Triq Santu Wistin) This large complex has 17 screens (on both sides of the road) showing first-run films. Adult tickets cost €7.90.

Shopping

St Julian's has several worth-a-browse small malls, such as the **Bay Street Complex** (www.baystreet.com.mt; Triq Santu Wistin; ⏰10am-10pm) and **Portomaso Shopping Complex** (Triq il-Knisja; ⏰8am-10pm), that sell clothes, swimwear and accessories, as well as foodstuffs.

Information

Be aware that there are occasional outbreaks of alcohol-fuelled violence in Paceville late at night. The nightlife zone is also noisy, so you may prefer to seek accommodation elsewhere.

Police Station (☎2133 2196; Triq San Ġorġ; ⏰24hr)

Post Office (Lombard Bank, Triq Paceville; ⏰8am-1.30pm Mon-Fri, to 12.30pm Sat)

Getting There & Around

Buses 202 and 13 (10 minutes, half-hourly) run from Sliema to St Julian's and Paceville. The main **bus terminus** for Paceville and St Julian's is located just north of Triq Gort.

Direct bus services to/from St Julian's and Paceville include the 202 to Ta'Qali Crafts Village, Rabat and Mdina (20 minutes, hourly); bus 212 along the coast to Buġibba (34 minutes, hourly); bus 222 (60 minutes, hourly) to Ċirkewwa (for Gozo ferries) via Buġibba; and bus X2 (55 minutes, hourly) to the airport. From Valletta catch buses 14, 15 or 16 (25 minutes, frequent).

Night buses, running between midnight and 3am or 4am on Friday and Saturday nights, include the N11 for Buġibba, Mellieħa and Ċirkewwa (for Gozo ferries); the N13 for Valletta and the N10 to/from the airport.

Wembleys (p181) provides a reliable 24-hour radio taxi service. There's also a busy **taxi rank** close to the intersection of Triq San Ġorġ and Triq il-Wilga in Paceville.

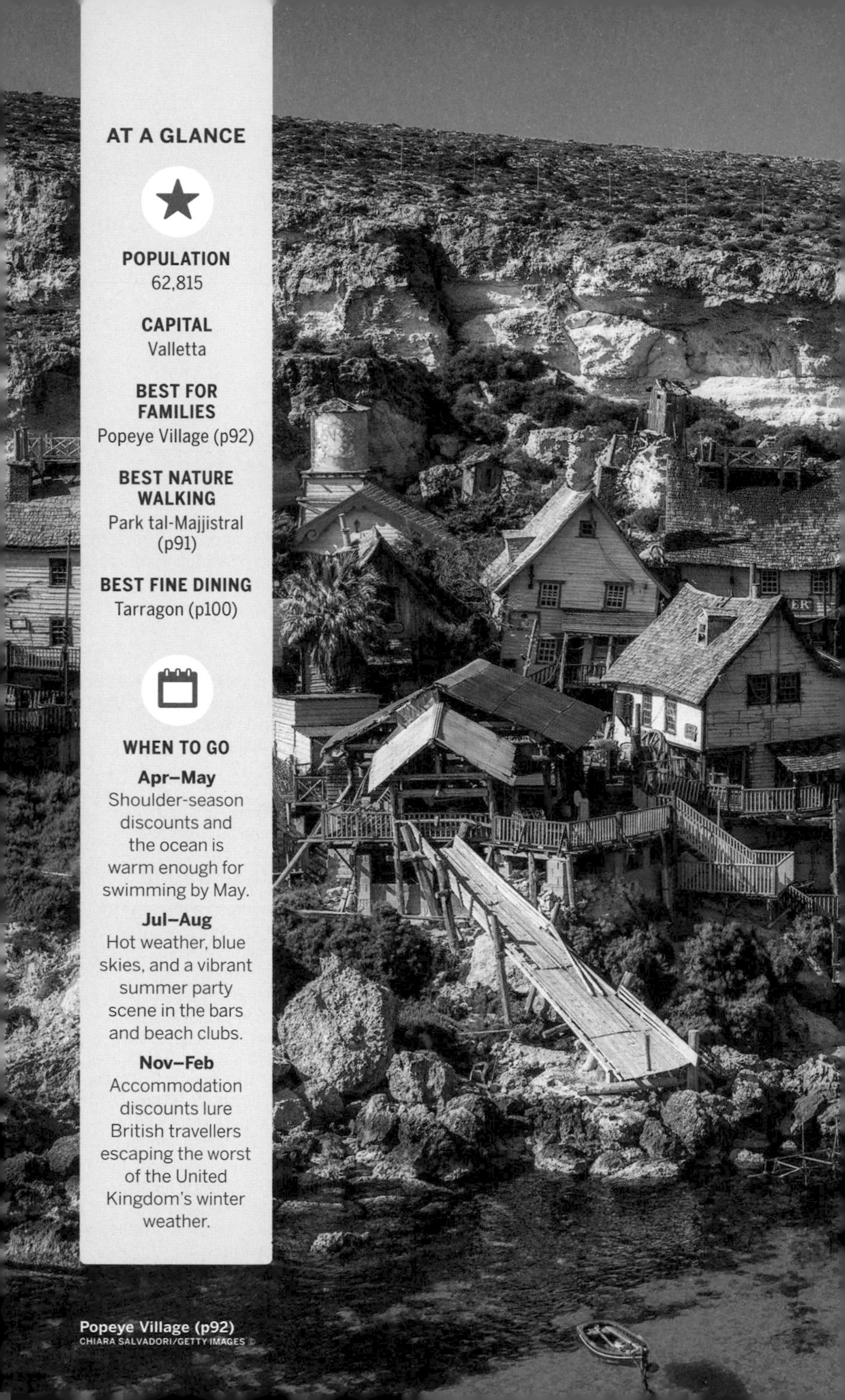

AT A GLANCE

POPULATION
62,815

CAPITAL
Valletta

BEST FOR FAMILIES
Popeye Village (p92)

BEST NATURE WALKING
Park tal-Majjistral (p91)

BEST FINE DINING
Tarragon (p100)

WHEN TO GO

Apr–May
Shoulder-season discounts and the ocean is warm enough for swimming by May.

Jul–Aug
Hot weather, blue skies, and a vibrant summer party scene in the bars and beach clubs.

Nov–Feb
Accommodation discounts lure British travellers escaping the worst of the United Kingdom's winter weather.

Popeye Village (p92)
CHIARA SALVADORI/GETTY IMAGES ©

Northern Malta

Sandy beaches, water sports, boat trips, birdwatching, horse-riding, and walks along the dramatic coastline – Malta's north is a prime location for holiday fun.

Buġibba and Qawra form Malta's largest resort area, and the area has the added attraction of the fabulous Malta National Aquarium on the beautifully landscaped Qawra promenade. Beaches range from the wonderfully accessible Mellieħa Bay, a long stretch of white sand speckled with sunbeds, kiosks and water sports, to the more remote Għajn Tuffieħa Bay, less crowded because of its steeply stepped approach.

You can go off the beaten track at Selmun Bay, or roam to discover splendid views from the cliffs at Ras il-Qammieħ. It's also the heartland of Malta's rural community, and the landscape is dotted with farms, orchards and vineyards.

INCLUDES

Northern Malta Highlights

1 Marfa Peninsula (p94) Exploring the dramatic underwater seascape while scuba-diving off this more rugged and remote part of Malta.

2 Ras il-Qammieħ (p94) Exulting in vast coastal views from this wild headland.

3 Għajn Tuffieħa Bay (p90) Making the long climb down to near-empty sands on a quiet spring day.

4 Malta National Aquarium (p97) Enjoying the setting on the Qawra promenade and the region's fabulous underwater inhabitants.

5 Golden Bay (p90) Taking a speedboat trip across cobalt waters, launching from this lovely bay and taking in the beautiful isle of Comino.

6 Rural Malta (p101) Discovering the best of northern Malta's hard-working farming community on a day trip with Merill Eco Tours.

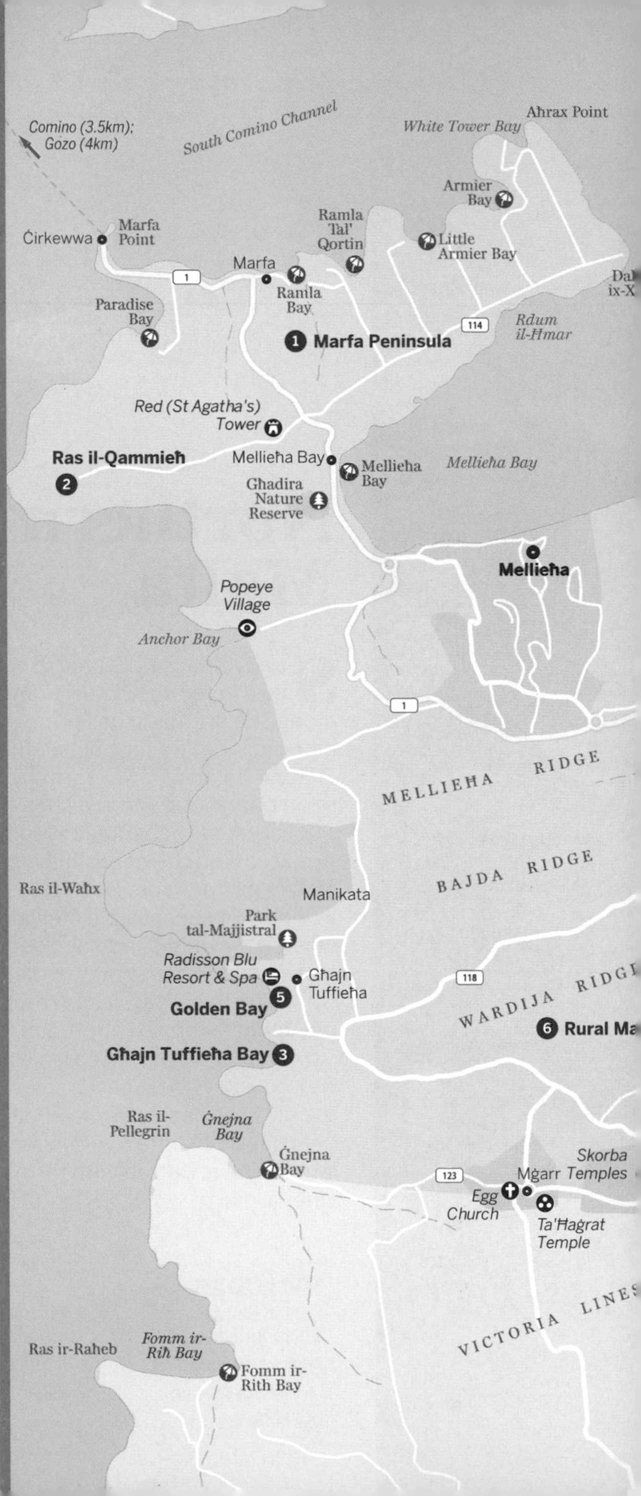

0 2 km
0 1 mile
MEDITERRANEAN SEA
Għajn Ħadid Tower
St Paul's Islands
Fort Campbell
Malta National Aquarium
4
St Paul's Bay
Qawra
Salina Bay
St Paul's Bay Village
Buġibba
Xemxija
Għajn Rasul
Salina Nature Reserve
Qalet Marku
Qalet Marku Tower
Baħar iċ-Ċagħaq Bay
Baħar iċ-Ċagħaq
Splash & Fun Park
St Julian's (250m)
Wardija
Burmarrad
VICTORIA LINES
San Pawl
Għargħur
Tat-Tarġa
Naxxar
Mosta
Balzan
1
16
17
18

Golden Bay & Għajn Tuffieħa

The fertile Pwales Valley stretches 4km from the head of St Paul's Bay to Għajn Tuffieħa. Here, two of Malta's best sandy beaches draw crowds of sun-worshippers. In close proximity, the Park tal-Majjistral offers excellent walking with sweeping coastal views.

◉ Sights & Activities

Għajn Tuffieħa Bay BEACH
Għajn Tuffieħa Bay (ayn too-*fee*-ha, meaning 'Spring of the Apples') is even lovelier than neighbouring Golden Bay – no buildings overlook it, and it's less busy, as it's reached via a long flight of 186 steps from the nearby car park. It's a 250m strip of red-brown sand, backed by slopes covered in acacia and tamarisk trees and guarded by a 17th-century watchtower. Sun loungers can be hired and snacks and drinks are available.

Golden Bay BEACH
The lovely sandy arc of Golden Bay has a beautiful setting, and is a popular place to hang out, with a few cafes, water sports and boat trips available. It's not too built up; there's just one mammoth five-star hotel rising above the shoreline.

Orangeshark H2O DIVING
(☑ 2356 1950; www.orangeshark.eu; Radisson Blu Resort & Spa, Golden Bay; courses from €80) This five-star PADI centre is attached to the five-star Radisson on Golden Bay. Snorkelling courses are also available.

Golden Bay Horse Riding HORSE RIDING
(☑ 2157 3360; www.goldenbayhorseriding.com; 1hr ride/90min sunset ride €20/30) Signposted from Golden Bay, this horse-riding centre offers enjoyable rides for all levels of experience on fields overlooking the northwest beaches. Book ahead.

Borg Watersports WATER SPORTS
(☑ 2157 3272; peterborg62@gmail.com; Golden Bay; ☺ 10am-6pm Apr-Nov) In Golden Bay, Borg Watersports has a range of activities: SUPs (stand-up paddle boards; €15 per hour), one-/two-person canoes (€14/18 per hour), powerboats (€200 per hour), sailboats (€35 per hour), jet skis (€60 per 20 minutes) and pedaloes (€20 per hour). It also operates trips to the Blue Lagoon, and parasailing (from €50) and waterskiing (from €40) are both available.

★ Charlie's Discovery Speedboat Trips BOATING
(☑ 9948 6949; www.facebook.com/charliesboat trips; adult/child €12/10, Comino trip €20/12; ☺ coastal trip noon & 2.30pm, Comino 4pm) Charlie is a knowledgable, award-winning guide. He'll take you on an exhilarating speedboat trip to view cliffs, bays and grottoes, including Għajn Tuffieħa, Ġnejna and Fomm ir-Riħ, and you'll get a chance to swim in Smurf-blue waters. Look out for Charlie, in his red hat and yellow T-shirt, on the Golden Bay beach.

From April to October Charlie also operates a daily trip, which includes a 1½-hour swim, to Comino's Blue Lagoon – a wonderful chance to visit once the crowds have left.

✖ Eating

Your best bet for a meal is to brush the sand off your toes and head to one of the upmarket options at the 10-storey **Radisson Blu Resort & Spa** (☑ 2356 1000; www.radissonblu.com; r low/high season from €130/245; ✱ @ ☏ ☲). Cheaper options include the fast-food kiosks near Golden Bay.

Agliolio MEDITERRANEAN €€
(☑ 2356 1000; Radisson Blu Resort & Spa, Golden Bay; mains €11-27; ☺ noon-4pm & 6.30-10pm) Cheery, noisy and aqua-coloured Agliolio has an appealing Med-flavoured menu heavy on pizza, pasta and salads; nab a table outside overlooking the beach.

Pebbles CAFE €€
(☑ 2356 1000; Radisson Blu Resort & Spa, Golden Bay; mains €10-15; ☺ 10am-10pm) The fab outdoor terrace here is perfect for coffee, cake, light meals or cocktails (€7 to €12). Platters (€17 to €34) are a good option for couples.

Essence MEDITERRANEAN €€€
(☑ 2356 1111; Radisson Blu Resort & Spa, Golden Bay; mains €22-32; ☺ 7-10pm Tue-Sat) Romantic Essence is this area's number-one pick for a fancy-pants dinner with beautiful sea views. Cooking is sophisticated with delicious and surprising combinations of flavours using seasonal ingredients. Menu highlights could include salmon ceviche with a citrus marmalade or duck breast with a pomegranate and walnut sauce. Bookings are recommended.

❶ Getting There & Away

Bus 223 serves Buġibba (25 minutes, hourly) via St Paul's Bay (10 minutes). Bus 225 runs to/from Sliema and St Julian's (50 to 70 minutes,

OFF THE BEATEN TRACK

PARK TAL-MAJJISTRAL

The area between Golden Bay and Anchor Bay was once earmarked for a golf course, but opposition from environmental groups led to the creation of **Park tal-Majjistral** (☎2152 1291; www.majjistral.org). Information boards show walking trails, and the park arranges guided walks (usually adult/child €5/3) from October to April, generally on Sundays, including sunset walks. Also available are 2½-hour snorkelling trips (adult/child €12/10; July to September; over-nines only). Check the website for upcoming events, and book walks and snorkelling via email (walks@majjistral.org).

The park protects a region of wild sea cliffs and limestone boulder scree, home to plants such as euphorbia, Maltese rock centaury and golden samphire, and wildlife such as Mediterranean chameleons. Bus 44 from Valletta (55 minutes, half-hourly) stops at the Tuffieħa stop at the park's southern end.

half hourly). Bus 44 goes to/from Valletta (one hour, hourly), while bus 101 run between here to Mellieħa (15 minutes) and Ċirkewwa (20 minutes) five times a day.

Mġarr & Around

POP 3629

The village of Mġarr (mm-*jarr*), 2km to the southeast of Għajn Tuffieħa (not to be confused with Mġarr on Gozo), is dominated by the dome of the famous Egg Church. Ancient and WWII historical sites are also features of the area, and it's a short drive from an excellent beach.

Sights

Egg Church CHURCH

Mġarr's Church of the Assumption was built in the 1930s with money raised by local parishioners, largely from the sale of local eggs. Some estimates put the number sold at more than 300,000.

Mġarr Shelter HISTORIC SITE

(☎2157 3235; www.il-barri.com.mt; Triq il-Kbira; adult/child €3/1.50; ⏲9am-1pm Tue-Sat, 10-11.30am Sun) The Mġarr Shelter was used by locals during the WWII bombings of Malta (enter through Il-Barri restaurant). You can only imagine the long uncomfortable hours spent down here in the humidity, 12m underground, but to show that life went on regardless, there are rooms on display that served as classrooms and hospitals.

Ta'Ħaġrat Temple ARCHAEOLOGICAL SITE

(☎2123 9545; www.heritagemalta.org; Triq San Pietru; adult/child incl the Skorba Temples €3.50/2.50; ⏲9am-5pm) The site of the Ta'Ħaġrat Temple, dating from around 3600 to 3300 BC, is concealed down a side street off Triq Fisher. There's not that much to see, except a few tumbled stones, but they represent some of the earliest temple buildings in Malta. Note that tickets are not available at the site and must be bought online, from any other Heritage Malta site, or from the Mġarr Snack Bar just off Mġarr's village square

Skorba Temples ARCHAEOLOGICAL SITE

(☎2158 0590; www.heritagemalta.org; Triq Sant'Anna; adult/child incl Ta'Ħaġrat Temple €3.50/2.50; ⏲9am-5pm) The excavation of the Skorba Temples, in the neighbouring village of Żebbiegħ, exposed two temples and some habitations dating to the temple builders' phase, and some even predating this, which are thus the oldest prehistoric structures discovered on the islands. Tickets are not available at the site and must be bought online, from other Heritage Malta sites, or from the Mġarr Snack Bar off Mġarr's village square.

Ġnejna Bay BEACH

This gentle red-sand beach is backed by terraced hillsides and has boathouses built into the rocks to one side. Built in 1637 by the Knights of St John, the Lippija Tower on the northern skyline makes a good target for a short walk.

Eating

Il-Barri MALTESE €€

(☎2157 3235; www.il-barri.com.mt; Triq il-Kbira; mains €9-22; ⏲9am-11pm Tue-Sun, 5.30-11pm Mon) Run by the same family since 1940, Il-Barri is on the Mġarr village square. The slick interior is a surprise, with its monochrome and wavy ceiling. It's a favourite local venue for a *fenkata* (rabbit casserole) and other Maltese-as-they-come local favourites such as *aljotta* (fish broth), quail and horsemeat, plus pizzas in the evening. Expect monster portions.

Getting There & Away

Bus 44 (48 minutes, half-hourly) runs from Valletta to Mġarr.

Mellieħa & Around

POP 10,090

The small town of Mellieħa (mell-*ee*-ha) perches picturesquely atop the ridge between St Paul's Bay and Mellieħa Bay. It's a popular resort, but hasn't been overdeveloped due to its distance from the beach, and outside the centre, the town has a laid-back, local feel. There are numerous large hotels in town, but Mellieħa retains a certain elegance, and is home to some excellent restaurants. A couple of friendly new guesthouses also provide a more local experience. A 15-minute walk leads down the steep hill to Mellieħa Bay (also known as Għadira Bay), the longest and most popular sandy beach in the Maltese Islands, with white sands, clear water, water sports, sunbeds and ice creams.

Sights

Mellieħa Bay BEACH

The warm, shallow waters and soft white sand of Mellieħa Bay are easily accessible (via bus or you can park on the road that backs the beach), safe for kids and great for swimming. Add the waterskiers, rental canoes, banana rides, parasailing boats, and the fact that the reliable northeasterly breeze blowing into the bay in summer makes it ideal for windsurfing, and you'll begin to realise that Mellieħa Bay is not the place to get away from it all.

Church of Our Lady of Victory CHURCH

(6.30-8.30am & 5-7.30pm, English-language Mass 10am Sun) The Church of Our Lady of Victory sits prominently on a rocky spur overlooking Mellieħa Bay. It's attached to the Sanctuary of Our Lady of Mellieħa, which has been a place of pilgrimage since medieval times – it is believed to have been blessed by St Paul himself. Its walls are covered with votive offerings, while the fresco of the Madonna above the altar is said to have been painted by St Luke.

Grotto of the Madonna CHURCH

(8am-6pm Sep-May, to 7pm Jun-Aug) Across the main street from the Church of Our Lady of Victory, a gate in the wall and a flight of steps lead down to the Grotto of the Madonna, a shrine dedicated to the Virgin. It is set deep in a cave lit by flickering candles, beside a spring with waters that are reputed to heal sick children. Baby clothes hung on the walls are votive offerings given in thanks for successful cures.

Mellieħa Air-Raid Shelters HISTORIC SITE

(7952 1970; Triq il-Madonna tal-Għar; adult/child €2.40/0.70; 9am-3pm Mon-Sat) The Mellieħa air-raid shelters were dug by hand to shelter the town's population from WWII bombs. It's one of the largest underground shelters in Malta, with a depth of 12m and a length of around 500m, and gives a haunting sense of what it was like to shelter down here. Spooky mannequins and some furnishings bring home the cramped environment, where each person was allotted 0.6 sq metres of space.

Għadira Nature Reserve NATURE RESERVE

(2134 7645; www.birdlifemalta.org; Triq Il-Marfa; donations welcome; 10am-4pm Sat & Sun Nov-May) FREE Close to Mellieħa Bay is the Għadira Nature Reserve, managed by BirdLife Malta volunteers. This area of shallow, reedy ponds surrounded by scrub is an important resting area for migrating birds (over 200 species have been recorded). The name, pronounced aa-*dee*-ra, means 'marsh'. Catch buses 42 and 49 from Valletta (90 minutes, half-hourly) to the Għadira stop. The entrance to the nature reserve is across the road from the beachfront Sundancer Kiosk.

Selmun (Imgiebah) Bay BEACH

Secluded Selmun Bay is an adventure to find, and a great place to escape the crowds; bring refreshments and sunshades. Take the road to Selmun Palace from Mellieħa, but turn left at Selmun chapel, before the palace. Follow the track for 1.75km, whereupon the road will bend to the right and you'll reach a crossroads. Take a left towards the coast and drive 200m, where you'll find a parking spot; you can walk to the beach from there.

Popeye Village AMUSEMENT PARK

(Anchor Bay; 2152 4782; www.popeyemalta.com; adult/child Jul & Aug €17/13.50, rest of year €15/12; 9.30am-5.30pm Mar-Jul, Sep & Oct, to 7pm Aug, to 4.30pm Nov-Feb) Steep-sided, pretty little Anchor Bay was named after the many Roman anchors that were found on the seabed by divers, some of which can be seen in the Maritime Museum (p69) at Vittoriosa. In 1979 Anchor Bay was transformed into the ramshackle fishing village of Sweethaven, the set for the 1980 Hollywood musical *Popeye,* starring Robin Williams. The vintage set still stands and houses an old-fashioned

Mellieħa

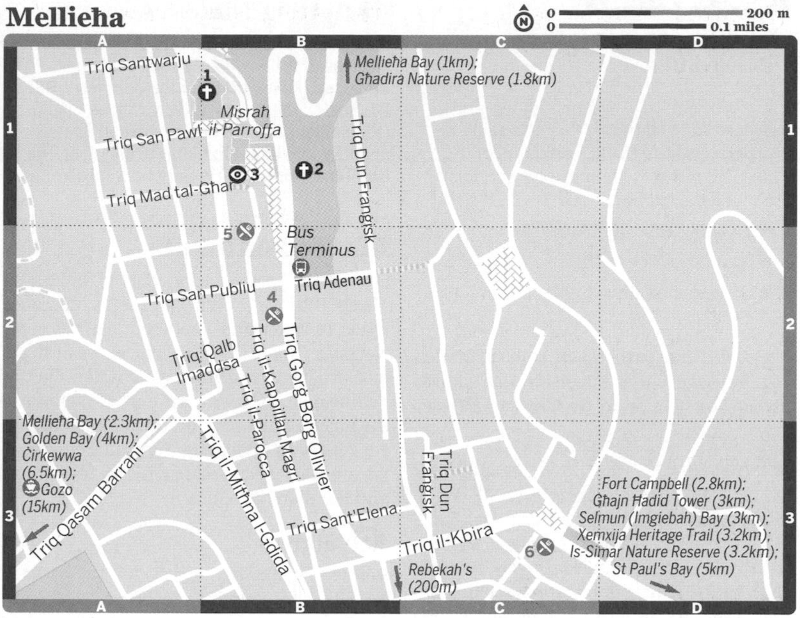

theme park. Admission includes animation shows, splash pools and a 15-minute boat ride. You can pay extra to make a movie (€6), which is particularly good fun.

Fort Campbell FORT

The derelict Fort Campbell is an abandoned coastal defence built by the British between WWI and WWII. To reach the fort, turn right just before you reach Selmun Palace and continue for around 1km. The headland commands a fine view over St Paul's Islands, and you can hike down to the coastal salt pans of Blata il-Bajda and around to Mistra Bay, or westwards along the cliff top to the ruined **Għajn Ħadid Tower** above the little beach at Mġieba Bay.

Activities

Sea Shell Dive Centre DIVING

(2152 1062; www.seashelldivingmalta.com; Adeera Beach Complex; introductory dives from €70; 8am-5pm Mon-Sat, to 2pm Sun) Helpful dive centre offering PADI courses and more.

Eating

★ **Munchies** MEDITERRANEAN €€

(2157 6416; www.munchies.com.mt; Marfa Rd, Mellieħa Bay; mains €10-25; 8am-11pm;) Multiple recommendations from local accommodation owners and an absolute waterfront location put Munchies near the top of Mellieħa's eateries. The menu covers the usual Mediterranean bases of *ftira,* pizza and pasta, and the views along Mellieħa's beach are superb.

There's also a private lido belonging to Munchies. Did we mention the ocean is less than 1m from some tables?

★ **Commando** MEDITERRANEAN €€€

(2152 3459; www.commandorestaurant.com; Misraħ Iz-Żjara tal-Papa; mains €17-27; 6-10.30pm Tue-Sat, noon-3pm Sun) Recently opened in a 300-year-old building on Mellieħa's heritage main square, the gutsy Mediterranean menu at Commando features a cassoulet of slow-cooked pork and beans, or braised-beef ravioli, as well as a risotto of local rabbit. Served with local honey, the *mqaret*

Mellieħa

Sights

1 Church of Our Lady of Victory B1
2 Grotto of the Madonna B1
3 Mellieħa Air-Raid Shelters B1

Eating

4 Arches B2
5 Commando B2
6 Il-Mitħna C3

LOCAL KNOWLEDGE

DIVING OFF THE MARFA PENINSULA

Some of Malta's most spectacular dive sites lie off the Marfa Peninsula, including Marfa Point, Tugboat Rozi and Ċirkewwa Arch. Local dive schools include the following:

- Sea Shell Dive Centre (p93)
- Dive Deep Blue (p99)
- Buddies Dive Cove (p99)

(deep-fried date pastries) are some of Malta's best. You can either sit inside the vaulted interior, or outside to take in the alfresco views.

★Rebekah's MEDITERRANEAN €€€
(☎2152 1145; www.rebekahs.com.mt; 12 Triq it-Tgham; mains €18-28; ⏰7-10.30pm Mon-Sat & noon-2.30pm Sun Nov-May, 7-10.30pm Mon-Sun Jun-Oct) Rebekah's is tucked away in Mellieħa's back streets, but it's worth seeking out (head south to the end of Triq Franġisk, then take a right). The menu ranges from local king prawns and pan-roasted salmon to a hearty and delicious rabbit stew.

Il-Mitħna MALTESE €€€
(☎2152 0404; www.mithna.com; 45 Triq il-Kbira; mains €18-29; ⏰6-10.30pm Mon-Sat, noon-3pm Sun) This is a lovely place to dine – the restaurant is housed in a 400-year-old windmill, the only survivor of three that once sat atop Mellieħa Ridge. There are outdoor tables in a pretty courtyard, and a menu of local dishes with a creative twist, such as rabbit in a coconut curry sauce.

The set menu (€25) served between 6pm and 7pm is a bargain.

Arches MEDITERRANEAN €€€
(☎2152 3460; www.archesrestaurant.com.mt; 113 Triq Ġorġ Borg Olivier; mains €26-31; ⏰7-11pm Mon-Sat) This acclaimed restaurant is large, elegant and stately, and decorated in white set against terracotta walls; the menu, prices and service all befit the chic decor and formality. The food is accomplished, delicious and adventurous, featuring dishes such as monkfish tortellini and quail with rosemary. Book ahead.

The tasting menu (with/without wine matches €47/67) is a leisurely and decadent experience.

Getting There & Away

Buses 41 and 42 from Valletta pass through Mellieħa (one hour, hourly), and continue to Ċirkewwa (20 minutes) for the Gozo ferry. Bus 221 also connects with Ċirkewwa, plus Buġibba (15 minutes). Bus 101 goes to Golden Bay (15 minutes) and Għajn Tuffieħa (18 minutes). The **Bus Terminus** is on Triq Ġorġ Borg Olivier.

Marfa Peninsula

On the far northeastern edge of Malta, the Marfa Peninsula offers access by unsealed roads to quiet and sheltered beaches – on weekdays anyway – excellent views of nearby Gozo, and pleasant coastal walks. On the peninsula's northwestern end, Ċirkewwa is the busy departure point for car and passenger ferries to Gozo, and for sightseeing boat trips to the much smaller island of Comino and the Blue Lagoon.

Sights

Red (St Agatha's) Tower FORTRESS
(☎2122 0358; www.dinlarthelwa.org; adult/child €2/free; ⏰10am-4pm mid-Sep–mid-Jun, to 7pm mid-Jun–mid-Sep) The chess-piece-like Red Tower was built in 1649 for Grand Master Lascaris, as part of the chain of signal towers that linked Valletta and Gozo; the view from its flat roof is stunning. This simple fortress is one of the more elaborate towers, and once housed a garrison of up to 49 men. The plaque above the entrance indicates that this is not a place of sanctuary, despite containing a chapel. It's staffed by volunteers and so is occasionally closed.

Ras il-Qammieħ AREA
The western headland, 129m at its highest point, commands fantastic views and feels like the end of the world. It's home to an old radar station.

Activities

Baia Beach Club BEACH
(☎2157 0942; www.baiabeachclub.com; Little Armier; ⏰lido 10am-6pm Tue-Sun May-Sep, restaurant 12.30-3.30pm Tue-Sun & 7-10.30pm Sat May-Sep) With a beautiful setting on Little Armier beach, this is a lido where you could go and hang out for a few hours or a day, with sunbeds to hire and beachside service, as well as a lovely restaurant with views upstairs offering Sicilian cooking and specialising in fresh fish and pasta.

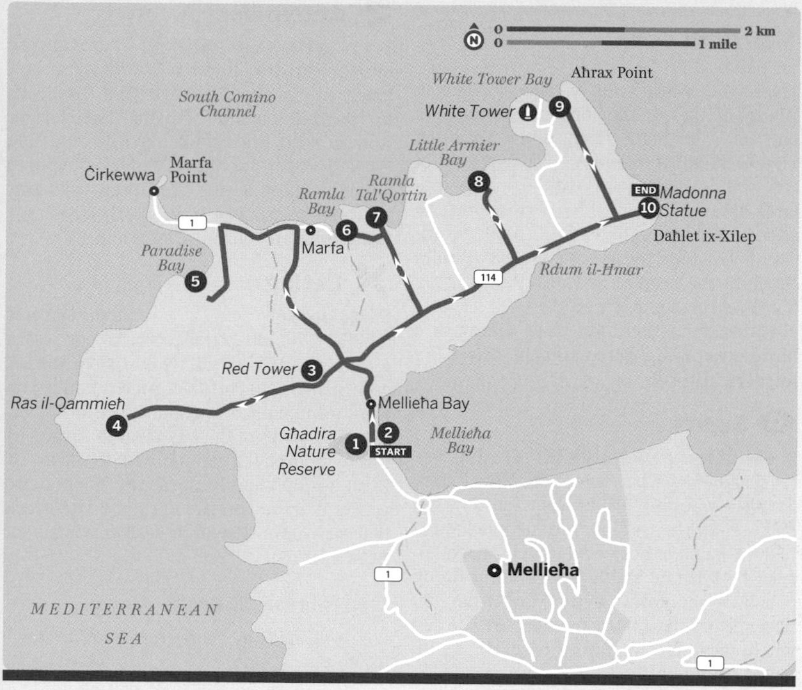

Driving Tour
Malta's Wildest Corner: The Marfa Peninsula

START GĦADIRA NATURE RESERVE
END DAĦLET IX-XILEP
LENGTH 22KM; 1½ TO TWO HOURS

This trip encompasses a nature reserve, an impressive tower, windswept coastal walks and some favourite local beaches.

Driving onto the peninsula, you'll pass the **1 Għadira Nature Reserve** (p92) on your left, with **2 Mellieħa Bay** (p92) on your right. When you reach the next junction, turn left, and aim uphill to the **3 Red Tower** (p94) and its dizzying views. From here the road gets bumpier. Drive until you reach the wild headland of **4 Ras il-Qammieħ** (p94), with more incredible views north to Gozo and south along Malta's western sea cliffs.

Next, return to the main road, following it down towards Ċirkewwa, the Gozo ferry terminal. Take the left before you reach the Paradise Bay Resort Hotel. This lane leads to **5 Paradise Bay** (🐾), a picturesque but narrow patch of sand backed by cliffs.

To access the rest of the peninsula, you'll need to drive back to the main road that runs along its spine. From here you can visit the area's little bays. First stop is **6 Ramla Bay**, its small, sandy beach monopolised by the resort of the same name; just east is **7 Ramla Tal'Qortin**, which has no sand and is surrounded by an unsightly sprawl of Maltese holiday huts.

Drive back to the main road, and you could take the second left down to **8 Little Armier Bay**, to hang out, eat and drink at the lovely Baia Beach Club. The fourth road leads to the **9 White Tower Bay**, which has another seaweed-stained patch of sand and a rash of holiday huts combining to form a small shanty town.

A track continues past the tower to the low cliffs of Aħrax Point, from which a pleasant coastal walk leads 1km south to a statue of the Madonna on **10 Daħlet ix-Xilep**. You can also reach the Madonna statue and a small chapel by following the main road east across the Marfa Peninsula.

Xemxija

POP 1100

The small, south-facing village of Xemxija (shem-*shee*-ya), on the north side of St Paul's Bay, takes its name from *xemx,* meaning 'sun' in Malti; it overlooks a lovely loop of bay, but is decked-out with low-rise custard-coloured apartment blocks that don't do a lot for the view. There are a couple of private lidos along the waterfront, but Pwales Beach at the head of St Paul's Bay is just a narrow strip of gravelly sand.

For walkers, there are trails taking in a bird-rich nature reserve and the area's Roman-era history.

Sights

Is-Simar Nature Reserve NATURE RESERVE

(☎2134 7646; www.birdlifemalta.org; Triq Il-Pwales; donations welcome; ⏰10am-4pm Sun Nov-May) FREE Is-Simar was opened in 1995 on a marshy patch of neglected land and is managed by BirdLife Malta (p35) volunteers on behalf of the government. More than 180 bird species have been recorded at the site where local and migratory bird life is protected from hunters.

The entrance is on the side street Triq Il-Pwales.

Activities

Xemxija Heritage Trail WALKING

Starting at Triq Raddet ir-Roti there is a lovely waymarked Heritage Trail that leads up the hill behind Xemxija. This former Roman road leads to Bajda ridge, passing ancient cave dwellings, Punic-Roman-era apiaries, and pilgrims' graffiti on what was a former pilgrimage trail, which takes anything from an hour to several hours.

Eating

Porto del Sol MEDITERRANEAN €€

(☎2157 3970; www.portodelsolmalta.com; Telghet ix-Xemxija; mains €9-25; ⏰6-10.30pm Tue-Sat, noon-3pm Fri-Sun) Porto del Sol is a family-run restaurant with a sunshaded outdoor terrace and views of the bay from its large picture windows. It's popular with locals for its fresh seafood and local dishes. There's also accommodation on-site in rooms with excellent sea views (low/high season apartment from €40/65).

Getting There & Away

Bus 49 (45 minutes, hourly) runs from Valletta to Xemxija.

From St Julian's and Sliema catch bus 222 (45 minutes, half hourly).

CATCHING THE FERRY FROM ĊIRKEWWA

Ċirkewwa is the port for car and passenger ferries to Gozo. Boats also leave from here to Comino.

Gozo Channel (☎2155 6114; www.gozochannel.com; foot passenger day/night €4.65/4.05, child €1.15, car & driver day/night €15.70/12.80) Operates the passenger and car ferry that shuttles between Malta's Ċirkewwa and Gozo's Mġarr. You pay on the return journey from Mġarr.

United Comino Ferries (☎9940 6529; www.unitedcominoferries.com; adult/child return €10/5; ⏰from Ċirkewwa & Marfa 8.30am-3pm, to 4pm in summer) Serves Comino island from Ċirkewwa and the Marfa jetty. Services take 35 minutes, and leave half-hourly in summer (hourly the rest of the year).

Ebsons Comino Ferries (☎2155 4991; www.cominoferryservice.com; adult/child €10/5; ⏰8.30am-3.40pm) Operates ferries from Ċirkewwa and Marfa, as well as between Mġarr and Comino.

By car, you can make the trip to/from Valletta in about 45 minutes. A taxi from Malta International Airport to Ċirkewwa costs €32.

Buses running from here to various destinations include the following:

41 & 42 Valletta (1¼ hours, every 20 minutes)

X1 Airport (70 minutes, hourly)

221 Buġibba (40 minutes, half-hourly)

221 Mellieħa (12 to 20 minutes, half-hourly)

222 Sliema & St Julian's (one hour, hourly)

SHARKLAB

If you visit the Malta National Aquarium (p97), you'll see some fascinating, alien-looking egg cases suspended in one of the tanks. These are shark eggs, rescued from the Pixxkerija (fish market), and some have been successfully hatched, helping to discover more about the development of oviparous (egg-laying) sharks.

Sharks tend to get bad press, but there is an organisation in Malta on their side. The NGO responsible is **Sharklab** (www.sharklab-malta.org), which is devoted to protecting elasmobranch species, namely sharks, rays and skates. Their activities include elasmobranch-spotting snorkelling trips, visits to the fish market to rescue eggs, and shark releases. If you want to protect one of the world's most misunderstood creatures, you can take part, or otherwise help by registering sightings on their website.

Buġibba, Qawra & St Paul's Bay

St Paul's Bay is named after the saint who was shipwrecked here in AD 60. Despite being a built-up area, there's a scenic view across the bobbing boats of the harbour. Although there are hotel developments, the promenade along the Qawra part of the coast is stunningly pretty, with the fantastic Malta National Aquarium at its tip. There are panoramic views from waterfront restaurants and cafes, and also some scenic rocks from which to swim. The Buġibba area is the most built up, entirely devoted to tourism, and has the most facilities.

This is the heartland of the island's cheap-and-cheerful package-holiday trade. Mobbed and lively in summer, it's full of hotels, bars and restaurants – the perfect base for a spell of inexpensive, sun-filled hedonism.

⊙ Sights

There's plenty to do along this bit of the coast, with the €15.6-million Malta National Aquarium, close to Qawra Tower, providing state-of-the-art wonder and a great focus for family fun. There are various diving and boating operators based in and around Buġibba, the free-of-charge Buġibba water park, along with a number of private lidos lining the waterfront, many offering sun lounges, water sports, swimming pools and cafe-bars.

★**Malta National Aquarium** AQUARIUM
(☑2258 8100; www.aquarium.com.mt; Triq it-Trunċiera; adult/child €13.90/7; ☉10am-6pm) Opened in 2013, this glass-and-metal starfish-shaped building perches in a sublime position on the Qawra headland, with endless blue views. It's great fun, with huge tanks showing environments that mimic the waters around the islands (for example, there's a replica of the bronze submerged Christ of the Abyss statue), as well as those further afield. There's a 12m underwater tunnel that allows visitors to walk through a huge tank, as well as another smaller tunnel to crawl through.

Daily educational sessions include learning about marine evolution and the aquarium's shark conservation program. Check the website for timings. The complex includes a children's playground (free of charge) and stunning views from its **La Nave** (www.lanave bistro.com; mains €11-26; ☉9.30am-10pm; ⊞) restaurant and outdoor cafe.

Malta Classic Car Collection MUSEUM
(☑2157 8885; www.classiccarsmalta.com; Triq it-Turisti; adult/child €9/4.50; ☉9am-6pm Mon-Fri, to 1.30pm Sat) Housed in purpose-built 3000-sq-metre premises, the Malta Classic Car Collection is a tribute to Carol Galea's love of cars. The privately owned collection of mint-condition vehicles (cars and motorbikes) includes plenty of 1950s and '60s British- and Italian-made classics, plus vintage jukeboxes and memorabilia from these eras to get you in the mood. Look for the classic blue Bugatti sports car outside.

Buġibba Water Park AMUSEMENT PARK
(☉9am-5pm Jun-Sep) FREE This is a small, fun, supervised (and free!) water park that kids will love, and includes various loopy colourful fountains that are perfect for kids running around on a hot day. There are different sections for different ages, and chairs so adults can relax (hopefully) around the edge.

Church of St Paul's Bonfire CHURCH
The old fishing village of St Paul's Bay, now merged with Buġibba, has retained something of its traditional Maltese character and has a few historical sights. The 17th-century Church of St Paul's Bonfire stands on the

Buġibba

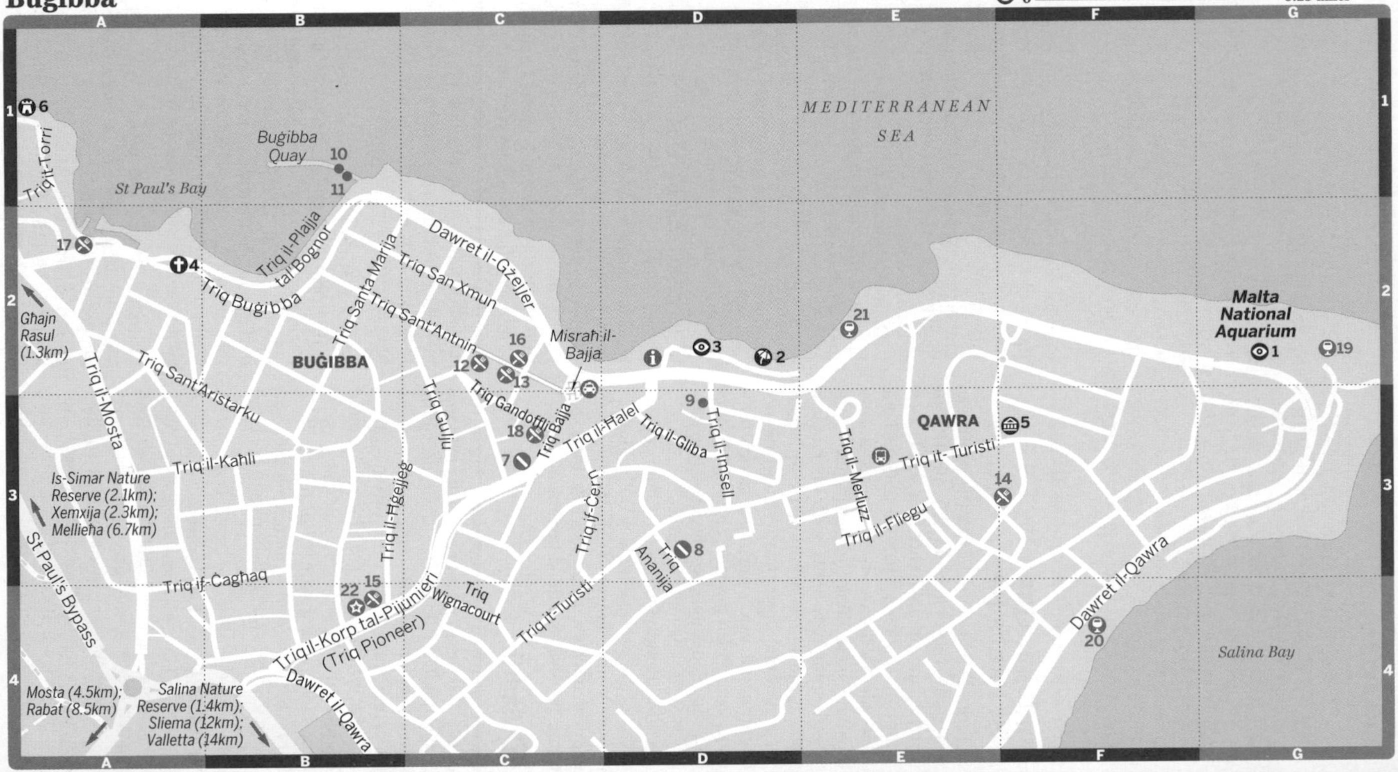
0 500 m
0 0.25 miles
MEDITERRANEAN SEA
St Paul's Bay
Buġibba Quay
Salina Bay
BUĠIBBA
QAWRA
Malta National Aquarium
Misraħ il-Bajja
Triq it-Torri
Triq il-Plajja tal'Bognor
Triq Buġibba
Dawret il-Gżejjer
Triq San Xmun
Triq Santa Marija
Triq Sant'Antnin
Triq Sant'Aristarku
Triq il-Mosta
Triq il-Kaħli
Triq Gulju
Triq Gandoffli
Triq Bajja
Triq il-Ħalel
Triq il-Gliba
Triq il-Imsell
Triq il-Merluzz
Triq it- Turisti
Triq il-Fliegu
Triq if-Ċern
Triq Ananija
Triq il-Ħġejjeġ
Triq if-Ċagħaq
Triq Wignacourt
Triq il-Korp tal-Pijunieri (Triq Pioneer)
Triq it-Turisti
Dawret il-Qawra
St Paul's Bypass
Għajn Rasul (1.3km)
Is-Simar Nature Reserve (2.1km); Xemxija (2.3km); Mellieħa (6.7km)
Mosta (4.5km); Rabat (8.5km)
Salina Nature Reserve (1.4km); Sliema (12km); Valletta (14km)
1
2
3
4
5
6
7
8
9
10
11
12
13
14
15
16
17
18
19
20
21
22
A B C D E F G

Buġibba

Top Sights
1 Malta National Aquarium G2

Sights
2 Buġibba Beach D2
3 Buġibba Water Park D2
4 Church of St Paul's Bonfire A2
5 Malta Classic Car Collection F3
6 Wignacourt Tower A1

Activities, Courses & Tours
7 Buddies Dive Cove C3
8 Dive Deep Blue D3
9 Eco Bikes Malta D3
10 Hornblower Cruises B1
11 Sea Adventure B1

Eating
12 Acqua Marina C2
13 Capuvino C2
La Nave .... (see 1)
14 Lovage F3
15 Salt Kitchen & Lounge B4
16 Sottozero C2
17 Tarragon A2
18 Venus C3

Drinking & Nightlife
19 Cafe del Mar G2
20 Cheeky Monkey F4
21 Mynt Club E2

Entertainment
22 Empire Cinema Complex B4

waterfront to the south of Plajja Tal'Bognor, supposedly on the spot where the saint first scrambled ashore. A bonfire is lit outside the church during the Festival of St Paul's Shipwreck (10 February). Mass times are listed at the front of the church.

Wignacourt Tower FORTRESS
(☎2122 0358; www.dinlarthelwa.org; Triq it-Torri; adult/child €2/free; ⏰10am-1pm Mon-Sat & 1st Sun of month) Built in 1609, the Wignacourt Tower was the first of the towers built by Grand Master Wignacourt. It guards the point to the west of the church, and houses a tiny museum with exhibits on local fortress history, including a small selection of guns and armour. There are stupendous views from here. It's volunteer-run, so opening hours can be flexible.

Salina Nature Reserve NATURE RESERVE
(www.birdlifemalta.org; Coast Rd; by donation) The newest of the nature reserves managed by Birdlife Malta is a haven for gulls and terns and migrating herons and egrets. Very occasionally, flamingos have been known to visit. The reserve is situated on the recently restored **Salina Salt Pans** built by the Knights of St John in the 16th century. Check the website for opening hours.

To reach the Salina Nature Reserve, catch bus 212 from Buġibba to the Salini stop (15 minutes, half-hourly).

Għajn Rasul FOUNTAIN
To the west of Buġibba, near the fishing-boat harbour at the head of the bay, is Għajn Rasul (Apostle's Fountain), where St Paul is said to have baptised the first Maltese convert to Christianity.

Activities

There are several dive operators in Buġibba that can help you explore the excellent nearby dive sites or those around the Maltese Islands.

Dive Deep Blue DIVING
(☎2158 3946; www.divedeepblue.com; 100 Triq Ananija; courses from €95) Well-regarded PADI dive centre for all levels, run by an experienced husband-and-wife team.

Buddies Dive Cove DIVING
(☎2157 6266; www.buddiesmalta.com; 24/2 Triq il-Korp Tal-Pijunieri; courses from €50; ⏰8am-5pm) Popular and well-regarded family-run dive centre. PADI certified.

Tours

Plenty of smaller operators offer tours from the jetty at Plajja Tal'Bognor. As well as shorter trips around St Paul's Bay, some operators offer trips to Comino for around €20. Head down to the jetty area to see what's available.

Sea Adventure BOATING
(☎9999 9387; www.seaadventureexcursions.com; Buġibba Jetty; tours €20-25; 👪) A water slide, an onboard kids' play zone and underwater viewing windows make this an excellent boat trip for families.

Tours include an all-day Comino itinerary, or the option of including three hours on Gozo with a visit to Victoria, Il-Kastell and Xlendi.

Hornblower Cruises BOATING
(☎7909 2764; www.hornblowerboat.com; Buġibba Jetty; ⏰Apr-Oct; 👪) Family-run Hornblower offers day trips to the Blue Lagoon and Comino via some of their caves (adult/child

€20/10), which includes a 4¼-hour stop on Comino, or a trip that stops for three hours on Gozo and an hour on Comino (€25/15).

Eco Bikes Malta MOUNTAIN BIKING
(☎9947 1627; www.ecobikesmalta.com; Triq il-Imsell; tours from €45, bike/e-bike per day from €15/20; ⏰9am-1pm & 5-7pm Mon-Sat) Mountain bike or e-bike tours with two four-hour itineraries taking in Mdina and the west coast (9am to 1pm, Tuesday and Friday) or around Valletta and the Three Cities (9am to 1pm, Wednesday and Saturday). Also recommended for independent hire of mountain bikes, touring bikes and e-bikes.

Eating

Sottozero ICE CREAM €
(☎2701 9339; www.sottozerofactory.com; 44 Triq Rebbiegha; ice cream from €2; ⏰9am-1am Mon-Thu, 9am-2am Fri-Sun) OK we're calling it: Sottozero sells the best ice cream and *gelati* in all of Malta. Our favourite flavours are the black chocolate, *cannella* (cinnamon) and liquorice, but with 115 flavours there's something for everyone. Fresh fruit milkshakes and icily refreshing *granita* are also very good reasons to hunt down this colourful spot a short walk from Buġibba's main square.

Capuvino MEDITERRANEAN €
(www.capuvino.com; Triq Sant Antnin; snacks €4-9; ⏰10am-11pm) Capuvino is near Buġibba's centre but feels slightly removed; the restaurant is shaded by tall palms and features chequered tablecloths and a few outside tables on a pedestrianised section of street. Food includes *ftira* (Maltese bread) sandwiches and pasta, and there's a backstreets-of-Rome vibe. Locals crowd in for occasional live music on Saturday nights from 8pm.

★**Lovage** BISTRO €€
(☎7959 4098; www.lovagebistro.com; 31 Triq l-Imhar; mains €17-24; ⏰7-11pm Wed-Sat & Mon, noon-3.30pm Sun) This corner bistro may be surrounded by tourist pubs, but it's a dining standout in the backstreets of Buġibba. The trio of lamb, beef and wild-boar sausages with onion marmalade is a hearty starter, while more delicate main dishes include the Moroccan-style spiced duck. Sit on the breezy terrace or near the bar in the cosy interior.

★**Acqua Marina** ITALIAN €€
(☎2703 4933; www.facebook.com/acquamarinamalta; 160 Triq Sant'Antnin; mains €10-17; ⏰11am-3pm & 7-11pm Wed-Mon) A tiny Italian restaurant that stands out for its attention to detail. It's a cut above, from the sea-hued decor and careful table decorations to the warm welcome from owner Carlo, to the simple yet delicious Italian cooking and daily fresh-fish specials.

Salt Kitchen & Lounge MEDITERRANEAN €€
(☎2157 8004; www.salt.com.mt; Triq Pioneer; mains €14-27; ⏰7-10.30pm Tue-Sat, noon-2.30pm Sun) A modern counterpoint to more traditional restaurants nearby, Salt's front patio segues to a spacious and contemporary interior. Mediterranean flavours prevail, but there's hints of Asian and Middle Eastern flavours. Try the Maltese pork with the house-made sausage or one of Salt's signature steak dishes with a choice of sauces.

★**Tarragon** MEDITERRANEAN €€€
(☎2157 3759; www.tarragonmalta.com; Triq il-Knisja; mains €23-32; ⏰6.30-11.30pm Mon-Sat, noon-3pm Sat & Sun, closed Sun Jul & Aug) Tucked above the harbour at St Paul's Bay, Tarragon combines sea views with a sophisticated Mediterranean-fusion menu. The white-tableclothed, wooden-floorboard style is both upmarket and informal, and seasonal standout menu items could include venison and pistachio ravioli or octopus with a cherry-tomato marmalade. The three-course degustation menu (per person €50) is a great way to experience the Tarragon magic.

THE VICTORIA LINES

The Victoria Lines are fortifications built by the British in the late 19th century. Named after Queen Victoria's Diamond Jubilee in 1897, they were intended to protect the island from any invaders landing on the northern beaches, but never saw any military action.

The lines run about 12km along a steep limestone escarpment from Fomm ir-Riħ in the west to Baħar iċ-Ċagħaq in the east and are great places for a walk, affording magnificent views. Three forts – Madliena Fort, Mosta Fort and Binġemma Fort – are linked by a series of walls, entrenchments and gun batteries. The best-preserved section, the Dwejra Lines, lies north of Mdina. For walking routes, see www.victorialinesmalta.com.

Venus MEDITERRANEAN €€€
(☎2157 1604; www.facebook.com/venusrestaurant; cnr Triq Bajja & Gandoffli; mains €18-28; ⏲6-11pm) Venus is where to go in Buġibba for a touch of romance and fine dining. There's a bright and sophisticated interior, and the modern fusion menu adds an imaginative twist to traditional ingredients. The homemade rabbit ravioli and the potato and cheese gnocchi with prawns are both very good, and the three-course set menu is great value at €25.

Drinking & Nightlife

Cheeky Monkey PUB
(☎7954 3853; www.cheekymonkeymalta.com; Dawret il-Qawra; ⏲noon-late; 📶) Our pick of the bars along the Qawra promenade. Ocean views southeast to the Ghallis Tower are best enjoyed from one of Malta's biggest decks. Bar snacks include burgers and platters (€18 to €21), and live music and DJs keep the party going at weekends.

Cafe del Mar BAR
(☎2258 8144; www.cafedelmar.com.mt; Triq Trunciera; sunbed €15-20, VIP sunbed €30-40, gazebo €80-120; ⏲10am-late Apr–mid-Oct) This glamorous open-air haunt alongside Malta's aquarium feels very Ibiza-esque, with its fantastic sea views, infinity pools and white sunshades.

Mynt Club CLUB
(☎2355 2410; Dawret il-Gżejjer; ⏲9pm-4am Jun-Sep, Fri-Sun only Oct-May) This pumping summer club, at the lido opposite the Dolmen Resort Hotel, is popular with tourists and locals happy to carry on all night in a lush waterfront setting. In the same complex is Batubulan Sunset Grill and Aqua Terrace Bar.

Entertainment

Empire Cinema Complex CINEMA
(☎2158 1787; www.empirecinema.com.mt; Triq il-Korp tal-Pijunieri; adult/child €6.60/3.50) A seven-screen multiplex showing new films. Some are discounted on Thursdays.

Information

Buġibba Tourist Information (☎2141 9176; www.visitmalta.com; ⏲9am-5.30pm Mon-Sat, to 1pm Sun) is a helpful information office.

Getting There & Away

There is a **taxi rank** on Misraħ il-Bajja, Buġibba.

From **Buġibba bus station** (Triq it-Turisti), buses 45 and 48 run to/from Valletta (every 20 minutes, one hour). Bus 31 also runs between Buġibba and Valletta (every 20 minutes), via Naxxar (30 minutes) and Mosta (40 minutes). Bus 223 goes from Buġibba to Għajn Tuffieħa Bay (25 minutes, hourly) via St Paul's Bay (10 minutes). Bus 221 heads to Ċirkewwa for ferries to Gozo (40 minutes, half hourly), via Mellieħa (30 minutes) and St Paul's Bay (15 minutes).

> **OFF THE BEATEN TRACK**
>
> **MERILL ECO TOURS**
>
> Focusing on Malta's rural north, these excellent **small-group tours** (☎9944 3118; www.merill.com.mt; per person €120; ⏲10am-4pm Wed) negotiate quiet back-roads to visit farmers and small-scale producers of cheese, wine, olives and preserves. Look forward to historical and cultural insights, lots of eating and drinking, and the opportunity to meet some interesting local characters.

Baħar Iċ-Ċagħaq

Baħar iċ-Ċagħaq (*ba*-har eetch *cha*-ag; aka White Rocks) lies halfway between Sliema and Buġibba. It has a scruffy rock beach and a hugely popular family-friendly water park.

Sights

Splash & Fun Park AMUSEMENT PARK
(☎2137 4283; www.splashandfunmalta.com; adult/child €22/15, from 3pm adult/child €15/10; ⏲9am-8pm mid-May–early Oct) This huge, if tired-looking, wave park is a fun place for a day out. Kids will love it, though be warned it's fresher and cleaner earlier in the season. That said, the wave pool constantly pumps 1.5m artificial waves; there are plenty of tunnels and spray jets; fibreglass waterslides; the 'Black Hole'; and a 240m-long 'lazy river' you can coast down on a rubber tube. Note that food can't be brought into the park.

Qalet Marku Tower FORTRESS
Qalet Marku Tower, on Qrejten Point, west of Baħar iċ-Cagħaq Bay, was built in a frenzy of fortified development ordered by Grand Master de Redin, which saw 13 such watchtowers built in a year along this coastline.

Getting There & Away

To get to Baħar iċ-Ċagħaq, take bus 13 from Valletta (60 minutes, every 20 minutes), which travels via Sliema (25 minutes) and St Julian's (10 minutes). Alight at the Splash bus stop.

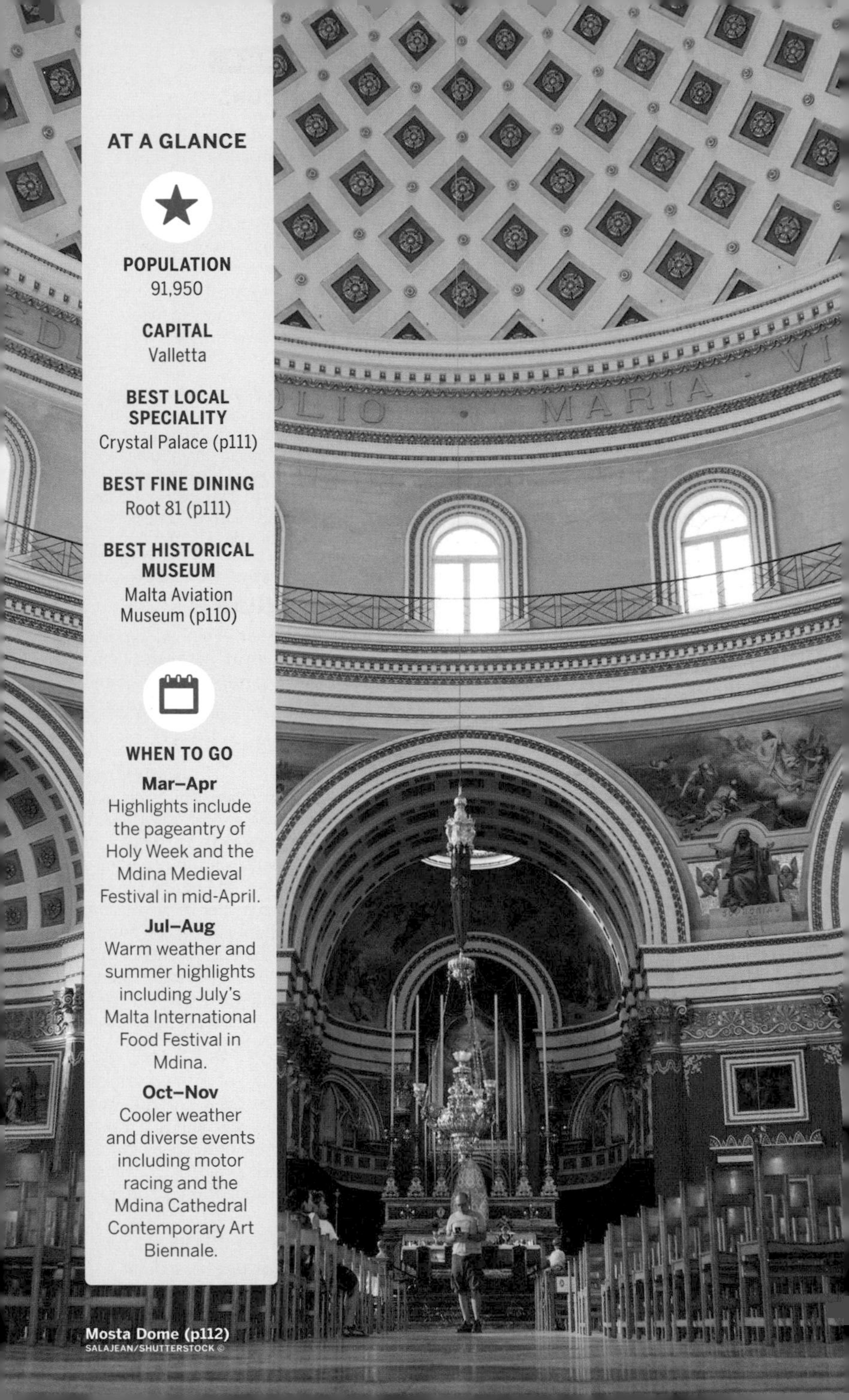

AT A GLANCE

POPULATION
91,950

CAPITAL
Valletta

BEST LOCAL SPECIALITY
Crystal Palace (p111)

BEST FINE DINING
Root 81 (p111)

BEST HISTORICAL MUSEUM
Malta Aviation Museum (p110)

WHEN TO GO

Mar–Apr
Highlights include the pageantry of Holy Week and the Mdina Medieval Festival in mid-April.

Jul–Aug
Warm weather and summer highlights including July's Malta International Food Festival in Mdina.

Oct–Nov
Cooler weather and diverse events including motor racing and the Mdina Cathedral Contemporary Art Biennale.

Mosta Dome (p112)
SALAJEAN/SHUTTERSTOCK ©

Central Malta

Central Malta combines beautiful historic centres with some of the island's most spectacular scenery. Here, you can explore Mdina, Malta's atmospheric ancient walled capital, perched on a hilltop with stupendous views over the hills and out to sea, visit remarkable medieval frescos in ancient catacombs, marvel at one of Europe's largest church domes, and spend the night worshipping the dance gods at some of Malta's best nightclubs. Natural attractions include stark cliffs (the perfect place to watch a sunset) and a scenic bay ideal for swimming (if only you can find it).

Sleeping and eating options range from luxurious five-star hotels to rustic village restaurants where locals come for their weekend feasts of rabbit, and the town of Rabat has several excellent restaurants. If you're after traditional Maltese traditional culture and a tranquil holiday that's a little off the well-worn path, this is the perfect base.

INCLUDES

Central Malta Highlights

❶ **Mdina** (p106) Strolling deserted thoroughfares to discover the haunting silence of this walled city after dark.

❷ **St Agatha's Crypt & Catacombs** (p110) Absorbing the local vibe of Rabat before going underground to admire amazing frescoes.

❸ **Diar il-Bniet** (p112) Lunching on traditional Maltese flavours at this excellent farmhouse restaurant.

❹ **Dingli Cliffs** (p112) Negotiating new walking trails to take in views of the coast and the tiny island of Filfla.

❺ **Mosta Dome** (p112) Questioning divine intervention while marvelling at the unexploded bomb in this church with one of the world's biggest domes.

❻ **Fomm ir-Riħ** (p115) Chilling out at this remote bay reached by a walking path.

San Pawl
Għargħur
Tat-Tarġa
Parish Church of Our Lady
Palazzo Parisio
Naxxar
Mosta Dome
5
Mosta
17
Valletta (5km)
Lija
Church of St Saviour
Balzan
Church of St Helen
16
Ta'Qali National Stadium
Malta Aviation Museum
San Anton Palace & Gardens
Birkirkara
Villa Bologna
Ta'Qali Crafts Village
Church of St Mary
Attard
Maria Rosa Winery
7
Mdina
1
Rabat
St Agatha's Catacombs
2
21
Our Lady of the Grotto
Hal Bajjada
Qormi
Żebbuġ
133
Verdala Palace
Buskett Gardens
117
Girgenti Valley
Siġġiewi
Malta International Airport
Tas Salvatur
Ta'Żuta (253m)
Tal Providenza
Tal Bajjada
Mqabba
Qrendi
Għar Lapsi
Żurrieq
Ħaġar Qim

Mdina

POP 290

The mysterious golden-stone Arabic walled city of Mdina crowns a hilltop, and is a world apart from modern Malta. Its hidden lanes offer exquisite architectural detail and respite from the day-tripping crowds, who largely stick to the main street. Today, with its massive walls and peaceful, shady streets, it is often referred to as the Silent City, a nickname that becomes appropriate after dark. Throughout the year, the Mdina area hosts excellent festivals and events ranging from food and art through to classic cars.

History

The citadel of Mdina was fortified from as long ago as 1000 BC when the Phoenicians built a protective wall and called their settlement Malet, meaning 'place of shelter'. The Romans built a large town here and called it Melita. It was given its present name when the Arabs arrived in the 9th century – medina is Arabic for 'walled city'. They built strong walls and dug a deep moat between Mdina and its surrounding suburbs (*rabat* in Arabic).

In medieval times Mdina was called Cittá Notabile – the Noble City. It was the favoured residence of the Maltese aristocracy and the seat of the *universitá* (governing council). The Knights of St John, who were largely a sea-based force, made Grand Harbour and Valletta their centre of activity, and Mdina sank into the background as a holiday destination for the nobility.

Sights

★St Paul's Cathedral CHURCH

(www.metropolitanchapter.com; Pjazza San Pawl; adult/child incl Cathedral Museum €5/free; 9.30am-4.45pm Mon-Sat, 3-4.45pm Sun) The cathedral is said to be built on the site of the villa belonging to Publius, the Roman governor of Malta who welcomed St Paul in AD 60.

The original Norman church was destroyed by an earthquake, and the restrained baroque edifice you see today was built between 1697 and 1702 by Lorenzo Gafa, who was influenced by the Italian master Borromini. Note the fire and serpent motifs atop the twin bell towers, symbolising the saint's first miracle in Malta.

Echoing St John's Co-Cathedral in Valletta, the floor of St Paul's is covered with the polychrome marble tombstones of Maltese nobles and important clergymen, while the vault is painted with scenes from the life of St Paul. The altar painting *The Conversion of St Paul* by Mattia Preti survived the earthquake, so too did the beautifully carved oak doors to the sacristy on the north side, and the apse above the altar, featuring the fresco *St Paul's Shipwreck*.

Cathedral Museum MUSEUM

(2145 4697; www.metropolitanchapter.com; Pjazza San Pawl; adult/child incl St Paul's Cathedral €5/free; 9.30am-4.30pm Mon-Fri, to 3.30pm Sat) The Cathedral Museum's outstanding highlight is a series of woodcut and copperplate prints and lithographs by the German Renaissance artist Albrecht Dürer. However, there are other items of interest, including Egyptian amulets dating from the 5th-century BC and a remarkable coin collection, which includes Carthaginian and Romana-Maltese examples. The museum is housed in a baroque 18th-century palace originally used as a seminary.

Mdina Ditch Garden GARDENS

Mdina's ditch was an important element of its fortifications. It was first created in the 15th century, but was rebuilt by the Knights of St John's military architect Charles François de Mondion. More recently, the Mdina city walls had become overgrown with ivy and vegetation; the ditch was filled by 273 citrus and seven olive trees.

Palazzo Falson HISTORIC BUILDING

(2145 4512; www.palazzofalson.com; Triq Villegaignon; adult/child €10/free; 10am-5pm Tue-Sun, last admission 4pm) The magnificent Palazzo Falson is a beautifully preserved medieval mansion, formerly the home of artist and philanthropist Olof Gollcher (1889–1962). A self-guided audio tour leads you from the beautiful stone courtyard through Gollcher's kitchen, studio, 4500-volume library, bedroom and chapel – all decorated with his impressive collections of art, documents, silver, weapons and rare rugs from Azerbaijan and Kazakhstan.

National Museum of Natural History MUSEUM

(2145 5951; www.heritagemalta.org; Pjazza San Publiju; adult/child €5/2.50; 9am-5pm) Housed in the elegant Palazzo de Vilhena is an interesting – if old-school fusty – array of displays. Of particular note is the geology section, which explains the origins of Malta's landscape and displays the wide range of local fossils. The tooth belonging to the ancient shark *Carcharodon megalodon* is food for thought – measuring 18cm on the edge, it belonged to a 25m monster that prowled the Miocene seas 30 million years ago.

Mdina Experience AUDIOVISUAL
(☎2145 4322; www.themdinaexperience.com; Misraħ Mesquita; adult/child €6.50/3; ⏲10am-5pm) These three presentations about Mdina's history of siege and embattlement come with an attendant waxwork display of knights to really bring the town's past to life. Options include the story of the Knights, the history of Mdina, and life during medieval times. Discount tickets (adult/child €14.50/3) incorporating all three are available.

Festivals & Events

Malta International Food Festival FOOD & DRINK
(www.maltainternationalfoodfestival.com; Mdina Ditch Gardens; ⏲Jul) The plazas and lawns of the recently restored Mdina Ditch Garden host stalls selling a wide range of local and international cuisine for four days in July.

Malta Classic SPORTS
(www.maltaclassic.com; ⏲Oct) Malta's premium motorsports event combines retro and vintage cars with an exciting hill climb, a classic-car Grand Prix, and the stylish display of beautifully restored cars at the Malta Classic Concours d'Elegance.

Eating

Fontanella Tea Gardens & Vinum Wine Bar CAFE €€
(☎2145 4264; www.fontanellateagarden.com; Triq is-Sur; mains €9-13; ⏲10am-late) Fontanella – a Maltese institution – has a wonderful setting atop the city walls, with sweeping views. It serves delicious home-baked cakes, *pastizzi,* sandwiches, pizzas and light meals, including particularly tasty *ftira* (traditional Maltese bread sandwiches). It also has an intimate wine bar, with flagstone walls and views from the ramparts.

Coogi's MEDITERRANEAN €€
(☎2145 9987; www.coogis.co; 5 Wesgħa Ta'Sant'Agata; mains €11-22; ⏲10.30am-3pm Sun-Thu, to 10pm Fri & Sat; 🌱) Coogi's attracts mainly tourists with its diverse Mediterranean menu ranging from octopus with garlic, apples and sultanas, through to rabbit livers or grilled swordfish. Lighter lunch options include pizza, pasta, and a good array of salads and vegetarian dishes. You can eat in the art-filled dining room, the small vine-draped courtyards, or out on the terrace atop the city walls.

Trattoria AD 1530 MEDITERRANEAN €€
(☎2145 0560; www.xarapalace.com.mt; Misraħ il-Kunsill; mains €11-26; ⏲noon-10.30pm) Part of boutique hotel **Xara Palace** (☎2145 0560; low/high season r from €143/192; ❄📶), this stylishly casual trattoria offers outdoor seating on the pretty square. There's a kids' menu, and the grown-ups can choose from pizza and pasta choices, plus more substantial mains.

De Mondion MEDITERRANEAN €€€
(☎2145 0560; www.xarapalace.com.mt; Misrah il-Kunsill; mains €30-45; ⏲7.30-10.30pm Mon-Sat) Romantic enough to inspire spontaneous marriage proposals, this place is set on the 17th-century rooftop of one of the island's loveliest hotels, Xara Palace. The French-inspired menu is seasonal, but expect esoteric delights such as Scottish scallops, foie gras and truffles. The pricey wine list is packed with big names and interesting vintages from around the world. .

Medina MEDITERRANEAN €€€
(☎2145 4004; www.medinarestaurantmalta.com; 7 Triq is-Salib Imqaddes; mains €18-25; ⏲7pm-late Tue-Sat, noon-2pm Sun) This pretty-as-a-picture romantic venue is in a medieval townhouse with vaulted ceilings and fireplaces. The garden courtyard is perfect for alfresco dining and sophisticated, artfully presented Maltese, Italian and French dishes. Maltese highlights on the menu include farmhouse-style rabbit, honey-lacquered quail and octopus stew.

Information

There is a helpful **Tourist Information Centre** (☎2145 4480; www.visitmalta.com; Torre dello Stendardo; ⏲9am-5.30pm Mon-Sat, to 1pm Sun) just inside Mdina's main gate.

Getting There & Away

The local bus terminus (p111) is in Rabat on Is-Saqqajja, 200m south of Mdina's main gate.

From Valletta, take buses 50, 51, 52 or 53 (30 minutes, every 10 minutes). Bus 52 goes on to Dingli. Bus 202 travels to/from Sliema (50 minutes, half-hourly) and St Julian's (one hour), going on to Dingli.

The X3 express bus travels between here and Buġibba (25 minutes, half-hourly) as well as the airport (55 minutes).

Mdina & Rabat

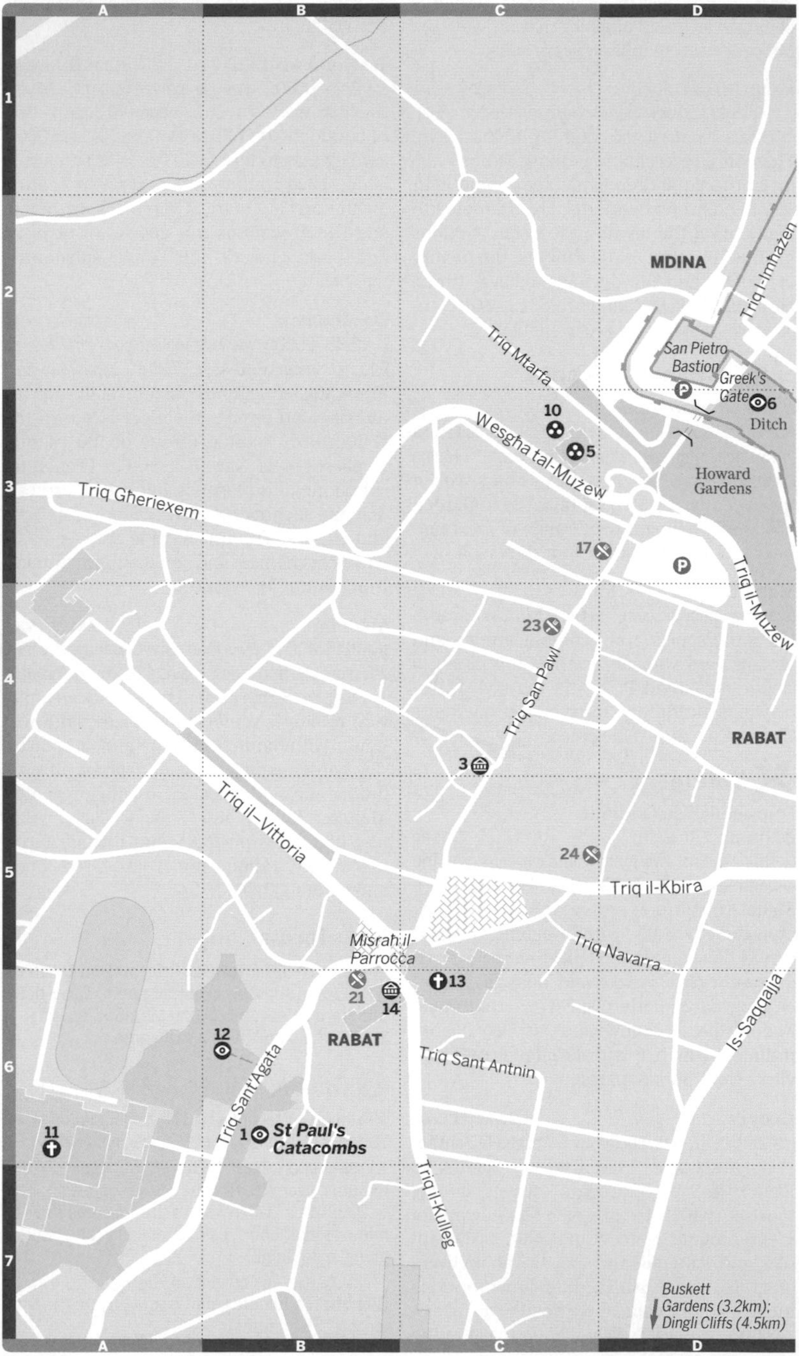
A
B
C
D
1
2
3
4
5
6
7
MDINA
Triq l-Imħażen
San Pietro Bastion
Greek's Gate
6
Ditch
Triq Mtarfa
10
5
Wesgħa tal-Mużew
Howard Gardens
Triq Għeriexem
17
Triq il-Mużew
23
Triq San Pawl
RABAT
3
Triq il-Vittoria
24
Triq il-Kbira
Misraħ il-Parrocca
Triq Navarra
13
21
14
Is-Saqqajja
12
RABAT
Triq Sant'Agata
Triq Sant Antnin
11
1
St Paul's Catacombs
Triq il-Kulleġ
Buskett Gardens (3.2km); Dingli Cliffs (4.5km)

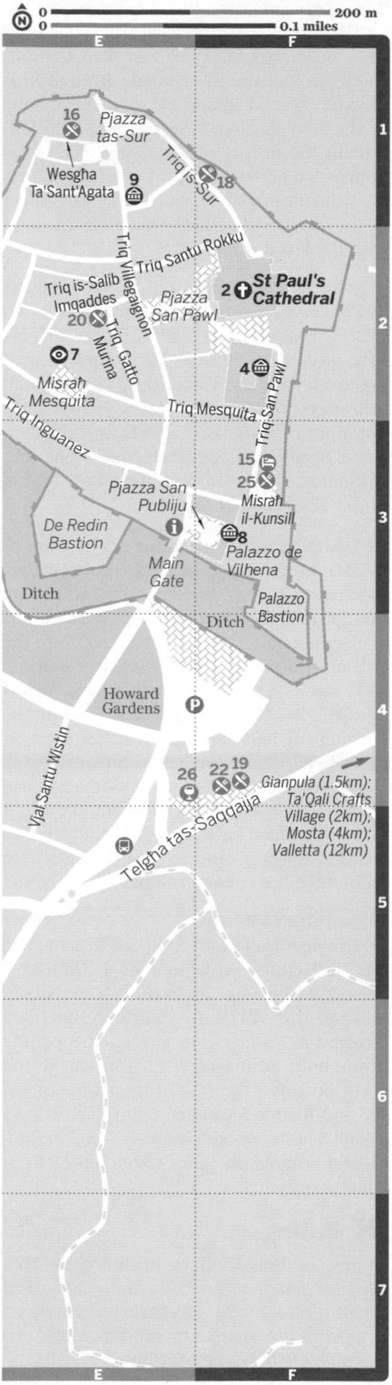

Mdina & Rabat

Rabat

POP 11,500

Rabat, sprawled to the south of Mdina, is a charming town in its own right, with narrow streets and wooden *galerijas* (Maltese balconies). It feels resolutely local despite its numerous sights of interest, particularly in the evening when the day trippers have ebbed away. Highlights include labyrinthine catacombs, important churches and stellar Roman mosaics.

Sights

★St Paul's Catacombs CATACOMB
(☎2145 4562; www.heritagemalta.org; Triq Sant'Agata; adult/child €5/1.50; ⏲9am-5pm) St Paul's Catacombs (named for their proximity

to the church) date from the 3rd century AD and were used for burial for around 500 years. Worship took place here in the Middle Ages, but later the complex was used as an agricultural store. It's an atmospheric labyrinth of rock-cut tombs, narrow stairs and passages. Admission includes a self-guided, 45-minute audio tour, available from the site's recently added visitor centre.

St Agatha's Crypt & Catacombs CATACOMB
(☎2145 4503; www.stagathamalta.com; Triq Sant'Agata; adult/child €5/2; ⏲9am-5pm Mon-Fri, to 2pm Sat) These catacombs contain a series of remarkable frescos dating from the 12th to 15th centuries. According to legend, this was the hiding place of St Agatha when she fled Sicily. Back at ground level is a quirky little museum containing everything from fossils and minerals to coins, church vestments and Etruscan, Roman and Egyptian artefacts. Regular tours are available.

St Agatha's Chapel CHURCH
First built in 1504, a newer church was built on this site in 1670, with further additions in the 19th and early 20th centuries. Highlights include the lovely shaded courtyard.

Domus Romana ARCHAEOLOGICAL SITE
(☎2145 4125; www.heritagemalta.org; Wesgħa tal-Mużew; adult/child €6/3; ⏲9am-5pm) The Roman House was built in the 1920s to incorporate the excavated remains of a large 1st-century-BC townhouse. There's a small but fascinating museum, which includes Roman glass perfume bottles and bone hairpins, as well as a display on the 11th-century Islamic cemetery that overlaid the villa. There are also some beautiful mosaics. At the centre of the original peristyle court there is a depiction of the *Drinking Doves of Sosos,* a fashionable Roman motif.

St Paul's Church & the Grotto of St Paul CHURCH
(www.wignacourtmuseum.com; Misraħ il-Parroċċa; adult/child incl Wignacourt Museum €5/2.50; ⏲9.30am-5pm Mon-Sat) St Paul's Church was built in 1675. Beside it, stairs lead down into the mystical Grotto of St Paul, a cave where the saint is said to have preached during his stay in Malta. The statue of St Paul was gifted by the Knights in 1748, while the silver ship to its left was added in 1960 to commemorate the 1900th anniversary of the saint's shipwreck. Come in the early morning or late afternoon to avoid the tour groups that congest the narrow space.

Casa Bernard HISTORIC BUILDING
(☎2145 1888; www.casabernard.eu; 46 Triq San Pawl; adult/child €8/4; ⏲10am-4pm Mon-Sat) You'll be personally guided through this privately owned 16th-century palace by one of the home's charming owners, who will explain the history of the mansion and the impressive personal collection of art, objets d'art, furniture, silver and china. Tours last 40 to 50 minutes and take place on the hour, with the last one at 4pm.

Wignacourt Museum MUSEUM
(☎2749 4905; www.wignacourtmuseum.com; Triq il-Kulleg; adult/child incl Grotto of St Paul €5/2.50, audio guide €2; ⏲9.30am-5pm) This sprawling museum has a gloriously hotchpotch collection that encompasses 4th-century Christian catacombs, a WWII air-raid shelter, a baroque chapel, religious icons and vestments, and paintings including Mattia Preti's *The Penitent St Peter.*

★Malta Aviation Museum MUSEUM
(☎2141 6095; www.maltaaviationmuseum.com; adult/child €7/2; ⏲9am-5pm Aug-May, to 5pm Mon-Sat & to 1pm Sun Jun-Sep) This is aircraft-enthusiast heaven, located on the former site of the Royal Air Force station, with stars of the show including a WWII Spitfire Mk IX and a Hawker Hurricane IIa, salvaged in 1995 after 54 years at the bottom of the sea off Malta's southwest coast. Other aircraft on display include a vintage Flying Flea, a De Havilland Vampire T11, a Fiat G91R and a battered old Douglas Dakota DC-3. Buses 52 and 53 (hourly) stop here on their routes between Rabat and Valletta.

Ta'Qali Crafts Village VILLAGE
(⏲9am-4pm Mon-Fri, to noon Sat & Sun) The arts and crafts workshops at Ta'Qali have been traditionally housed in old Nissen huts on this WWII RAF airfield, but they received a modern and permanent upgrade throughout 2018 and 2019. You can watch glass-blowers at work, and shop for gold, silver and filigree jewellery, paintings by local artists, leather goods, Maltese lace, ceramics and ornamental glass. Catch bus 52 from Valletta or Rabat.

Eating

Dining in Rabat offers a choice of Malta's best *pastizzi,* good daytime cafes, and evening meals with excellent terrace views of most of the island. On Sundays many restaurants are only open for lunch.

★ Crystal Palace PASTRIES €
(Triq San Pawl; pastizzi €0.30; ⏲3am-11pm) Spot it by the hordes outside, this hole-in-the-wall *pastizzerija* close to Mdina's city walls is renowned as one of Malta's best, as it freshly bakes the little moreish pastry parcels throughout the night. It's a favourite with local coach and taxi drivers.

Parruċċan Confectionery SWEETS €
(Misraħ il-Parroċċa; sweets from €1; ⏲10am-5pm) Here you can pick up samples of Maltese specialities such as nougat, delicious nut brittle and fig rolls.

★ Root 81 MEDITERRANEAN €€
(☎7949 2083; www.facebook.com/root81malta; 21 Telgħa tas-Saqqajja; mains €15-28; ⏲noon-2.45pm Wed-Sun, 6.30-10.30pm Mon & Wed-Sat) Root 81 is one of the more modern bistros enlivening the dining scene around traditionally conservative Mdina and Rabat. It's worth booking an outside table for an early dinner, and combining spectacular valley views with dishes such as goat-cheese fritters or a risotto of local red prawns.

Ta' Doni CAFE €€
(☎2762 5170; 73 Triq San Pawl; snacks €5-6; ⏲9am-6pm) Fresh *ftira* sandwiches bulging with local produce, including cheese, pickled onions and Maltese sausage, are the speciality at this cool cafe also offering Maltese wine and craft beer. An energetic young team provides excellent service, and Ta' Doni is a good place for shared platters (€18) and to pick up home-grown produce such as jams, honey, olive oil and liqueurs.

★ Townhouse No 3 MEDITERRANEAN €€€
(☎7900 4123; www.townhouseno3.com; 3 Triq il-Kbira; mains €20-25; ⏲4-11pm Tue-Sat, noon-3pm & 4-10pm Sun) Concealed in the backstreets of Rabat, Townhouse No 3 offers a modern take on Maltese and Mediterranean flavours. Dishes could include rabbit ravioli with a thyme jus, or gnocchi with grilled squid and chilli and lime fennel. Service is informal but professional.

Fork & Cork MEDITERRANEAN €€€
(☎2145 4432; www.forkandcork.com.mt; 20 Telgħa tas-Saqqajja; mains €21-26; ⏲6.30-10.30pm Mon-Sat) One of several new restaurants making Rabat an emerging dining hub, the Fork & Cork is perched above the road with excellent views of the surrounding countryside. Traditional Maltese flavours linger throughout the menu – including a terrine of rabbit and quail – but main dishes like lamb with a swede fondant, falafels and Moroccan spices echo a broader provenance.

THE TRAGEDY OF ST AGATHA

St Agatha was a 3rd-century Christian martyr from Sicily who fled to Malta to escape the amorous advances of a Sicilian governor. On returning to Sicily she was imprisoned and tortured, her breasts were cut off with shears, and she was burnt at the stake. In Rabat there's a church, St Agatha's Chapel (p110), dedicated to her, near the catacombs (p110), which are said to have been her hiding place in Malta.

Drinking & Nightlife

Tat Tarrag WINE BAR
(☎9942 7404; 25 Telgħa tas-Saqqajja; ⏲6pm-late Tue-Sat, 10.30am-late Sun) Head here for excellent views, good-value shared platters and a wide selection of Maltese and international wines. On balmy summer evenings, Tat Tarrag's outside tables are the best place to top off an afternoon exploring Mdina and Rabat.

Gianpula CLUB
(☎9947 2133; www.gianpulavillage.com; ⏲Groove Gardens 11pm-4am Sat, Marrakech 10pm-4am Sat & Sun, Phoenix 11pm-4am Fri & Sat) The sprawling open-air Gianpula Village, just east of Rabat, is more than just a club. Areas include 'Groove Gardens', with an underground vibe; 'Marrakech', with a 'VIP' look; and 'Phoenix', with R&B and house. It also has a rooftop club and an outdoor arena for hosting occasional festivals.

Uno CLUB
(☎2141 5241; www.facebook.com/unomalta; Ta'Qali Crafts Village; ⏲11pm-4am Fri & Sat Jun-Sep) In Ta'Qali Crafts Village, this popular open-air local club hauls in Malta's beautiful people, who shake it to house and R&B on Friday and Saturday nights in summer. Recent events have included global superstars like Armin van Buuren. Check Facebook for what's planned.

Getting There & Away

Buses 201 and 202 (60 minutes, hourly) run from the airport, while bus 52 (33 minutes, every half hour) runs from Valletta. The **bus stop** (Is-Saqqajja) is just south of Mdina.

Dingli Cliffs

Dingli was named after either the Maltese architect Tommaso Dingli (1591–1666) or his 16th-century English namesake Sir Thomas Dingley, who lived nearby. It's a quiet village with not much to it apart from a very good farm-to-table restaurant.

Less than 1km to the southwest the land falls away at the spectacular 220m-high Dingli Cliffs. A road runs along the top of the cliffs, and well-marked walking trails lead past the incongruous radar tower to the lonely little 17th-century **Chapel of St Mary Magdalene** and onwards to Ta'Żuta (253m). This is the highest point on the Maltese Islands, and you'll enjoy excellent views along the coast to the tiny island of Filfla.

◎ Sights

The Cliffs NATURE CENTER
(☑ 7964 2380; www.thecliffs.com.mt; Triq Panoramika; donations appreciated; ☺ audiovisual 11am, noon, 7pm Mon, Thu, Sat Oct-May & 7pm Mon, Wed, Fri, Sun Apr-Sep, guided walks 11am Wed, Fri Oct-May & 6.30pm Thu Apr-Sep) Beyond being an excellent restaurant, The Cliffs also acts as a local nature centre supporting the ecology, history and culture of the area. There's the opportunity to experience a free audiovisual display and also go on a guided walk along the cliffs. Group sizes are limited, so booking ahead is necessary. Walks include a troglodyte cave, wildflowers and sensational views.

✖ Eating

★ Diar il-Bniet MALTESE €€
(☑ 2762 0727; www.diarilbniet.com; 121 Triq il-Kbira, Ħad-Dingli; mains €11-27; ☺ noon-2.30pm daily & 6.30-9pm Mon-Tue & Thu-Sat) Located in a historic farmhouse in the centre of Dingli village, this family-run farmhouse restaurant is something special. All produce is sourced from 'the house of the girls', or their farm 200m away, or other local producers. Dishes include stuffed aubergines or courgettes, homemade pies and fried rabbit, followed by desserts such as date and anisette tart. Platters also available.

The Cliffs MALTESE €€
(☑ 2145 5470; www.thecliffs.com.mt; Triq Panoramika; mains €7.50-19.50; ☺ 10.30am-4pm & 7-10.30pm Fri & Sat Oct-May, Wed-Mon Jun-Sep; 🛜) Close to Dingli's radar tower, on the cliffs, this place is run by two local brothers and is an attractive, contemporary, brasserie-style restaurant with a narrow glass-framed terrace running around it. It specialises in local food using local produce, such as wild asparagus and garlic, local cheeses and honey, and Maltese wines.

ⓘ Getting There & Away

Bus 52 runs from Valletta (45 minutes; at least hourly) to Dingli. Bus 201 connects Dingli Cliffs with Rabat (15 minutes, hourly), and, in the other direction, runs along the coast to Ħaġar Qim (20 minutes), the Blue Grotto and the airport (45 minutes). For Dingli Cliffs alight bus 201 at the Maddalena or Cliffs stop.

Mosta

POP 20,240

A busy and prosperous town spread across a level plateau, Mosta is famous for its splendid domed church. It's also an ideal starting point for exploring the Victoria Lines (p100).

◎ Sights & Activities

Mosta Dome CHURCH
(☑ 2143 3826; www.mostachurch.com; Pjazza Rotunda; €2; ☺ 9.30am-5pm Mon-Fri, to 4.30pm Sat, noon-4pm Sun) The Parish Church of Santa Maria, better known as the Rotunda or Mosta Dome, was designed by the Maltese architect Giorgio Grognet de Vassé and built (1833–60) and boasts a stunning blue, gold and white interior.

The church's circular design with a six-columned portico was closely based on the Pantheon in Rome, and the great dome – a prominent landmark (its external height is 61m) – is visible from most parts of Malta. With a diameter of 39.6m, it's one of the world's largest domes.

Bidnija Horse Riding School HORSE RIDING
(☑ 7999 2326; www.bidnijahorseriding.com; Bidnija; ☺ 9am-dusk) Just northwest of Mosta, on the road to St Paul's Bay, Bidnija offers horse rides ranging from one to seven hours, accompanied by qualified instructors. If you're staying in the north of the island, it offers free pick-up.

✖ Eating

Ta'Marija Restaurant MALTESE €€
(☑ 2143 4444; www.tamarija.com; Triq il-Kostituzzjoni; mains €18.50-30; ☺ noon-2.30pm Tue-Sun, 6.30-11pm daily) Ta'Marija Restaurant is highly rated for its authentic Maltese cuisine,

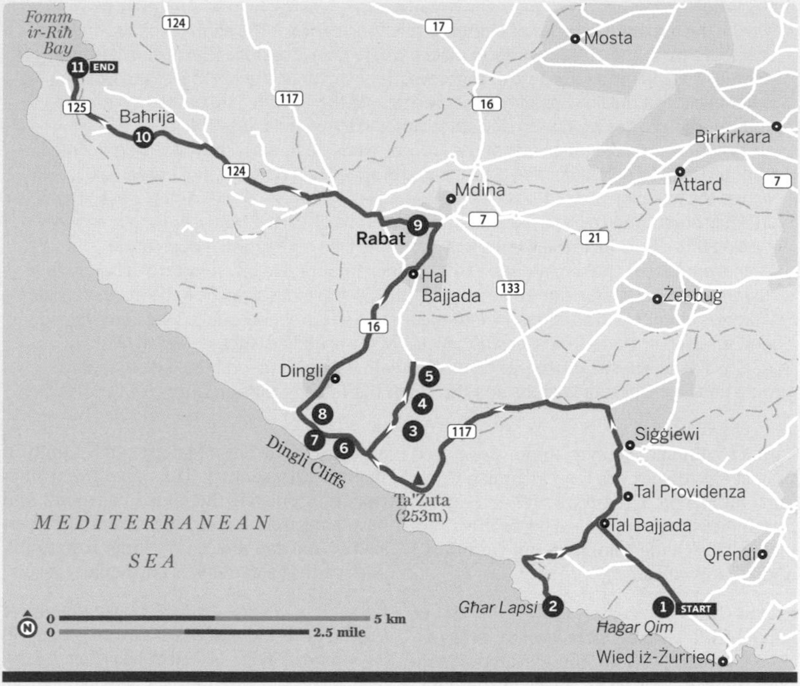

Driving Tour
Temples, Sea Cliffs & Gardens

START ĦAĠAR QIM & MNAJDRA
END FOMM IR-RIĦ
LENGTH APPROX 15KM; ONE HOUR

In this most traditional region you can experifine prehistoric temples, breathtaking coastlines, grand palaces and mysterious cart ruts.

Start your tour at the megalithic temples of ❶ **Ħaġar Qim & Mnajdra,** (p124) with sweeping views over the coast. From here, drive to ❷ **Għar Lapsi** (p125) for excellent swimming, then take the road inland through the Girgenti Valley. Next, veer towards the coast again, along the southern end of Dingli Cliffs. After about a kilometre, turn inland to visit the ❸ **Cart Ruts** (p114) – mysterious prehistoric tracks – at Clapham Junction.

From here it's a short drive to ❹ **Buskett Gardens** (Triq il-Buskett), Malta's only extensive woodland. Planted by the Knights as a hunting ground, today the groves of pine, oak, olive and orange trees provide picnic sites in summer and orange-scented walks in winter.

Close by you'll see ❺ **Verdala Palace**, built in 1586 as a summer residence for Grand Master Hugues Loubeux de Verdalle. It was designed by Gerolamo Cassar in the form of a square castle with towers at each corner, but only for show – it was intended to be a hunting retreat. It became first the British Governor of Malta's summer residence, and is now that of the Maltese president.

Next, double back to the cliffs to rejoin the panoramic road, passing the ❻ **Chapel of St Mary Magdalene** (p112). After travelling a short distance to the north you'll see the outlandish ❼ **Radar Tower** perched on the edge of the cliffs. Right by here is ❽ **The Cliffs** (p112); stop for lunch.

After lunch, drive inland to ❾ **Rabat** (p109), from where you can take Triq Ghajn Qajjet west towards the traditional village of ❿ **Baħrija**. Where the village's road splits, take the right-hand fork and follow the road towards the coast. When the road forks, turn right; this will lead you down to a viewpoint over ⓫ **Fomm ir-Riħ Bay** (p115).

THE RIDDLE OF THE RUTS

One of the biggest mysteries of Malta's prehistoric period is the abundance of so-called 'cart ruts' throughout the islands. In places where bare limestone is exposed, it is often scored with a series of deep parallel grooves, looking for all the world like ruts worn by cartwheels. But the spacing of the ruts varies, and their depth – up to 60cm – means that wheeled carts would probably get jammed if they tried to use them.

A more likely explanation is that the grooves were created by a travois – a sort of sled with two parallel poles joined by a frame and dragged behind a beast of burden. This still leaves the question of what was being transported. Suggestions have included salt and building stone, but it's more likely to have been topsoil, carted from low-lying areas to hillside terraces to increase the area of cultivable land for a growing population.

In some places the ruts are seen to disappear into the sea on one side of a bay, only to re-emerge on the far side. In other spots they seem to disappear off the edge of a cliff. This has given rise to all sorts of weird theories, but is probably due to long-term erosion and sea-level changes due to earthquakes – Malta is riddled with geological faults.

Good places to see the ruts and come up with your own theories include Clapham Junction near Buskett Gardens and the top of the Ta'Ċenċ cliffs on Gozo (p137).

with a traditional *kenura* (stone) stove used to heat side dishes. It's a great choice if you don't mind a bit of (dare we say?) cheesy entertainment with your meal, as it offers regular folkloric entertainment and traditional Maltese folk music.

Pjazza Café CAFE **€€**

(☎2141 3379; 1st level, Pjazza Rotunda; mains €7-18; ⏰9am-11pm; 📶) At the elevated Pjazza Café you can enjoy great views of the dome from a table by the window, while downing a light lunch or snack, pizza or pasta.

ℹ Getting There & Away

Numerous buses pass through Mosta; alight at the Rotonda 1 stop. From Valletta take bus 41, 42 or 44 (30 minutes). Buses 41 and 42 continue to St Paul's Bay (25 minutes), Mellieħa (40 minutes) and then Ċirkewwa (for Gozo, 55 minutes). Bus 31 connects with Buġibba.

Naxxar

POP 13,445

Naxxar, a couple of kilometres northeast of Mosta (so close the towns almost merge), is a graceful, stately town that is off the tourist trail and has a few important historic sights, including the **Parish Church of Our Lady**, one of the tallest baroque edifices in Malta.

Palazzo Parisio HISTORIC BUILDING

(☎2141 2461; www.palazzoparisio.com; Pjazza Vittorja; adult/child incl audio guide €15/5, garden only €5; ⏰9am-6pm) The glorious Palazzo Parisio was originally built in 1733 by Grand Master Antonio Manoel de Vilhena, then acquired and refurbished by a Maltese noble family in the late 19th century. The magnificent interior (in particular the gilded ballroom) and baroque gardens resemble a miniature Versailles. You can also eat at Luna restaurant, and tea in the gardens is particularly lovely.

Luna RESTAURANT **€€€**

(☎2141 2461; www.palazzoparisio.com; Pjazza Vittorja; mains €16-28; ⏰9-11am, noon-3pm & 3.30-6pm Mon-Sun, dinner 7pm-late Wed-Sun) In the aristocratic surroundings of Palazzo Parisio you'll find the excellent Luna restaurant, patrolled by gracious, white-clad staff serving relaxed breakfast and lunch specials, and a more refined dinner menu. Afternoon tea from around 3.30pm every afternoon is a delightful selection of scones and dainty sandwiches. You can also eat out in the gardens. Children are welcome during the day.

Old Charm WINE BAR

(☎7906 4298; www.facebook.com/pg/theoldcharm; Sqaq Nru 6; platters €15-18; ⏰7-11pm Tue-Sun) Something slightly different for Malta, the Old Charm is a cosy wine bar with a snacks and platters menu offering a mix of Mediterranean and Indian flavours. It's in a very quiet residential area a short walk from Naxxar's main square. Try the Spiced Up platter with homemade pakoras and samosas.

ℹ Getting There & Away

To get to Naxxar, take bus 31 (30 minutes, every 20 minutes) from Valletta, or bus 202 (25 minutes, hourly) from St Julian's, which goes on to Rabat.

Birkirkara & the Three Villages

POP 40,000

The main road from Valletta to Mosta passes through the town of Birkirkara (population 22,247), one of the biggest population centres on the island. Just west of Birkirkara is an upmarket residential area known as the Three Villages, centred on the medieval settlements of **Attard**, **Balzan** and **Lija**. The old village centres still retain their narrow streets, and interesting sites include Attard's grand mansions and gardens, and local parish churches, including the **Church of St Saviour** (Misraħ tat-Trasfigurazzjoni; ⊗7am-7pm) in Lija, the **Church of St Mary** (www.attard-parish.org; Pjazza Tommaso Dingli; ⊗7am-6pm) in Attard, and the **Church of St Helen** (Is-Santwarju; ⊗6.45-9.45am & 5.30-7pm Mon-Sat, 6.45-noon & 5.30-7pm Sun) in Birkirkara.

⊙ Sights

San Anton Palace & Gardens GARDENS
(Triq Birkirkara; ⊗7am-6pm) The early-17th-century San Anton Palace in Attard onec served as the official residence of the British Governor of Malta, and is now that of the Maltese president. The lovely walled gardens contain groves of citrus and avocado, as well as an aviary. The Eagle Fountain, just inside the main gate, dates from the 1620s.

Villa Bologna HISTORIC BUILDING
(☑2141 7973; www.villabologna.com; Triq Sant'Anton; adult/child €6/free; ⊗9am-5pm Mon-Fri, to 1pm Sat) This baroque, 18th-century mansion in Attard has wonderful gardens with greenery that is like balm to the eyes; there were some lovely features added in the 1920s such as the sunken pond and the dolphin garden. The villa also contains a shop selling marvellous Ceramika Maltija pottery: handmade ceramics made to traditional designs.

Maria Rosa Winery WINERY
(☑7900 4330; www.mariarosawineestate.com; Sqaq Il-Ħofra; wine & food pairing €25; ⊗9am-4pm Mon-Fri) The small, family-run Maria Rosa estate just south of Attard stands on 4.2 hectares of agricultural land, and runs regular tours and tastings; call for details.

✕ Eating

There's plenty of choice at the gracious **Corinthia Palace Hotel** (Vjal de Paule) in Attard: the elegant **Villa Corinthia** (☑2144 0301; mains €22-38; ⊗7-10pm) for fine dining; **Rickshaw** (☑2544 2190; www.facebook.com/rickshawrestaurant; mains €16-28; ⊗7-11pm Tue-Sat) offering pan-Asian cuisine; and the **Summer Kitchen** (☑2544 2738; mains €10-18; ⊗11am-4pm & 7-11pm May-Oct), a seasonal alfresco pizza-and-pasta eatery that's good for families. Cheaper neighbourhood restaurants also abound.

★**Bahia** MEDITERRANEAN €€
(☑9999 1270; www.bahia.com.mt; Triq Preziosi, Lija; mains €15-23; ⊗7-11pm Tue-Sat, noon-3pm Sun) Named after a variety of oranges grown locally, Bahia is an innovative and stylish bistro near Lija's compact village square. Look forward to just 12 seasonal dishes. Seafood highlights could include red prawn and crab with confit potato and *dashi* (Japanese-style broth), while local fish with *kimchi* and burnt lemon introduces Asian flavours.

ⓘ Getting There & Away

Buses 54 and 56 travel to Attard (30 minutes, frequent) from Valletta. Many regular buses travel from Valletta to Birkirkara (25 minutes) and the X3 travels from the airport to Birkirkara (20 minutes) and Attard (30 minutes) via Paola.

Fomm ir-Riħ

Fomm ir-Riħ (meaning 'mouth of the wind') is one of Malta's most remote and difficult-to-reach bays, and is an essential destination for travellers wishing to see a more wild side of the island. Note that walking access to the bay is relatively wild too, and only confident hikers with good balance and average fitness should consider it.

Ta'Gagin (☑2145 0825; www.facebook.com/tagaginbahrija; Triq Is-Sajf ta' San Martin; mains €15-24; ⊗5-11pm Mon-Sat, 11am-3pm Sun) is a popular local restaurant serving traditional Maltese cuisine such as rabbit and snails. Or try **North Country Bar & Restaurant** (☑2145 6688; www.facebook.com/northcountryresbahrija; Triq Is-Sajf ta' San Martin; mains €15-20; ⊗6pm-midnight Tue-Sat, noon-midnight Sun), which offers generous portions of rabbit and sausages.

ⓘ Getting There & Away

Fomm ir-Riħ is best visited with a car or scooter, but it is definitely doable on public transport. To get to Baħrija, catch bus 109 (17 minutes, hourly) from Rabat. From Baħrija to the car park near the bay it's a walk of around 2km.

AT A GLANCE

POPULATION
43,632

CAPITAL
Valletta

BEST PLACE TO SWIM
Il-Kalanka Bay (p121)

BEST SEAFOOD RESTAURANT
Tartarun (p120)

BEST LOCAL BAR
Bongo Nyah (p122)

WHEN TO GO

May–Jun
Spring weather and less visitors to St Peter's Pool.

July–Aug
The busiest time of the year. Visit on a weekday for a table at the best restaurants and always book ahead.

Sep–Oct
Warm waters still and a quieter time at the Marsaxlokk Sunday market.

Marsaxlokk (p120)
CALIN STAN/SHUTTERSTOCK ©

Southern Malta

Several of Malta's most extraordinary historical sites lie in the less-visited southeast of the country, including its most breathtakingly located prehistoric temples (Ħaġar Qim and Mnajdra), which date back more than 5000 years, and the Għar Dalam cave, full of fossilised remains of prehistoric animals. There's splendid coastal scenery, too, boat trips to visit grottoes, and fabulous swimming spots off the tourist trail. It's also the base of much of the country's heavy industry, which means tourism is less developed here, though many locals head to the south to eat out at the weekend. Many people visit the sometime fishing village of Marsaxlokk for its Sunday fish market, and to eat seafood at the small town's many restaurants, which front a harbour full of bobbing, colourful boats. The nearby coastal port of Marsaskala is also very popular as a dining destination, especially on weekends.

INCLUDES

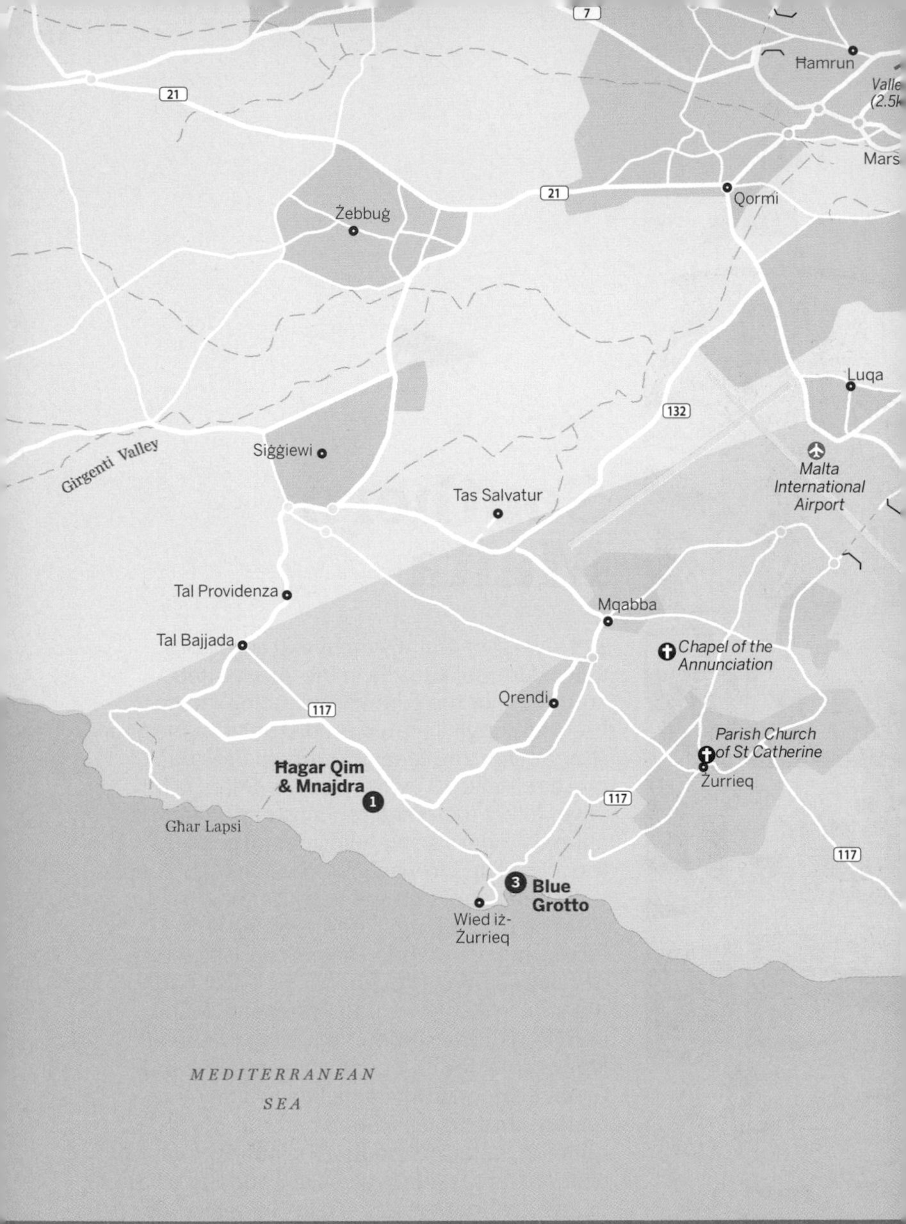

Southern Malta Highlights

❶ **Ħaġar Qim & Mnajdra** (p124) Questioning who, when, how and why, while drinking in the scenery at these mysterious temples.

❷ **St Peter's Pool** (p120) Negotiating walking trails to take a giant leap of faith into the glittering royal-blue waters of this coastal gem.

❸ **Blue Grotto** (p123) Taking a mid-morning boat trip to marvel at this natural formation's shimmering play of light and shadow.

4 Għar Dalam Cave & Museum (p121). Exploring a mysterious underworld of prehistoric bones and ancient history.

5 Marsaxlokk (p120) Devouring fresh seafood with a view of bobbing fishing boats.

6 Marsaskala (p122) Meeting the friendly locals amid the weekend eating and drinking scene at this southern Maltese port.

Marsaxlokk

POP 3535

The ancient fishing village of Marsaxlokk (marsa-shlock; from *marsa sirocco,* meaning 'southeasterly harbour') at the head of Marsaxlokk Bay resolutely remains a slice of real Maltese life, despite the encroachment of industry and the descent of hundreds of tourists every Sunday for its weekly fish and souvenir market.

Old low-rise houses ring the waterfront, and a photogenic fleet of brightly coloured *luzzu* (fishing boats) dance in the harbour attended by their weather-worn owners. The town is home to around 70% of the Maltese fishing fleet, and is renowned for its top-notch seafood restaurants, making it a magnet for long-lunching locals and bus-loads of day trippers.

It makes for a relaxed base once the Sunday hordes have left. If you're after nightlife into the wee small hours, you'll be disappointed. But if you're looking to chill out (and regularly tuck into all manner of fishy morsels), you'll be happy.

History

Marsaxlokk Bay is Malta's second natural harbour. It was here that the Turkish fleet was moored during the Great Siege of 1565, and Napoleon's army landed here during the French invasion of 1798. In the 1930s the calm waters of the bay were used as a staging post by the huge, four-engined Short C-Class flying boats of Britain's Imperial Airways as they pioneered long-distance air travel to the far-flung corners of the Empire. During WWII Marsaxlokk Bay was the base for the Fleet Air Arm, and in 1989 the famous summit meeting between Soviet and US leaders Mikhail Gorbachev and George Bush (senior) was held on-board a warship anchored in the bay. Today the harbour is framed by the fuel tanks and chimney of a power station and the huge cranes of the Kalafrana Container Terminal – eyesores that dominate this once entirely scenic part of the Maltese coast.

Sights & Activities

★St Peter's Pool BAY

St Peter's Pool is a fantastic swimming spot, a natural lido in the rocks with large areas of flat slab for sunbathing between swims. Follow the narrow road out towards Delimara Lighthouse until you are just past the power station chimney (about 1.5km from the main road), and you'll see a low building on the left with 'St Peter's Pool' signposted on it.

A rough track leads down to a small parking area – if you meet a car coming the other way it'll be a face-off over who'll back up. Don't leave valuables in your car.

Sunday Fish Market MARKET

At Marsaxlokk's colourful, packed-to-the-gills Sunday Fish Market, you can admire the riches of the Med before they're whisked off to Malta's top hotels and restaurants. The market starts early in the morning and the best stuff is long gone by afternoon. Note that parking is at an absolute premium, so consider catching the bus. Expect it also to be very full.

Delimara Point AREA

Delimara Point, southeast of Marsaxlokk, is blighted by a huge power station whose chimney can be seen for miles around, but there are a few good swimming places on the eastern side of the peninsula, where the power station isn't in view, and this is a pleasant place to walk. You can access St Peter's Pool from here, and walk on to a large scoop of bay called Ħofra Iz-Zghira, which has some **salt pans**.

Waterfront Market MARKET

The Sunday fish stalls are far outnumbered by the stalls of this daily market, which mainly sells kitsch aimed at tour groups visiting the town.

Eating

★Tartarun SEAFOOD €€

(☎2165 8089; www.tartarun.com; Xatt is-Sajjieda; mains €12-28; ⊙noon-3.30pm Tue-Sun, 7.30-10.30pm Tue-Sat) Locals love upmarket Tartarun, which offers a more sophisticated take on all things fishy. Dishes such as sea bream, roasted prawn and cherry tomatoes are perfectly executed. The 'fish snacks' menu (€4 to €13) is a good option for a leisurely lunch of shared tapas-style plates. Try the swordfish tataki. There are a few outside tables, though they're somewhat traffic-plagued on Sunday.

Roots MEDITERRANEAN €€

(☎2165 3205; Xatt is-Sajjieda; mains €10-15; ⊙11am-3pm & 7-10.30pm Tue-Sun) This modern eatery in Marsaxlokk may not have harbourfront tables like other nearby establishments, but that means it works harder on service and in the kitchen. Menu highlights include just maybe Malta's best *calamari fritti* (fried calamari), and delicate seafood pasta dishes like *panzerotti* stuffed with prawns and scallops.

T'annamari SICILIAN €€
(☎2744 6211; www.tannamari.com; 28 Xatt is-Sajjieda; mains €11-25; ⏲11.30am-3pm & 7-11pm Wed-Mon) A Slow Food ethos meets Sicilian flavours at this relaxed restaurant away from the hubbub of Marsaxlokk's tourist strip. Locals and in-the-know Italian tourists crowd into the heritage interior for dishes including squid-ink ravioli, pappardelle with lobster, and fillet of swordfish with breadcrumbs, pine nuts and raisins.

★**Terrone** MEDITERRANEAN €€€
(☎2704 2656; www.terrone.com.mt; 1 Triq il-Wilga; mains €20-28; ⏲noon-9pm Mon-Fri, 8am-10pm Sat & Sun, closed Wed Jan-Feb) Seasonal, sustainable and local are all important at Terrone, where the menu is adjusted on a daily basis. Sit inside the chic interior enlivened with colourful tiles, or outside with fishing boat views, and enjoy dishes like tuna tartare, kingfish carpaccio and chargrilled octopus. A six-course seafood degustation menu is €55 per person. Angus rib-eye is available for steak fans.

Information

There is a helpful **Tourist Information Office** (☎21651151; www.visitmalta.com; Xatt is-Sajjieda; ⏲9am-5pm Mon-Sat, to 2pm Sun) on the northern (left hand) edge of the harbour.

Getting There & Away

Buses 81 and 85 run from Valletta to Marsaxlokk regularly (35 minutes, every 40 minutes), via Paola. The 119 runs between Marsaxlokk and Marsaskala (20 minutes, hourly) and continues to the airport.

Getting Around

Boat trips around the harbour on a traditional *luzzu* cost €5 per person. Local boat owners also offer transfers around Delimara Point to St Peter's Pool (€10 per person).

Birżebbuġa

POP 13,453

Birżebbuġa (beer-zeb-*boo*-ja, meaning 'well of the olives') lies on the western shore of Marsaxlokk Bay. It began life as a fishing village, but today it's a dormitory town for workers from the nearby Malta Freeport. A couple of interesting natural and historic sights make it worthy of a visit.

OFF THE BEATEN TRACK

IL-KALANKA BAY

St Peter's Pool is deservedly popular as a swimming and sunbathing destination, but you can continue down the same road (Triq Delimara) to quieter Il-Kalanka Bay, where the bay's natural swimming hole is reached via a stepped path of around 50m. Care should be taken when jumping into the water as the distance is higher than at St Peter's Pool. Easier access is from the right-hand side of the pool.

Sights

★**Għar Dalam Cave & Museum** ARCHAEOLOGICAL SITE
(☎2165 7419; www.heritagemalta.org; Għar Dalam; adult/child €5/2.50; ⏲9am-5pm) This is the reason to head to Birżebbuġa. Around 500m north on the main road from Valletta, Għar Dalam (aar-da-lam; the name means 'cave of darkness') is a 145m-long cave in the Lower Coralline Limestone. It has yielded a magnificent harvest of fossil bones and teeth. The lowermost layers of the cavern, more than 500,000 years old, yielded remains belonging to dwarf elephants, hippopotamuses, micro-mammals and birds.

The animals are all of European type, suggesting that Malta was once joined to Italy, but not to northern Africa. It's also where the first signs of human habitation on Malta, from 7400 years ago, have been discovered, with remains including pottery dating back to 5200 BC and Neanderthal teeth found in the top layer.

The museum at the entrance contains an exhibition hall with displays on how the cave was formed and how the remains of such animals came to be found here and their development in response to local conditions, as they evolved in different ways to such creatures elsewhere. In the older part of the museum are display cases mounted with thousands and thousands of bones and teeth. Beyond the museum a path leads down through gardens to the mouth of the cave, where a walkway leads 50m into the cavern. A pillar of sediment has been left in the middle of the excavated floor to show the stratigraphic sequence.

Għar Ħasan Cave CAVE

Għar Ħasan Cave lies within the cliff-bound coastline south of Birżebbuġa. From Birżebbuġa follow the road towards Żurrieq, then turn left on the minor road at the top of the hill to reach a cliff-top parking area just before an industrial estate; the cave entrance is down some steps in the cliff-face to the left. Access to the actual cave has been fenced off for safety reasons, but it is still worth visiting for the coastal views and surrounding area. The 'Cave of Ħasan' is supposed to have been used as a hideout by a 12th-century Saracen rebel.

Getting There & Away

To get to Għar Dalam and Birżebbuġa, take regular buses 82 or 85 (30 minutes, half-hourly) from Valletta, which run via Paola. The cave museum is on the right-hand side of the road at a small, semicircular parking area 500m short of Birżebbuġa. There is no public transport to Għar Ħasan – it's a 2.5km walk south of Birżebbuġa.

Marsaskala

POP 15,504

Marsaskala (also spelt Marsascala), gathered around the head of a long, narrow bay, was originally a Sicilian fishing community: the name means 'Sicilian Harbour'. Today it is an increasingly popular residential area and seaside resort among the Maltese. It appeals because of its great restaurants, local feel and bustling, boat-bobbing little harbour.

Sights

St Thomas Bay BEACH

St Thomas Bay is a deeply indented bay to the south of Marsaskala, lined with concrete and breeze-block huts and a potholed road, and surrounded by apartments. It has a sandy beach, and the place is popular with local people and windsurfers. A few local bars are busy at weekends. It's about a 10-minute walk from Marsaskala along Triq tal-Gardiel. From St Thomas Bay you can continue walking along the coast to Marsaxlokk (about 4km).

Eating

Locals travel across Malta to enjoy the many restaurants of Marsaskala. The town is particularly famed for its seafood. Sunday night is especially busy with families.

Coffee Circus CAFE €

(☎9974 6537; www.coffeecircus.eu; 29 Triq ix-Xatt; snacks €4-7; ⏰9am-11pm) Rustic mismatched furniture, an informed and diverse approach to both tea and speciality coffee, and healthy food including wraps and salads all make Coffee Circus stand out amid the more raucous bars and pubs along Marsaskala's harbourfront main drag.

★**Bongo Nyah** CAFE €€

(☎9965 9472; www.bongonyah.com.mt; Triq il-Gardiel; mains €10-13, platters €19; ⏰6.30pm-1am Tue-Fri, noon-1am Sat & Sun;) Asian, Middle Eastern and Mediterranean flavours all mingle on Bongo Nyah's eclectic menu. A quirky cocktail list, Gozo's Lord Chambray craft beers on tap, and regular music and comedy events conspire to make the bar-eatery one of southern Malta's most fun places to relax. The shared Ottoman, Mumbai and Al-Magħreb platters travel from North Africa to India via Istanbul.

Tal-Familja SEAFOOD €€

(☎2163 2161; www.talfamiljarestaurant.com; Triq il-Gardiel; mains €10-28; ⏰11am-11pm Tue-Sun) A local favourite, with a huge menu and daily specials, at the heart of which are fresh seafood and classic Maltese cuisine. There's a set menu of four courses (€30), which

MALTESE BOATS

The brightly coloured fishing boats that crowd the harbours around the coast have become one of Malta's national symbols. Painted boldly in blue, red and yellow, with the watchful 'Eyes of Osiris' on the bows to ward off evil spirits, the *luzzu* (*loots*-zoo) is a large double-ended fishing boat (for nonsailors, that means it's pointed at both ends). The *kajjik* (*ka*-yik) is similar in appearance, but has a square transom (it's pointed at the front end only). The *dgħajsa* (*dye*-sa) is a smaller and racier-looking boat, with a very high stem and stern-posts – a bit like a Maltese gondola. These are not solid, seaworthy fishing boats, but sleek water taxis. They were once all powered by oars, but today's *dgħajsas* generally carry an outboard engine.

should set you back most of the afternoon. Bookings recommended for evenings and also weekend lunches.

Getting There & Away

Buses 91, 92 and 93 run frequently from Valletta to Marsaskala (one hour) and bus 119 runs to the airport (50 minutes, hourly). The **bus terminus** is on Triq Sant'Antnin at the southern end of the waterfront promenade.

Żurrieq

POP 11,140

The town of Żurrieq sprawls across a hillside on the south coast, in a sort of no man's land to the south of the airport. This part of Malta feels cut off from the rest of the island, and although it's only 10km from Valletta as the crow flies, it seems much further. Signage from Żurrieq to neighbouring towns is poor, but this region is small and it shouldn't take long to find the direction you need (ask locals for guidance if you get stuck).

Sights

Parish Church of St Catherine CHURCH
(Misrah Ir-Repubblika) The Parish Church of St Catherine was built in the 1630s and houses a fine altarpiece of St Catherine – painted by Mattia Preti in 1675, when the artist took refuge here during a plague epidemic. There are several 17th- and 18th-century windmills dotted about the town.

Chapel of the Annunciation CHURCH
(☎2122 5952; www.dinlarthelwa.org; ⏲9am-noon 1st Sun of month) On a minor road between Żurrieq and Mqabba is the Chapel of the Annunciation, in the deserted medieval settlement of **Ħal Millieri**. This tiny church, set in a pretty garden, dates from the mid-15th century and contains important 15th-century frescos – the only surviving examples of medieval religious art in Malta.

Blue Grotto NATURAL FEATURE
This huge natural arch is in the sea cliffs 400m to the east of the seaside hamlet of Wied iż-Żurrieq. Thirty-minute boat trips also take in seven caves, including the **Honeymoon Cave**, **Reflection Cave** and **Cat's Cave**. The best viewing time is before mid-morning when the sun is shining into the grotto.

You can also see the Blue Grotto from a viewing platform beside the main road east of the turn-off to Wied iż-Żurrieq.

> **THE ISLET OF FILFLA**
>
> Filfla is the smallest of Malta's archipelago of five islands. It's 5km off the south coast of Malta, and was separated from the mainland as the result of the geological Maghlaq Fault. Its name probably comes from the Arabic *filfel*, which means chilli or pepper, and it was possibly so-named because of its shape. It suffered the ignominy of being used for target practice by the British armed forces until it was declared a nature reserve in 1970.
>
> The islet supports important breeding colonies of seabirds, including an estimated 5000 to 8000 pairs of storm petrels, as well as two species of lizard and snail not found elsewhere. It's also off-limits due to unexploded shells lying in the surrounding waters.

Tours

Wied iż-Żurrieq BOATING
(☎9945 5347; adult/child €8/4; ⏲9am-5pm Apr-Oct, 9.30am-3.30pm Nov-Mar) About 2km west of Żurrieq lies the tiny harbour of Wied iż-Żurrieq, set in a narrow inlet in the cliffs and guarded by a watchtower. Here, boats depart, weather permitting, for enjoyable 30-minute cruises to the **Blue Grotto**, a huge natural arch in the sea cliffs 400m to the east.

Eating

Il Corsaro MEDITERRANEAN €€
(☎7725 8895; Triq Wied iż-Żurrieq; mains €12-16; ⏲noon-3.30pm Tue-Sun, 7-11pm Fri & Sat) Ignoring the maxim that restaurants at popular tourist destinations are often not very good, Il Corsaro offers both excellent food and stellar views. It's a compact space, just enough for a few tables and an open kitchen, but menu highlights include mussels with fragrant pepper, and local seafood including calamari and prawns.

There are only six tables, so it's worth booking ahead.

Getting There & Away

Bus 201 (50 minutes, hourly) runs from Rabat to Wied iż-Żurrieq via Dingli Cliffs and Ħaġar Qim, and goes on to the airport, via Żurrieq . Bus 71 connects Żurrieq (which is about 1.5km from the Blue Grotto) with Valletta (35 minutes, half hourly).

Ħaġar Qim & Mnajdra

The megalithic temples of **Ħaġar Qim & Mnajdra** (☎2142 4231; www.heritagemalta.org; Triq Ħaġar Qim; adult/child €10/5.50; ⏰9am-6pm Apr-Sep, 9am-5pm Oct-Mar) are the best preserved and most evocative of Malta's prehistoric sites, and have an unparalleled location atop sea cliffs, looking over to the islet of Filfla.

There's an informative hands-on visitors centre to explain the background to the structures, a children's room where kids can build a temple out of blocks, and an atmospheric if not all that informative 4D film introduction.

Ħaġar Qim (*adge*-ar eem; 'standing stones') is the first temple you reach after the visitors' centre. The facade, with its trilithon entrance (two upright stones with a third across the top as a lintel), has been restored, and gives an idea of what it may once have looked like. The temples were originally roofed over, probably with corbelled stone vaults, but these have long since collapsed.

Before going in, look round the corner to the right – the megalith here is the largest in the temple, weighing more than 20 tonnes. The temple consists of a series of interconnected, oval chambers with no uniform arrangement, and differs from other Maltese temples in lacking a regular trefoil plan. In the first chamber on the left is a little altar post decorated with plant motifs, and in the second there are a couple of pedestal altars. The 'fat lady' statuettes and the 'Venus de Malta' figurine that were found here are on display in the National Museum of Archaeology (p172) in Valletta.

Mnajdra (mm-*nigh*-dra), a 700m walk downhill from Ħaġar Qim, is more elaborate. There are three temples side by side, each with a trefoil plan and a different orientation. The oldest temple is the small one on the right, aligned towards the southwest and Filfla Island. The central temple, pointing towards the southeast, is the youngest. All date from between 3600 and 3000 BC.

In the right-hand apse there is a separate chamber entered through a small doorway, with an 'oracle hole' to its left. The function of this is unknown.

It has been claimed that the southern temple is full of significant solar alignments. At Ħaġar Qim at sunrise during the summer solstice, a sunbeam enters a circular opening in the back of the right-hand apse in the left rear chamber. Around the summer (June) and winter (December) solstices and the spring (March) and autumn (September) equinoxes, Heritage Malta (www.heritage

Ħaġar Qim Temple

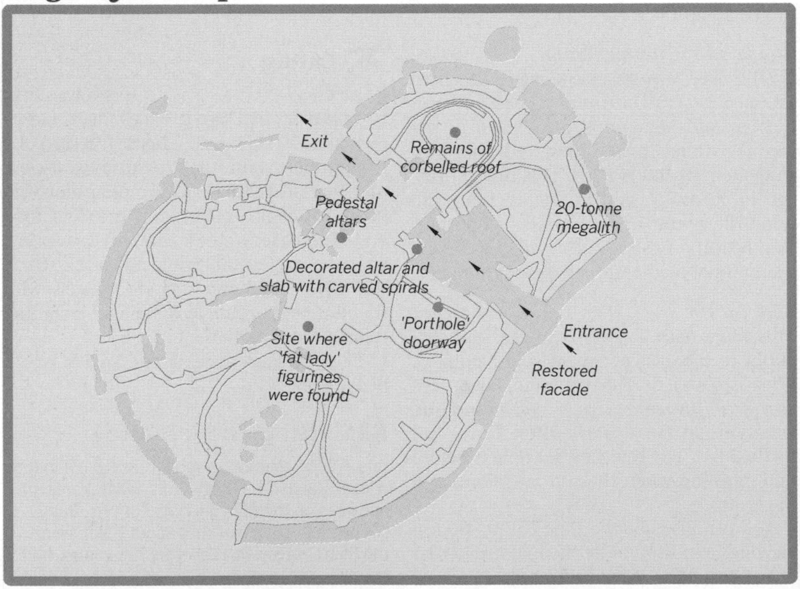

MEGA-ATTRACTIONS

The megalithic temples of Malta, which date mainly from the period 3600 to 3000 BC, are among the oldest free standing stone structures in the world. They pre-date the pyramids of Egypt by more than 500 years. The oldest surviving temples are thought to be those of Ta'Ħġrat and Skorba near the village of Mġarr (p91) on Malta. Ġgantija (p143) on Gozo and Ħaġar Qim and Mnajdra on Malta are among the best preserved. Tarxien (p67) is the most developed, its last phase dating from 3000 to 2500 BC. The subterranean tombs of the Hypogeum (p67) date from the same period as the temples and mimic many of their architectural features below ground.

The purpose of these mysterious structures is the subject of much debate. They all share certain features in common – a site on a southeasterly slope, near to caves; a spring and fertile farmland; a trefoil or cloverleaf plan with three or five rounded chambers (apses) opening off the central axis, which usually faces between south and east; megalithic construction, using blocks of stone weighing up to 20 tonnes; and holes and sockets drilled into the stones, perhaps to hold wooden doors or curtains made from animal hide. Most temple sites have also revealed spherical stones, about the size of cannonballs – it has been suggested that these were used like ball bearings to move the heavy megaliths more easily over the ground.

malta.org) organises special guided tours to experience these alignments at the Mnajdra Temples (€25 per person).

On the cliff top to the southeast of Mnajdra is a 17th-century watchtower and a memorial to Sir Walter Congreve (Governor of Malta 1924–27), who was buried at sea off this point. You can hike west along the cliffs to Għar Lapsi. The tiny uninhabited island Filfla (p123), 5km offshore, is clearly visible.

Eating

Ħaġar Qim Restaurant MALTESE €€
(☎2142 4116; mains €11-27; ⏲10am-4pm & 7-10.30pm Tue-Sun, to 3pm Mon Jun-Sep, to 3pm Tue-Sun, 7-10.30pm Fri-Sun Oct-May) This pleasingly spacious restaurant, just above the Ħaġar Qim and Mnajdra car park, has a large open-air terrace shaded by a bamboo-slatted canopy. It serves excellent beef, rabbit and fish dishes plus the usual suspects (pizza and pasta).

Getting There & Away

Bus 74 runs from Valletta to Ħaġar Qim (35 minutes, half-hourly) continuing on to Wied iż-Żurrieq (five minutes) and the Blue Grotto. From Rabat and Mdina, bus 201 (45 minutes, hourly) goes to Ħaġar Qim via the Dingli Cliffs. From Ħaġar Qim it also continues on to Wied iż-Żurrieq.

Għar Lapsi

On the road west of the Ħaġar Qim and Mnajdra temples is a turn-off (signposted) to Għar Lapsi. The name means 'Cave of the Ascension', and there was once a fishermen's shrine here. The road winds steeply to the coast and ends at a car park beside a couple of restaurants and boathouses. The main attraction here is the **swimming** – a little cove in the low limestone cliffs has been converted into a natural lido, with stone steps and iron ladders giving access to the limpid blue water. It's a popular spot for bathing and picnicking among locals, and is well frequented by divers and fishermen.

Eating

Carmen's Bar & Restaurant MEDITERRANEAN €€
(☎2146 7305; www.facebook.com/carmensbarlapsi; mains €10-17; ⏲11am-10pm Wed-Mon) This tiny bar-restaurant is set in a fisherman's boat hut, among fishing boats, just above the Għar Lapsi swimming hole, and is a splendid, simple place to sit and have a drink or tuck into some fresh fish.

Ta'Rita Lapsi View MALTESE €€
(☎2164 0608; www.taritalapsiview.co; mains €6-18; ⏲11am-3pm & 6.30-10.30pm Tue-Sun) This 1950s-style restaurant has the look of a '50s municipal swimming pool, its exterior fronted by trestle tables, but inside it's retro Malta, an echoing place with high ceilings. As you'd expect, old-fashioned home-cooking is the order of the day, with burgers, sandwiches, rabbit, steak, *lampuka* and stewed octopus.

Getting There & Away

At the time of writing, there was no public transport to Għar Lapsi.

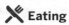

AT A GLANCE

POPULATION
34,430

CAPITAL
Valletta

BEST FOR LOCAL CRAFT BEER
Lord Chambray (p137)

BEST FOR OUTDOOR ACTIVITIES
Gozo Adventures (p130)

BEST ARCHAEOLOGICAL SITE
Ġgantija Temples (p143)

WHEN TO GO

May–Jun
Lower visitor numbers and fine and settled spring weather.

Jul–Aug
Party time at the island's outdoor venues, especially at the popular Blue Lagoon on Comino.

Sep–Oct
Lower visitor numbers at the Blue Lagoon, and the cultural showcase of the Mediterranea festival from mid-October.

Malsaforn salt pans (p140)
ANIBALTREJO/GETTY IMAGES ©

Gozo & Comino

Gozo, called Għawdex (*aow*-desh) in Malti, is a gloriously pretty island, with what the 19th-century nonsense poet Edward Lear called a 'pomskizillious and gromphibberous' landscape. He coined the words to describe the island's fairy-tale hillocks topped by enormous churches, its hidden, glittering coves, and its sculptured coastal cliffs.

Gozo moves at a much slower pace than its bigger, busier neighbour. Although it is more than one-third the size of Malta, it has less than one-tenth of the population – only about 35,000 Gozitans live here (and they are Gozitans first, Maltese second). This is a lovely place to kick back, with sandy beaches, rocky coves, excellent scuba-diving and snorkelling, plus history in the form of megalithic temples and medieval citadels.

For foodies, there's the appeal of vineyard visits and great oceanfront dining on fresh seafood, and just a short boat ride away is the glorious Blue Lagoon on tiny Comino.

INCLUDES

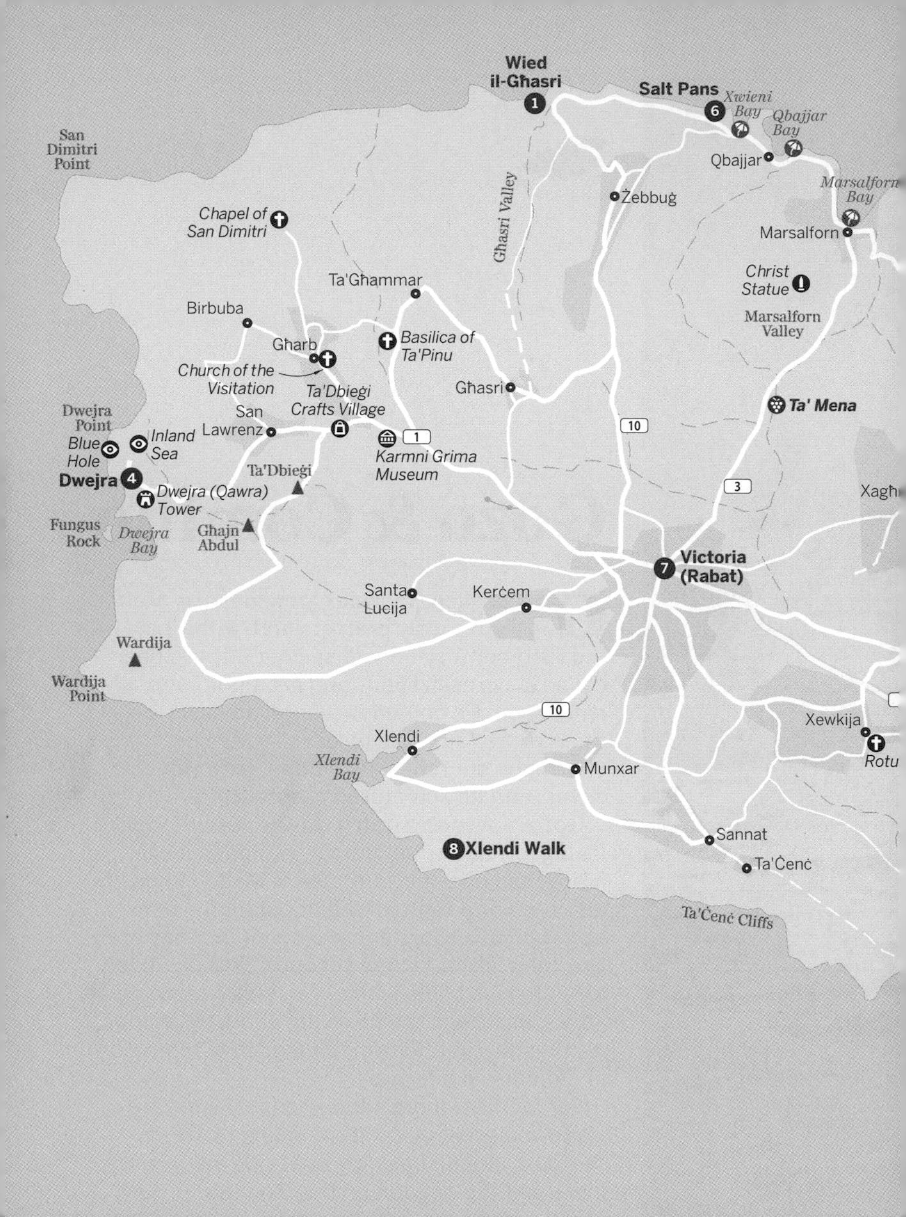

Gozo & Comino Highlights

❶ **Wied il-Għasri** (p144) Swimming from the pebbled beach at this remote and compact cove.

❷ **San Blas Bay** (p146) Getting red sand in your shorts at one of Gozo's best swimming and snorkelling beaches.

❸ **Comino** (p148) Taking in the incredible 360-degree views from atop this tiny island.

❹ **Dwejra** (p140) Admiring a coastal moonscape and negotiating the Inland Sea by fishing boat.

5 Mġarr ix-Xini (p136) Having a seafood lunch at this tiny bay, ideally having arrived by boat.

6 Salt Pans (p140) Seeing the sun sparkle and waves crash at Gozo's historic salt pans.

7 Victoria (p131) Exploring the recently restored Il-Kastell citadel.

8 Xlendi Walk (p35) Negotiating this stunning coastal hike from Mġarr to Xlendi.

GOZO

For such a small island, Gozo packs in a wide variety of experiences and attractions. Travelling history fans shouldn't miss the megalithic temples at Ġgantija, and the recently restored Il-Kastell fortress towering above Gozo's compact capital of Victoria is one of Malta's finest sights. Mountain biking, kayaking and clifftop hiking are all opportunities for active visitors, while Gozo's food and wine scene focuses strongly on fresh local produce and briny-fresh seafood. While Malta can sometimes feel busy and crowded, sleepy and laid-back Gozo offers the perfect opportunity to breathe out and relax.

Activities

Gozo Fun WATER SPORTS
(☎7714 3393; www.gozofun.com; adult/child €35/25) Stand-up paddleboarding (SUP) tours taking in Gozo and Comino, including a popular sunset departure. Also offers lessons (from €20).

Gozo Adventures ADVENTURE SPORTS
(☎9999 4592; www.gozoadventures.com) Offers a half-/full-day sea-kayaking excursion to Comino and Gozo (€45/65), half-/full-day walks (€45/65) on Gozo, and rock-climbing, bouldering and abseiling trips.

Sea Kayak Malta KAYAKING
(☎9999 4592; www.seakayakmalta.com; day trips €65) Offers sea-kayaking day trips to Comino or St Paul's Island as well as longer kayaking holidays.

Tours

Gozo Segway Tours TOURS
(☎9944 8901; www.gozosegway.com; Segway tours €20-69, e-bike hire from €15) Segway tours ranging from one to four hours, including a popular itinerary taking in the Marsalforn salt pans. E-bikes are also available for hire, and the operators conveniently drop them off at your accommodation.

City Sightseeing Gozo BUS
(www.city-sightseeing.com; adult/child €18/10; ⏱every 45min 9.45am-6.30pm) Hop-on-hop-off bus tours of Gozo. The full circuit takes two hours.

Malta Sightseeing Gozo BUS
(www.maltasightseeing.com; adult/child €20/13; ⏱every 45min 9.40am-3pm) Malta Sightseeing Gozo offers hop-on-hop-off bus tours.

Getting There & Away

Gozo Channel (p179) runs the car and foot passenger ferry connecting Ċirkewwa on Malta with Mġarr on Gozo (every 45 minutes from 6am to 10.30pm, and roughly every 90 minutes overnight). Pay for your return ticket in Mġarr on the return trip, not on the way out. At the time of writing, a fast ferry service was planned to link Gozo and Valletta.

Getting Around

BUS

Buses tend to run daily, about hourly, and most pass through Victoria. You can buy your ticket aboard the bus, or at the ticket machines at the **Victoria bus station** (Triq Putirjal), which is close to the town centre. A two-hour ticket costs €2 between July and September (€1.50 between October and June); a block of 12 tickets costs €15, and a seven-day Explore pass €21. City Sightseeing Gozo and Malta Sightseeing Gozo offer hop-on-hop-off bus tours.

CAR & BICYCLE

If you want to see as much of the island as possible, then it makes sense to rent a car. It's also even cheaper than in Malta, though in high season you'll need to book ahead as supply is limited. Options for car rental – both based in Victoria – include Mayjo Car Rentals (p181) and **Victoria Garage** (☎2155 6414; www.victoriagaragegozo.com; Triq Putirjal; car per day from around €22). At the Mġarr ferry terminal, Mġarr Tourist Services (p136) rents cars and jeeps.

Cycling is also a great option on Gozo as the roads are mostly quiet. See Mġarr Tourist Services (p136) for bikes, e-bikes and scooters. In Victoria, **Victoria Garage** (bicycle per day from €5) also rents bikes.

TAXI

Approximate taxi fares from Victoria include €10 for Marsalforn or Mġarr, €8 to Xagħra and €8 to Xlendi. There are taxi ranks near Victoria's **bus station** and at **Pjazza Indipendenza**.

Victoria (Rabat)

POP 6900

Victoria, the chief town of Gozo, sits in the centre of the island, 6km from the ferry terminal at Mġarr and 3.5km from the resort town of Marsalforn. It's crowned by the tiny citadel Il-Kastell, which appears to grow out of its rocky outcrop. The small walled city houses numerous interesting museums and, following a careful 2016 restoration, is now one of Malta's essential sights.

Victoria

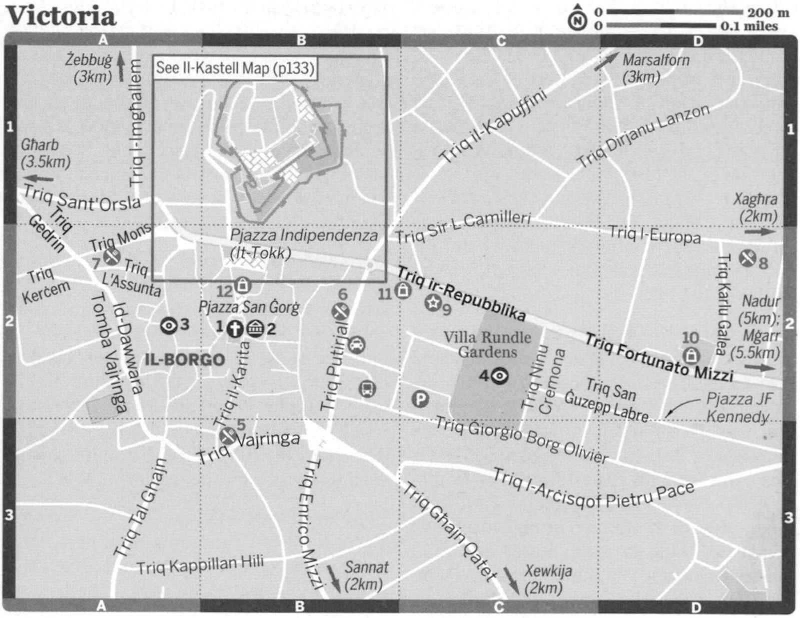

Gozo's capital is the island's main hub of shops and services. Named for the Diamond Jubilee of Queen Victoria in 1897, it was originally known as Rabat, and is still called that by many of the islanders (and on several road signs).

Sights

Il-Kastell & Around

★Il-Kastell FORTRESS

(Ċittadella; adult/child €5/3.50) While the walls surrounding Il-Kastell date from the 15th century, there have been fortifications atop this flat-topped hill since the Bronze Age: it developed under the Phoenicians and later became a Roman town. After terrible raids on Gozo by the Turks, it became customary for all the island's families to stay within Il-Kastell overnight, a practice that lasted into the 17th century. You can walk almost all the way around the city walls for astounding views over Gozo and towards the sea.

Also known locally as the Ċittadella, an excellent new visitor centre experience opened in 2016 to complement Il-Kastell's compact array of interesting museums. Inside the walls are also arts and crafts shops specialising in silver jewellery and traditional Gozitan lace.

Entry to Il-Kastell includes the Ċittadella Visitors' Centre (p132) and entry to four museums falling under the Heritage Malta banner: the Archaeology Museum (p132), the Old Prison (p132), the Gozo Nature Museum (p132) and the Gran Castello Historic House (p132).

Victoria

Sights

1 Basilica of St George B2
2 Heart of Gozo B2
3 Il-Borgo A2
4 Villa Rundle Gardens C2

Eating

5 Black Cat Cafe B3
6 Bon Bon B2
7 Maldonado Bistro A2
8 Patrick's D2

Entertainment

9 Aurora Opera House C2

Shopping

10 Arkadia Supermarket D2
11 Bookworm C2
12 La Bottega del Sole e della Luna B2

Ċittadella Visitors' Centre VISITOR CENTRE
(www.facebook.com/cittadellagozo; Telgħa tal-Belt; adult/child 4 museums €5/3.50; ⏲9am-5pm) Inaugurated in mid-2016 as part of the excellent restoration of Victoria's Il-Kastell, this award-winning visitors' centre includes a poignant and informative audiovisual presentation of the history of the site, and other interactive displays covering the history of Gozo and Malta. The spectacular architectural makeover cunningly makes use of capacious former water reservoirs built by the British in the 1870s.

Cathedral of the Assumption CHURCH
(www.gozocathedral.org; Misraħ il-Katidral; adult/child incl museum €5/2; ⏲5am-8pm) Built between 1697 and 1711 to replace a church destroyed by a 1693 earthquake (which was in southern Italy but caused damage as far Gozo), the cathedral was designed by Lorenzo Gafa, also responsible for St Paul's Cathedral (p106) at Mdina. The elegant facade is adorned with the escutcheons of Grand Master Ramon de Perellos and Bishop Palmieri. Due to a lack of funds the dome was never finished, but a trompe l'œil painting makes it look as if it were.

Cathedral Museum MUSEUM
(☎21556087; www.gozocathedral.org; Triq il-Fossos; adult/child incl cathedral €5/2; ⏲10am-4pm Mon-Sat) This jumble of objects within the Cathedral Museum includes a *zucchetto* (skull cap) worn by Pope Francis, church gold and silver, some religious art (including a disturbing 19th-century painting depicting the martyrdom of St Agatha) and a 19th-century bishop's carriage.

Archaeology Museum MUSEUM
(☎2155 6144; www.heritagemalta.org; Triq Bieb il-Mdina; adult/child incl Visitors' Centre & 4 museums €5/3.50; ⏲9am-5pm) Victoria's Archaeology Museum houses some incredible finds. There are some 'fat lady' carvings from Ġgantija Temples and Xagħra, around 3000 to 4000 years old. There are also Roman anchors, a 3rd-to-5th-century skeleton that was found buried in an amphora, Bronze Age jugs dating from 2400 to 1500 BC, and some fascinating Phoenician amulets in the form of the Eye of Osiris – an ancient link to the symbols seen on Maltese fishing boats of today.

Gozo Nature Museum MUSEUM
(☎2155 6153; www.heritagemalta.org; Triq il-Kwartier; adult/child incl Visitors' Centre & 4 museums €5/3.50; ⏲9am-5pm) This gracious old building houses a series of low-key exhibits explaining the geology of the island and its water supply. There are some interesting fossils downstairs, including huge megalodon shark teeth. Parts of the building were used as an air-raid shelter during WWII.

St John's Demi-Bastion FORTRESS
There is a good panorama from here. Look for the huge dome of the Rotunda at Xewkija, with Comino and Malta in the background; the distant Gothic spire of the church above Mġarr Harbour; the watchtower of Nadur, and the dome and twin clock towers of its parish church; and the view of Xagħra on its hilltop to the east, capped by Ta'Kola Windmill and the Church of Our Lady of Victory.

Old Prison HISTORIC BUILDING
(☎2156 5988; www.heritagemalta.org; Triq il-Kwartier; adult/child incl Visitors' Centre & 4 museums €5/3.50; ⏲9am-5pm) The Old Prison served as a jail from the late 1500s to 1904, and proved particularly useful for locking up hot-tempered Knights until they cooled off. The cells here once held Jean Parisot de la Valette for a few months for beating up a layperson. His punishment included two years service in Tripoli before he later became Grand Master. Particularly fascinating is the historic graffiti etched into the walls by the inmates, including crosses, ships, hands and the cross of the Knights.

Gran Castello Historic House MUSEUM
(☎2156 2034; www.heritagemalta.org; Triq Bernardo de Opuo; adult/child incl Visitors' Centre & 4 museums €5/3.50; ⏲9am-5pm) This folklore museum is a lovely maze of stairs, rooms and courtyards. The fine, rambling old building itself, dating to 1500, houses a collection of domestic, trade and farming implements, which give an insight into rural life on Gozo.

IL-KASTELL & MALTA PASS

If you have a Heritage Malta multisite pass or a Malta Pass (www.maltapass.com.mt), all entry is covered. Note, however, that neither pass covers entry to the Cathedral of the Assumption or the Cathedral Museum. Entry to these must be purchased separately from the **Cathedral Ticket Office** (www.gozocathedral.org; adult/child incl cathedral & museum €5/2; ⏲10am-4pm Mon-Sat).

Il-Kastell

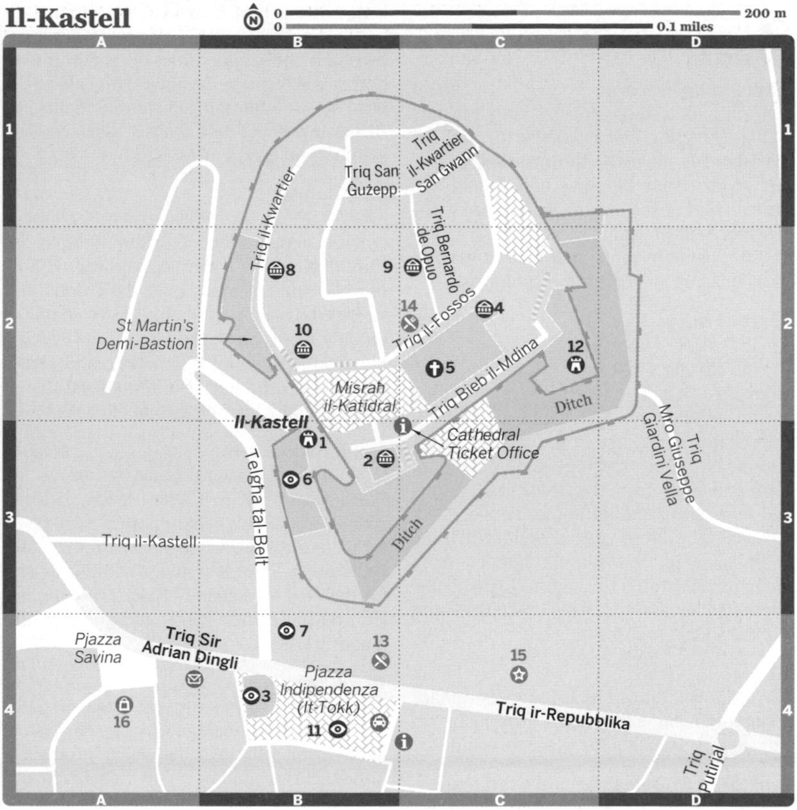

Il-Kastell

Top Sights
1 Il-Kastell ... B3

Sights
2 Archaeology Museum ... B3
3 Banca Giuratale ... B4
4 Cathedral Museum ... C2
5 Cathedral of the Assumption ... C2
6 Ċittadella Visitors' Centre ... B3
7 Gozo 360° ... B4
8 Gozo Nature Museum ... B2
9 Gran Castello Historic House ... C2
10 Old Prison ... B2
11 Pjazza Indipendenza ... B4
12 St John's Demi-Bastion ... C2

Eating
13 Café Jubilee ... B4
14 Ta'Rikardu ... C2

Entertainment
15 Astra Theatre ... C4

Shopping
16 Pio's Antiques ... A4

Gozo 360° AUDIOVISUAL
(☎2155 9955; www.gozo360.com.mt; entrance on Telgħa tal-Belt; adult/child €7/3; ⌚10am-3pm Mon-Sat) Gozo 360° is a 30-minute audiovisual show that gives a good, basic introduction to the island's history and sights before veering off into tourist board–style fluff.

Shows take place every 30 minutes, and the commentary can be experienced in 15 languages.

The show is held at the Citadel Cinema, which also screens a concise and up-to-date program of international blockbuster and arthouse films.

Pjazza Indipendenza & Around

Pjazza Indipendenza PIAZZA

Victoria's main square hosts a daily **market** (6.30am to 2pm) and is known throughout the island as **It-Tokk** (the meeting place). The semicircular baroque building at the western end of the square is the **Banca Giuratale**, built in 1733 to house the city council. After being restored in 2016, it now hosts occasional art and cultural exhibitions.

Heart of Gozo MUSEUM

(2155 7504; www.heartofgozo.org.mt; Triq il-Karita; donations welcome; 9am-5pm) This innovative small museum was founded by the Fondazzjoni Belt Victoria to exhibit treasures belonging to the Basilica of St George as well as other artefacts, including coins and lamps from the Herod era in Israel and scrap silver amounting to the weight of a shekel. A column runs through all three floors showing the island's history from prehistoric Ġgantija through to British rule. There's an audio room, where you can listen to traditional local music.

Il-Borgo AREA

The old town, known as Il-Borgo, is a maze of narrow, meandering alleys around Pjazza San Ġorġ. It's a beguiling place to wander.

Basilica of St George CHURCH

(2155 6377; www.stgeorge.org.mt; Pjazza San Ġorġ; 4.30am-12.30pm & 2.30-7.30pm) The well-attended original parish church of Rabat dates from 1678, and the lavish interior contains a fine altarpiece of *St George and the Dragon* by Mattia Preti. Note that wearing shorts inside the church is not allowed.

Villa Rundle Gardens GARDENS

(7am-10.30pm Apr-Oct, 7.30am-8.30pm Nov-Mar;) The Rundle Gardens, south of Triq ir-Repubblika, were laid out around 1914 by General Sir Leslie Rundle (Governor of Malta, 1909–15), and are pleasant and shady for walking around. Occasional concerts and festivals are held throughout spring and summer, and there is a children's playground.

Eating & Drinking

Black Cat Cafe CAFE €

(2156 9240; www.facebook.com/blackcatcafe19; 19 Triq Vajringa; snacks & mains €3-8; 8am-4pm Mon-Sat;) Owned by a Maltese-Australian, the exceptionally cosy Black Cat Cafe brings a touch of Down Under cafe culture to the backstreets of Victoria. That means excellent coffee, smoothies and artisan teas, homestyle baking – try the carrot cafe or the bliss balls – and more substantial mains like BLT sandwiches and bagels with smoked salmon and cream cheese.

Café Jubilee CAFE €

(2155 8921; www.cafejubilee.com; Pjazza Indipendenza; mains €5.75-16.75; 8am-10.30pm;) This cafe-bar has a nice atmosphere, with its marble counter, brass rails, dark wood and vintage ads on the walls, and has a couple of outside tables on the square. In the evening it becomes a popular wine bar and serves good local drops. It also offers local dishes such as rabbit, as well as other snacks.

Maldonado Bistro BISTRO €€

(9901 9270; www.maldonado.com.mt; 18 Triq Mons; mains €9-18; 6.30pm-late daily, 11.30am-3pm Sat & Sun) This cellar bistro is a fun place for an *aperitivo* or dinner – it's intimate and welcoming – and is popular with locals and tourists for its delicious Italian cooking, including handmade pasta, and good accompanying wines.

Ta'Rikardu GOZITAN €€

(2155 5953; 4 Triq il-Fossos; mains €7.50-15; 10am-8pm) Tucked away in Il-Kastell, Ta'Rikardu sells excellent local produce – honey, cheese and wine (with particularly good rosé) – along with souvenirs and paintings. Take a seat and order a cheap, delicious platter, which includes cheese, bread, tomatoes, capers and olives. Vegetable soup or homemade ravioli is also available; wash it all down with the owners' Gozitan wine.

Patrick's MEDITERRANEAN €€€

(21566667; www.patrickstmun.com; Triq l-Ewropa; mains €16.90-32.50, 6-course tasting menu with wine matches €90; 6.30-10.30pm Mon-Sat year round & noon-2.30pm Sun Dec-Jun;) From the linen-covered tables to the extensive wine list and menu of complex fusion dishes, Patrick's is polished and professional. Asian influences, New Zealand beef and fresh local fish all come together wonderfully in a nautical yet elegant blue-and-white dining room. The restaurant is consistently a worthy contender for one of Gozo's most popular eateries.

Entertainment

Despite its diminutive size, Victoria has two theatres compared to Valletta's one.

Aurora Opera House THEATRE
(☎2156 2974; www.teatruaurora.com; Triq ir-Repubblika; 📶) The Aurora Opera House stages productions including opera, ballet, comedy, drama, cabaret, pantomime, celebrity concerts and exhibitions.

Astra Theatre THEATRE
(Teatru Astru; ☎2155 0985; www.lastella.com.mt; Triq ir-Repubblika) Astra Theatre is the 19th-century home of Soċjetà Filarmonika La Stella, and stages predominantly opera, music and ballet.

Shopping

La Bottega del Sole e della Luna FOOD & DRINKS
(☎24700742; www.facebook.com/bottegasoleluna; Pjazza San Ġorġ; ⏲9.30am-6.30pm Mon-Fri, to 4pm Sat) This pleasantly overstocked store is divided into two parts: one side sells a cornucopia of local Gozitan food specialities and interesting souvenirs, while the other is a deli crammed with gourmet food and drink products from Italy and France. Drop in for goodies to be enjoyed on the deck at your farmhouse.

Pio's Antiques ANTIQUES
(☎9906 6101; Pjazza Savina; ⏲8am-12.30pm Mon-Sat) An Aladdin's cave of Gozitan and Maltese bric-a-brac, including candlesticks and tradtional door knockers. There's two separate rooms of heritage finds waiting to be discovered.

Bookworm BOOKS
(☎2155 6215; 105 Triq ir-Repubblika; ⏲7.30am-7pm Mon-Fri, to 1pm Sat) Well-stocked shop with a good range of fiction and guidebooks, plus local and British newspapers.

Arkadia Supermarket FOOD & DRINKS
(www.arkadia.com.mt; Triq Fortunato Mizzi; ⏲7am-8pm) Gozo's best supermarket, with some Waitrose products and an excellent deli section.

Information

Aurora (Opera House, Triq ir-Repubblika; ⏲7am-midnight; 📶) There is free wi-fi offered at the Aurora cafe in the Opera House.

Free wi-fi is also available around the Il-Kastell precinct.

Bank of Valletta (102 Triq ir-Repubblika; ⏲8.30am-2pm Mon-Thu, to 5.30pm Fri, to 12.30pm Sat)

General Hospital (☎2156 1600; Triq l-Arċisqof Pietru Pace)

Gozo Police Headquarters (p174) Gozo's main police station is located near the corner of Triq ir-Repubblika and Triq Putirjal.

Post Office (5 Triq Sir Adrian Dingl; ⏲8.15am-4.30pm Mon-Fri, to 12.30pm Sat)

Tourist Information Office (☎2291 5452; www.visitgozo.com; Pjazza Indipendenza; ⏲9am-5.15pm Mon-Sat, to 12.45pm Sun & public holidays) A very helpful office with maps and brochures.

Getting There & Away

From the Mġarr ferry terminal to Victoria is around 7km. A taxi is around €10. Most buses (€1.50) on Gozo also run through Victoria's bus station (p130).

Mġarr

POP 3650

Mġarr is Gozo's main harbour and the point of arrival for ferries from Malta. It's home to a cluster of restaurants and is a fun and scenic place to dine on fresh fish. There are also a few bars, including the characterful Gleneagles. The hill above the town is capped by the ramparts of Fort Chambray, formerly a fortress built by the Knights of St John, but now housing an apartment complex.

Sights & Activities

Church of Our Lady of Lourdes CHURCH
(☎2166 6537; Triq Lourdes) This 20th-century neo-Gothic church appears almost to hang over the village. Begun in 1924, a lack of funds meant that its construction was not completed until the 1970s.

Viewpoint VIEWPOINT
Triq iż-Żewwiega leads to a stunning viewpoint just south of Qala. It's worth the effort to get here – 1.8km uphill from the harbour; once here you can enjoy the magnificent panorama over Gozo and out to sea.

Bethlehem Village AREA
(Għajnsielem) On the right after the first roundabout as you leave Mġarr is this life-sized Bethlehem-style village, where 150 actors create a living nativity, which attracts thousands of people each December. It's a fun place to explore even when it's not in use.

Boat Trips

You can arrange boats to Comino at stands along the main road through Mġarr and around the harbour. For a small supplement, most offer a quick trip to view some of Comino's caves.

Xlendi Pleasure Cruises BOATING
(☎9911 1909; www.xlendicruises.com; c/o Mġarr Tourist Services; ⏱Apr-Oct) This outfit offers boat trips around Gozo and/or Comino. A four-hour trip taking in Gozo and Comino costs €30/15 per adult/child, while an 8½-hour trip is €40/20 (with a buffet lunch for either costing €8/5). Private charters are €280 for three hours. Trips depart from Mġarr Harbour, but transfers can be arranged.

Eating & Drinking

Bugeja Fish Market MARKET €
(⏱8.30am-12.30pm & 4.30-7pm Mon-Sat) Head to Bugeja, just outside Mġarr, to purchase your fresh fish for a barbecue. It has a great range of local fish and seafood, and attracts queues of locals.

Bancinu MEDITERRANEAN €€
(☎2155 5656; www.bancinu.com; Triq ix-Xatt; mains €13-22; ⏱11.30am-2.30pm & 6.30-11pm Thu-Tue) Named after a historic ferry that used to cross between Gozo and Malta, Bancinu offers knockout renditions of traditional Mediterranean flavours. Begin with a delicate starter of whitebait fritters on rucola (rocket) then move on to homemade octopus *panzotti* (a stuffed pasta). Leave room for apple and cinnamon tart.

Tmun Mġarr MEDITERRANEAN €€
(☎2156 6276; www.tmunmgarr.com; Triq Martino Garces; mains €16-24; ⏱noon-2.30pm & 6.30-10.30pm Wed-Mon) Family-run Tmun Mġarr offers a menu rich in seafood dishes such as bouillabaisse and fresh-from-the-sea fish. Set behind the fishing boats at the water's edge, it has an outdoor terrace. If you're tiring of Malta's usual focus on Mediterranean flavours, Tmun Mġarr also offers a few Asian-inspired dishes such as calamari with chilli, ginger and lemongrass.

★**Gleneagles Bar** PUB
(☎2155 6543; Triq ix-Xatt; ⏱3pm-late Mon-Sat, noon-late Sun) This is the social hub of the village and a glorious place to head for a sundowner, with views over the harbour. It fills up in the early evening with a lively mix of locals, fishermen, yachties and tourists. It's named after the first ferry-service ship (1885).

Information

Mġarr Harbour Info Booth (Ferry Terminal; ⏱9am-2pm) Helpful information office for when you arrive in Gozo.

Getting There & Away

From the **Vapur bus stop** near the ferry terminal, buses 301, 303 and 323 all depart frequently for Victoria (20 minutes).

Getting Around

Mġarr Tourist Services (☎2155 3678; www.gozomgarrtouristservice.com; Shop 4, Ferry Terminal; bicycle/e-bike/scooter rental from €8/20/25 per day) Versatile operation right near the ferry terminal offering bicycle rental (from €8 per day), e-bikes (from €20 per day), scooter rental (from €5 per day) and quad bike rental (per day €90). Cars and jeeps can also be hired,

Mġarr ix-Xini

The narrow, cliff-bound inlet of Mġarr ix-Xini (Port of the Galleys) was once used by the Knights of St John as their main harbour on Gozo. One of their watchtowers still guards the entrance.

The Turkish admiral Dragut Reis also sheltered in the bay when he raided Gozo in 1551 and took most of the island's population into slavery.

A more recent invasion was when Brad Pitt and Angelina Jolie used Mġarr ix-Xini as the location for the film *By the Sea* in 2014, building a hotel set on the cliffs and taking over the bay for five months.

There's a tiny shingle beach at the head of the inlet, and a paved area where tourists and locals stake out their sunbathing territories. It's a gorgeous place to swim and snorkel, particularly on weekdays when fewer people come. It's also home to a classic Gozo restaurant.

Sights

Torri ta'Mġarr ix-Xini TOWER
(www.wirtghawdex.org; ⏱11am-1.30pm Sat & when tower flag is flying) This watchtower built by the Knights of St John in the 17th century guards the entrance to Mġarr ix-Xini's tiny harbour.

Eating

★**Rew Rew** SEAFOOD €€
(☎7985 4007; mains €17-25; ⏱11am-6pm Mar-Nov) This simple, pine-shaded place has 10 tables beside a beachside shack and serves up delicious seafood, including calamari, prawns and fish. Mains are served with salad and deliciously chunky homemade chips, and it's the perfect place for a leisurely lunch

looking out to sea. The restaurant appears as an old-fashioned grocery in the 2015 movie *By the Sea*. Cash only.

Phone ahead for a reservation.

Getting There & Away

There is no public transport to Mġarr ix-Xini, and it is accessed via a narrow winding road. It's well signposted, though, and perfectly accessible in a normal car. Try not to visit at the weekend when car parking at the bay is at an absolute premium. Another way is to arrive by boat; charter one from Xlendi or Mġarr. From Xewkija, it's also a pleasant walk of around 2.5km (30 minutes).

Xewkija

POP 3300

The village of Xewkija – and most of southern Gozo – is dominated by the vast dome of the Parish Church of St John the Baptist, which is better known as the Rotunda. The 74m-high dome is the third-largest in the world. Visible throughout the island, the dome has a gallery offering superb views across Gozo.

Sights

Rotunda CHURCH

(Parish Church of St John the Baptist; ☎2155 6793; ⏰5am-noon & 3-8pm) The Rotunda is built around a 17th-century church that was too small for the community's needs, and this more recent structure can seat around three times the village's population. The austere interior impresses through sheer size. Paintings of scenes from the life of St John the Baptist adorn the six side chapels. To the left of the altar is a museum displaying baroque sculptures and relics from the old church. Work on the church began in 1951 and was completed in 1971.

It was built mainly with the volunteer labour of parishioners and paid for by local donations. A small lift (€3) takes visitors up to the gallery surrounding the dome, for great panoramas – the 74m dome is higher than St Paul's Cathedral in London.

Shopping

Lord Chambray FOOD & DRINKS

(☎2155 4324; www.lordchambray.com.mt; Triq Mġarr, Gozitano Agricultural Village, Xewkija; ⏰10am-6pm) Pop into Lord Chambray's compact tasting room to try the full range of craft beers and occasional seasonal releases. Our favourite is the Blue Lagoon Belgian-style wheat beer. Tours are available, but you'll need to phone ahead to check it's not too busy. You'll find its beers in many outlets around Malta and Gozo.

Getting There & Away

Bus 323 (hourly, seven minutes) travels from Victoria to the Dome bus stop right outside the Rotunda.

Ta'Ċenċ

The quiet village of Sannat, once famed for its lace-making, lies 2km south of Victoria, and gives access to the Ta'Ċenċ plateau. Signs from the village square point the way to Hotel Ta'Ċenċ, one of Gozo's finest; its bar is a great place for a sundowner. Around the Ta'Ċenċ plateau, tracks lead to ancient signs of human civilisation.

Sights

Ta'Ċenċ Sea Cliffs NATURAL FEATURE

A track to the left of the entrance to Hotel Ta'Ċenċ leads to the high plateau of Ta'Ċenċ. Views north to Victoria, Xewkija and Xagħra are good, especially towards sunset. Wander off to the left of the track, near the edge of the limestone crag, and you will find a prehistoric dolmen – a large slab propped up on three smaller stones like a table. Keep your eyes peeled – the dolmen is not signposted and is a little tricky to spot.

The best walking is off to the right, along the top of the huge Ta'Ċenċ sea cliffs. These spectacular limestone crags, more than 130m high, were once the breeding ground of the Maltese peregrine falcon. Near the cliff top you can see traces of prehistoric cart ruts, origins unknown.

Eating

Il-Kantra Lido Bar & Restaurant MEDITERRANEAN €€€

(☎7987 3787; www.tacenc.com; Hotel Ta'Ċenċ; mains €15-26; ⏰noon-3pm & 7-10pm Jun-Aug) Rent sunbeds, eat and drink at the Hotel Ta'Ċenċ's gorgeously set summer-only restaurant. Look forward to incredible views towards the inlet of Mġarr ix-Xini. From the hotel, it's around 3km down an unsealed road to the restaurant. It's fine for ordinary cars but parking is limited. During the peak of the summer season, the hotel provides shuttle-bus transport.

Getting There & Away

Bus 305 runs between Victoria and Ta'Ċenċ (10 minutes, hourly).

Xlendi

POP 800

The sometime fishing village of Xlendi is now also a popular resort town. The cluster of hotels are low-rise and unobtrusive, and it's a beautiful bay. For weekending Maltese and tourists, it's a favourite place to chill out by the sea, with good swimming, snorkelling and diving, and plenty of rocks for sunbathing. In the 19th century, this was known as 'women's harbour', as it was reserved for women-only bathing. Around Xlendi there is excellent coastal walking.

Activities

At the head of the bay, steps lead over the cliff above the little fishing-boat harbour to a tiny cove in the rocks where you can swim. This was apparently once reserved for the local nuns. Alternatively, you can keep walking up the hillside above and then hike over to Wardija Point and Dwejra Bay. On the south side of Xlendi Bay, a footpath winds around to the 17th-century watchtower, **Torri ta'Xlendi**, on Ras il-Bajjada. Below here you can scramble down to some **salt pans** with fantastic, windswept views. From here you can hike east to the Sanap cliffs, and on towards Ta'Ċenċ.

Another alternative is the 12km (largely coastal) Xlendi Walk (p35), linking Xlendi with Mġarr Harbour, one of eight walking routes around Gozo and Comino. See 'Country Walks/Rambling' on www.visitgozo.com to download route maps and track information.

Water Sports

Moby Dives (☎2156 4429; www.mobydives.net; Triq il-Gostra; introductory dives from €45) and **St Andrews Divers Cove** (☎2155 1301; www.gozodive.com; Triq San Ximun; introductory dives from €45) can help you explore the excellent nearby dive sites, offering 'taster' dives, beginners' courses and excursions for those who already know what they're doing.

Xlendi Pleasure Cruises BOATING
(☎9911 1909; www.xlendicruises.com; ⏲Apr-Oct) Waterside Xlendi Pleasure Cruises offers motorboats, canoes and paddleboats for hire, as well as fishing trips (€45 per person), snorkelling and cave tours. The company also has a menu of cruises leaving from Mġarr Harbour and will provide transfers.

Xlendi Water Sports WATER SPORTS
(☎9942 7917; www.xlendicruises.com) Xlendi offers self-drive boats, jet skis (from €40 per 20 minutes), guided kayak tours (1½-hour trip €15 per person), hour-long trips along the coast to Dwejra (adult/child €15/7), and four-hour and longer trips to Comino and the Blue Lagoon (€23/12).

Eating

★**Boat House** MEDITERRANEAN €€
(☎2156 9153; www.theboathousegozo.com; Xatt ix-Xlendi; mains €11.50-30; ⏲noon-10.30pm; 📶👪) This is a highly rated restaurant where you can eat fresh fish with the sea almost lapping at your toes – there's a seafront, tented terrace. Seafood is the obvious choice, prices are reasonable and it's a great choice for families. If you're a squid fan, push the boat out with the Boat House's Trio de Calamari featuring squid three ways.

Sofia Bar & Restaurant BALKAN €€
(☎9971 2623; www.facebook.com/pg/SofiaBarRestaurantGozo; Triq ix-Xlendi; mains €9-14; ⏲noon-2.30pm & 6.30-11pm) Balkan flavours come to Xlendi at this restaurant decked out in blue and white, referencing a Greek island taverna. The menu travels from Greece to Serbia and Bulgaria, and the grilled lamb dishes, stuffed vine leaves and robust shepherd's salads are all good value. There's no views of the sea, but a hearty welcome and decent Bulgarian wines easily compensate.

Ta' Karolina MEDITERRANEAN €€
(☎2155 9675; www.karolinarestaurant.com; Triq Marina; mains €7-24; ⏲12.30-3pm & 6.30pm-late Feb-Dec) This long-running seafront restaurant is named after the nun Karolina Cauchi, who raised money to have the steps cut into the cliffs at Xlendi in the 19th century. These days it features a covered terrace, and a great range of soups, pasta and Gozitan specialities. Outdoor tables framed by aquamarine waters have an absolute waterfront location. Booking ahead is recommended.

Iċ-Ċima Restaurant MEDITERRANEAN €€
(☎2155 8407; www.cimarestaurant.com; Triq San Xmun; mains €10-25; ⏲noon-2.30pm & 6.30-10.30pm Wed-Mon) This friendly restaurant is situated a short walk uphill from the village and has an outstanding view over the bay

LOCAL KNOWLEDGE

CLIMBING GOZO

The British Army first pursued rock climbing on Gozo and Comino in the 1950s and '60s, even producing a guidebook of the islands' routes. After independence, climbing was subsequently forgotten as a local sport, but in recent years has been rediscovered. There are now more than 300 climbs in 12 locations across the island in amazingly dramatic yet accessible locations. Dwejra has good-quality rock and some incredible climbs, although climbers have to be aware of not disturbing nesting sea birds in spring. Another important area is between Xlendi and Munxar, with 21 new bolted routes in a coastal gorge. You can learn to climb here, or there are multiple climbs at grades 7 to 8 for experts looking for a challenge. For more information, see **Gozo Climbing** (www.gozo-climbing.com).

and the coastal cliffs from its rooftop. It's an excellent choice, with the emphasis on seafood, plus dishes like *fenek stuffat tan-nanna Sylvia* (rabbit cooked to Nanna Sylvia's recipe). Thanks Nanna Sylvia! The pizzas are also very good.

Drinking & Nightlife

La Grotta CLUB

(www.lagrottaleisure.com; Triq ix-Xlendi; admission varies; 10pm-dawn Fri & Sat May-Oct) On the road to Victoria about 600m east of Xlendi, La Grotta has a unique setting with amazing views. It's housed in a limestone cave in the cliffs above the valley, with two large dance areas (indoors and out), and hosts big-party nights, DJs and live music.

Getting There & Away

Bus 306 (hourly, 25 minutes) runs between Xlendi and Victoria. By car, follow signs from the roundabout at the southern end of Triq Putirjal in Victoria. Alternatively it's a 3km walk from Victoria bus station.

Għarb & San Lawrenz

The village of Għarb (pronounced 'aarb', meaning 'west') in the northwest of Gozo has one of the most beautiful churches on the Maltese Islands.

The charming village of San Lawrenz is where novelist Nicholas Monsarrat (1910–79) lived and worked for four years in the early 1970s. His love for the Maltese Islands is reflected in his novel *The Kappillan of Malta*.

Between San Lawrenz and Santa Lucija is **Ta'Dbieġi Crafts Village** (www.gozoartisans.com; Triq Franġisk Portelli; 10.30am-4pm Mon-Fri, to 12.30pm Sat), where artisans sell handicrafts, lace, glass and pottery.

Sights

Basilica of Ta'Pinu CHURCH

(2155 6187; www.tapinu.org; Triq ta'Pinu; 7am-7pm Mon-Sat, 6am-12.15pm & 1.30-7pm Sun) The Basilica of Ta'Pinu, accessible via a short, scenic walk from Għarb, is an extraordinary sight – a huge, lone church on a Gozitan hillock, towering over the countryside. Malta's national shrine to the Virgin Mary is an important centre of pilgrimage. It was built in the 1920s on the site of a chapel where a local woman, Carmela Grima, claimed to have heard the Virgin speak to her in 1883.

Thereafter, numerous miracles were attributed to the intercession of Our Lady of Pinu, and it was decided to replace the old church with a grand new one.

Built in a Romanesque style, with an Italianate campanile, it has a tranquil interior of pale golden stone. Part of the original chapel, with Carmela Grima's tomb, is incorporated behind the altar. The rooms to either side of the altar are filled with votive offerings, including children's clothes, hoists and plaster casts. The basilica's name comes from Filippino Gauci, who used to tend the old church – Pinu is the Malti diminutive for Filippino. Visitors should dress appropriately. A free smartphone audio tour is available over he church's wi-fi network.

It's well worth walking up the track leading to the top of the hill of Ta'Għammar opposite the church, which is punctuated by marble statues marking the Stations of the Cross.

Karmni Grima Museum MUSEUM

(2155 6045; www.tapinu.org; 2 Triq-l-Għarb; €3; 9am-4pm Tue-Sat, 9am-12.30pm Sun) In the former house of Carmela Grima, whose vision gave rise to the Ta'Pinu Basilica, there's a small museum that gives an insight into rural 19th-century life.

OFF THE BEATEN TRACK

MARSALFORN SALT PANS

The salt pans set just outside Marsalforn are the island's most spectacular system. The northern coast of Gozo was particularly suited to salt production, as its area of flat limestone could be cut into by hand. Seawater ran into the shallow basins and the wind and sun did the rest; the salt pans on Gozo apparently date from Roman times. Small caverns were cut into the rock to store the salt. The Knights were in charge of salt harvesting and fined anyone who produced salt without permission. Nowadays the salt is still harvested between May and September, but only for local use. The sea and wind can be wild here, as it hammers the surrounding cliffs into sculptural shapes.

Church of the Visitation CHURCH
(www.gozodiocese.org/churches/parishes/gharb) Għarb's baroque Church of the Visitation was built between 1699 and 1729, with an elegant curved facade and twin bell towers. Three female figures adorn the front: Faith, above the door; Hope, with her anchor, to the right; and Charity. Inside, there is an altarpiece, *The Visitation of Our Lady to St Elizabeth,* which was gifted to the church by Grand Master de Vilhena.

Chapel of San Dimitri CHURCH
A drive or pleasant walk of about 30 minutes (just over 2km) from Għarb leads to the tiny Chapel of San Dimitri (signposted on the road to the left of the church). This small, square church with its baroque cupola dates from the 15th century, though it was rebuilt in the 1730s. It stands in splendid isolation amid terraced fields. You can continue the walk down to the coast, and return via the Basilica of Ta'Pinu.

Eating

Tatita's MEDITERRANEAN €€
(2156 6482; www.facebook.com/tatitas2; Pjazza San Lawrenz; mains €9.50-28; 6-10.30pm Wed-Mon) Tatita's occupies what was once San Lawrenz police station. When it's warm, you can dine alfresco on the postcard-perfect square. It's very welcoming – and family-friendly, too, despite the formal look and snow-white tablecloths. The kitchen prepares local treats like roasted and stuffed quail or a mixed grill of fish and king prawns.

Getting There & Away

Bus 312 connects Għarb with San Lawrenz (six minutes, hourly) and Victoria (16 minutes), while the 308 runs between Victoria and Ta' Pinu (10 minutes, hourly). For the Ta'Dbieġi Crafts Village catch bus 311 (10 minutes, hourly) from Victoria.

Dwejra

Geology and the sea have conspired to produce some spectacular coastal scenery at Dwejra on the west coast. Two vast, underground caverns in the limestone have collapsed to create two circular depressions now occupied by Dwejra Bay and the Inland Sea. The **Azure Window**, a huge natural arch in the sea cliffs that drew throngs of tourists, collapsed into the sea in March 2017 as a result of natural erosion. Huge underwater sections of the arch can be seen on 15-minute boat trips leaving from the Inland Sea, and the surrounding coastal landscapes are still wildly scenic and definitely worth visiting.

Sights

★**Dwejra Bay & Dwejra Point** AREA
The collapsed cavern of Dwejra Bay has been invaded by the sea, and is guarded by the brooding bulk of Fungus Rock. A path below Dwejra (Qawra) Tower leads to a flight of stairs cut into the rock, leading down to a little slipway on the edge of the bay. There is good **swimming** here.

For even more peace, you can hike right around to the cliff top on the far side of the bay, for a view encompassing Fungus Rock and Dwejra Point and, between them, Crocodile Rock (seen from near Dwejra Tower it looks like a crocodile's head).

The broad horizontal shelf of rock to the south of Dwejra Point has been eroded along the geological boundary between the globigerina limestone and the lower coralline limestone – the boundary is marked by a layer of fossilised scallop shells and sand dollars (a flattened disc-shaped sea urchin).

Blue Hole DIVE SITE
The Blue Hole is a vertical chimney running down into the limestone, about 10m in diameter and 25m deep, that connects

with the open sea through an underwater arch about 8m down. Understandably, it's a very popular dive site and the snorkelling is also excellent. While diving, the underwater remains of the Azure Window, which collapsed in 2017, can often be seen.

Moby Dives (p138) and St Andrews Divers Cove (p138), both located in Xlendi, are available for lessons and equipment hire.

Inland Sea LAGOON
The Inland Sea is a cliff-bound lagoon connected to the open sea by a tunnel that runs for 100m through the headland of Dwejra Point. The tunnel is big enough for small boats to sail through in calm weather, and the Inland Sea has been used as a fishermen's haven for centuries. These days, fishers supplement their income by taking tourists on **boat trips** (per person 15min €4) through the tunnel. Trips pass over the remains of the Azure Window in the crystalline waters.

Dwejra Marine Environmental Education Centre NATURE CENTRE
(2155 0429; www.facebook.com/dwejramarineenvironmentaleducationcentre; Dwejra Bay; 11am-3pm Tue-Fri & 10am-3pm Sat & Sun Jan-Apr & Oct-Dec, to 5pm May-Sep) FREE While at the Inland Sea, stop in at this interesting centre to learn about the natural history and underwater marine life of the area.

Dwejra (Qawra) Tower CASTLE
(www.dinlarthelwa.org; adult/child €2/free; 10.30am-12.30pm & 1.15-3.30pm Sun-Fri & when flag is flying) Visit this restored tower for breathtaking views.

Getting There & Away

Bus 311 runs between Victoria and Dwejra (16 minutes, hourly). Alternatively, catch bus 312 to San Lawrenz (10 minutes) and walk the 1.5km down to the bay.

Marsalforn

POP 750

Former fishing village Marsalforn (the name is possibly derived from the Arabic for 'bay of ships') is Gozo's main holiday resort. It's small-scale and has a pleasant feel; the promenade, lined by restaurants, is backed by developments of low-rise hotels and apartments.

At the head of Marsalforn's bay is a tiny scrap of sand, but better swimming and sunbathing can be found on the rocks out to the west. You could also hike eastward over the hill a couple of kilometres to Calypso's Cave (p144) and Ramla Bay (p144).

Sights & Activities

Żebbuġ VILLAGE
Żebbuġ is a quiet Gozitan village in the hills west of Marsalforn. It is mainly residential as accommodation and services for travellers are largely gathered around Marsalforn Bay. Żebbuġ is renowned for excellent lace-making, however, and onyx found locally has been used to decorate the village's Parish Church.

Xwieni Bay BEACH
Around 1.5km from Marsalforn, Xwieni Bay is separated from neighbouring Qbajjar Bay by a headland with a small fort. Xwieni combines a sandy beach for good swimming with a few simple food and drink kiosks. Slightly further west, Gozo's fascinating coastal strip of salt pans begins.

Christ Statue STATUE
As you enter Marsalforn from Victoria, you'll see the figure of Christ on a hill. The statue was erected in the 1970s, replacing earlier statues and a wooden cross from around the 1900s; the 96m-high hill is known as Tas-Salvatur (the Redeemer).

Eating & Drinking

★Qbajjar MEDITERRANEAN €€
(2155 1124; www.qbajjarrestaurant.com; Triq ix-Xwejni; mains €13-22; 10.30am-3.30pm & 5.30-10.30pm Wed-Mon) Around 1km west of Marsalforn in quieter Qbajjar Bay, ocean views and excellent seafood blend at this locals' favourite. Combine views of nearby rocky headlands with dishes including a great spaghetti pescatore crammed with seafood, and delicate ravioli stuffed with local Gozitan cheese.

Look forward to good service, which has just the right mix of informality and efficiency.

Arzella MEDITERRANEAN €€
(21554662; www.facebook.com/ristorantearzella; Triq Għar Qawqla; mains €11-23; noon-3pm & 6.30-10.30pm Wed-Mon Apr-Oct, Fri-Sun Nov-Mar) Set high up to the east of the bay, family-run Arzella has a covered terrace with great views out to sea, and buzzes with locals who come for its fresh fish and convivial atmosphere.

Marsalforn

0 — 200 m
0 — 0.1 miles

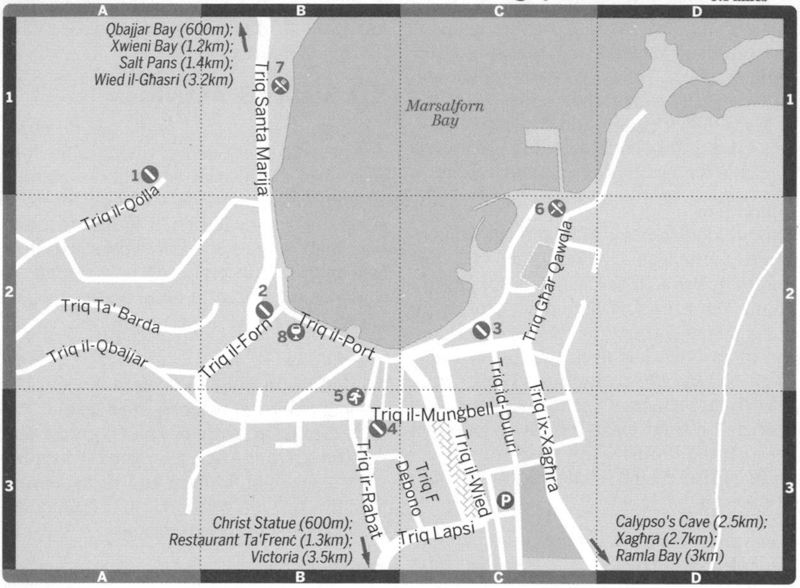

Otters Bistro GOZITAN, ITALIAN €€
(☎2156 2473; www.facebook.com/ottersbistroandlounge; Triq Santa Marija; mains €9-21; ⏰11.30am-10.30pm; 📶) Waterfront Otters has a glorious, shady, outdoor terrace overlooking the bay. The menu has some great Gozitan choices, including braised lamb shank with fig and orange sauce, or spaghetti Gozitana (tossed with Maltese sausage, olives, capers, tomatoes and chilli).

Restaurant Ta'Frenċ MEDITERRANEAN €€€
(☎2155 3888; www.tafrencrestaurant.com; Triq ir-Rabat; mains €28-38, 7-course degustation €80; ⏰noon-2pm & 7-10pm; 🍷) About 1.5km south of Marsalforn, this restaurant is in a beautiful setting (a 200-year-old converted farmhouse surrounded by garden) and has an impressive menu of French, Italian and Maltese dishes created from fresh local ingredients. There's also an extensive, award-winning wine list.

A more affordable option is the Market Menu, with two-/three-/four-course options (€25/40/50) . The two-course option is available at lunchtimes only.

Piutrentanove WINE BAR
(☎7755 0039; www.piutrentanovebar.com; 65 Triq il-Port; ⏰4pm-3am; 📶) This small lounge bar on the waterfront has a sleek interior and a couple of outside tables, and is a lively place to be in the summer months. It also serves decent pizzas.

Marsalforn

Activities, Courses & Tours
1 Atlantis A1
2 Bubbles B2
3 Calypso C2
4 Nautic Team B3
5 On 2 Wheels Gozo B3

Eating
6 Arzella C2
7 Otters Bistro B1

Drinking & Nightlife
8 Piutrentanove B2

Getting There & Away

Bus 310 runs between Marsalforn and Victoria (17 minutes, hourly). Bus 322 travels to/from Mġarr (38 minutes, every 1½ hours) via Ramla Bay (20 minutes) and Xagħra (14 minutes).

Hire scooters or bikes from **On 2 Wheels Gozo** (☎2156 1503; www.on2wheelsgozo.com; Triq ir-Rabat; bike/scooter rental from €15/30).

The best option for car **parking** is south of the bay along Triq il-Wied.

Xagħra

POP 4885

The pretty village of Xagħra (*shaa*-ra), one of Gozo's largest, spreads across the flat summit of the hill east of Victoria. The 19th-century Church of Our Lady of Victory looks down benignly on the tree-lined **Pjazza Vittorja**, where old men sit and chat in the shade of the oleanders – there's always something gossip-worthy going on in the village square.

Other attractions include two incongruous caverns concealed under locals' houses, and another nearby cave offering excellent ocean views.

Sights & Activities

★Ġgantija Temples ARCHAEOLOGICAL SITE

(☎2155 3194; www.heritagemalta.org; access from Triq i-Imqades; adult/child incl Ta'Kola Windmill €9/5; ⏰9am-5pm) Perched on the crest of the hill to the south of Xagħra, the awe-inspiring megalithic Ġgantija Temples command soaring views over most of southern Gozo. As the name implies (*ġgantija* – pronounced dje-gant-ee-ya – means 'giantess'), these are the largest of the megalithic temples found on the Maltese Islands – the walls stand over 6m high, and the two temples together span over 40m.

The site has a wonderful visitor's centre, with displays putting the temples into context and showcasing many of the extraordinary carvings discovered here, including the famous 'fat ladies'.

Along with Ta'Ħaġrat and Skorba in Malta, the Ġgantija Temples are thought to be Malta's oldest, dating from 3600 to 3000 BC. Both temples face towards the southeast, and both have five semicircular niches within. The south temple (on the left) is the older, and is entered across a huge threshold slab with four holes at each side, thought to be for libations. The first niche on the right contains an altar with some spiral decoration – there was once a pillar here with a snake carved on it, but the pillar now lives in Victoria's Archaeology Museum (p132). The left-hand niche in the inner chamber has a well-preserved trilithon altar; on the right is a circular hearth stone and a bench altar.

The outer wall of the later north temple complex is particularly impressive in scale. The largest of the megaliths measures 6m by 4m and weighs around 57 tonnes, and the wall may originally have stood up to 16m tall – it's incredible to contemplate how these huge stones were put in place. The exterior walls were built of harder-wearing coralline limestone, while the interiors were built of the lighter globigerina limestone – brought here from around a kilometre away.

MARSALFORN DIVING

A number of Marsalforn dive operators can help you explore Gozo's great dive sites, including:

➡ **Atlantis** (☎2155 4685; www.atlantisgozo.com; Atlantis Hotel, Triq il-Qolla; introductory drives from €40; ⏰7.30am-6.30pm)

➡ **Bubbles** (☎2702 8299; www.diving-gozo.com; 17 Triq il-Forn; introductory dives fron €40; ⏰8am-6pm)

➡ **Calypso** (☎2156 1757; www.calypsodivers.com; Triq il-Port; introductory dives from €40)

➡ **Nautic Team** (p27)

Ta'Kola Windmill HISTORIC BUILDING

(☎2156 1071; www.heritagemalta.org; Triq il-Bambina; adult/child incl Ġgantija Temples €9/5; ⏰9am-5pm) Built in 1725 at the instigation of the Knights, who built many such windmills to encourage the production of flour (this is one of the few left standing), Ta'Kola now houses a cute museum of country life, with displays of tools and living quarters. Best, though, is the climb up the narrow stairs to see the original milling gear, complete with huge millstones.

Xerri's Grotto CAVE

(☎7906 9718; www.facebook.com/pg/xerrisgrotto; l'Għar ta'Xerri; adult/child €2.50/1; ⏰10am-4.30pm Sep-May, to 6pm Jun-Aug) In the back streets to the north of the village square lies Xerri's Grotto. This underground cavern, complete with stalactites and stalagmites, is unusual in that it is entered through a private house. Having discovered the cave beneath his home, the owner decided to cash in on the tourist potential. Xerri's Grotto was discovered in 1923 when Antonio Xerri was digging a well.

It's big, deep and interesting. If no one is there, just wait and someone will quickly show up.

OFF THE BEATEN TRACK

WIED IL-GĦASRI

A 5km hike west along the coast from Marsalforn is the narrow, cliff-bound inlet of Wied il-Għasri. Here a staircase cut into the rock leads down to a tiny shingle beach at the head of the inlet. It's a gorgeously picturesque place and there is good swimming and snorkelling when the sea is calm, but it's best avoided in rough weather when the waves come crashing up the narrow defile.

You can also drive or walk to Wied il-Għasri from the village of Għasri, about 2km south. If you're coming from Marsalforn, there is a signposted turn-off about 300m after the coast road heads inland, where a rough track drops down to the right and leads to a rocky parking area; it's accessible in a regular car.

Ninu's Cave CAVE

(Triq Jannar; donations appreciated; ⌚9.30am-6pm) In the back streets to the north of the village square lies Ninu's Cave, beneath an unassuming-looking house. This underground cavern, discovered by the current owner's grandfather in 1888, is complete with stalactites and stalagmites.

★Ta' Mena WINERY

(☎2156 4939; www.tamena-gozo.com; Triq Rabat; ⌚10am-5pm) This winery near Xagħra en route from Victoria to Marsalforn sells good wine under the Marsamena and Ancient Gods labels, and has a well-stocked farm shop with its own Gozo sea salt, honey, olive oil, chutneys, capers and sun-dried tomatoes. Occasional food and wine tours (per person €16 including lunch) are held at 1pm on Saturdays. Booking ahead is essential.

Ramla Bay BEACH

(Ir-Ramla) Ramla Bay is one of the prettiest sandy beaches on Gozo, with red-gold sand. The minimal remains of a Roman villa are hidden amid the bamboo behind the beach, and Calypso's Cave looks down from the hilltop to the west. It also has a cafe-restaurant and sunbed/sunshade hire.

Bus 322 travels to Ramla Bay from Mġarr (15 minutes, half-hourly) and on to Xagħra (10 minutes) and Marsalforn (25 minutes). The 302 runs between here and Nadur (five minutes, hourly) and Victoria (30 minutes).

The walk here from Nadur takes between 15 and 20 minutes. The beach is usually heaving with people in summer; it's more tranquil in spring and autumn, and in winter you can have the place almost to your (goose-pimpled) self.

From Xaghra it's a walk of around 30 minutes.

Calypso's Cave CAVE

Calypso's Cave overlooks the sandy beach of Ramla Bay – it's a 30-minute walk from Xagħra's village square. The cave itself is hardly worth the hike – it's just a hollow under an overhang at the top of the cliff – but the views are.

On a calm day you can see the remains of an artificial reef extending into the sea. This was part of the defences built by the Knights of St John to prevent attackers landing on the beach. In theory, the enemy ships would run aground on the reef, where they would be attacked using primitive mortar-like weapons.

Pomskizillious Museum of Toys MUSEUM

(☎2156 2489; Triq Ġnien Xibla; adult/child €2.80/1.50; ⌚10.30am-1pm Thu-Sat Apr, Oct & Nov, 10.30am-1pm Mon & Sat May, 10.30am-1pm daily Jun-Sep, 10.30am-1pm Sat Dec-Mar) This small labour of love has an impressive array of 19th-century and 1930s doll houses, toy soldiers, and spooky china dolls, mostly in glass cases.

There's a display case devoted to nonsense poet Edward Lear, who coined the word 'pomskizillious' to describe Gozitan scenery.

Lino's Stables HORSE RIDING

(☎2156 2477; www.linostables.com; 16 Triq is-Spiera; ⌚by appointment) These stables offer one- and two-hour horse rides to Marsalforn for €15/30 for both beginners and more experienced riders. Children over 10 may ride their own horses, but younger children ride with their accompanying adult or in a gig. Book in advance.

Eating & Drinking

★Oleander GOZITAN €€

(☎2155 7230; www.oleandergozo.com; Pjazza Vittorja; mains €11-25; ⌚11.30am-3pm & 6.30-10pm) The much-loved Oleander, located on the pretty village square with tables outside, has a menu specialising in Maltese cuisine, with dishes including rabbit cooked in various ways, homemade ravioli with Gozitan

Xagħra

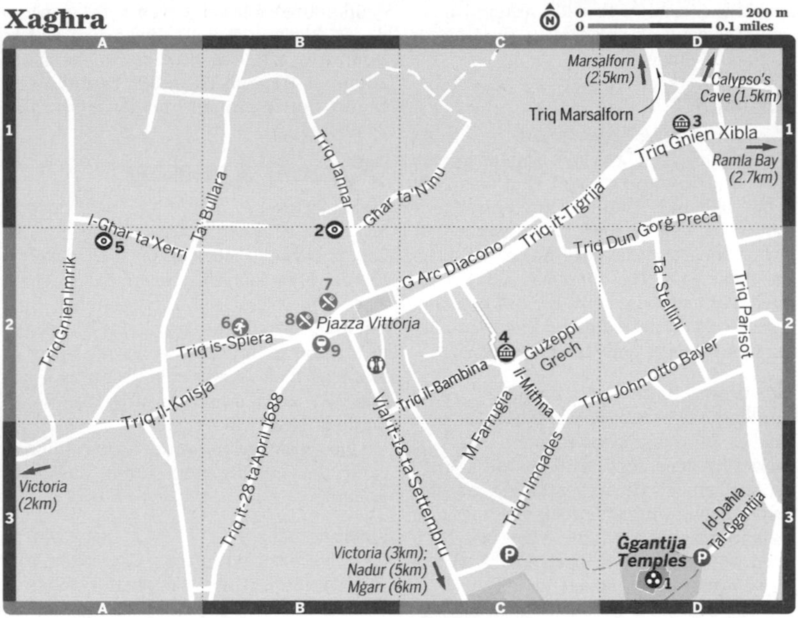

cheese, and fresh fish of the day. Boneless quail stuffed with local figs and pistachios is a definite menu highlight.

D-Venue MEDITERRANEAN €€
(☎7955 7230; www.dvenuerestaurant.com; Pjazza Vittorja; mains €8-21; ⊙noon-3pm & 7-11pm Tue-Sun) D-Venue has blonde-stone arches downstairs, and a great glass-covered terrace on the 1st floor. Food is equally stylish, with choices like spaghetti with prawns and rocket, calamari, rabbit and crispy duck breast.

73 in the Square WINE BAR
(☎7788 9966; www.facebook.com/73inthesquare; Pjazza Vittorja; ⊙3pm-late) Adding a touch of after-dark energy to Xagħra's pretty main square, this modern wine bar does good-value platters and also draws locals from around Gozo to regular live-music events on weekends. Check the Facebook page for what's scheduled.

Getting There & Away

Bus 307 runs between Victoria and Xagħra (35 minutes, hourly). Bus 322 connects the town with Marsalforn (13 minutes, every 1½ hours), Ramla Bay (10 minutes) and Mġarr (25 minutes). **Parking** is best near the Ġgantija Temples, from where it is an easy walk to Xagħra's main square and the Ta'Kola Windmill.

Xagħra

Top Sights
1 Ġgantija Temples D3

Sights
2 Ninu's Cave B2
3 Pomskizillious Museum of Toys D1
4 Ta'Kola Windmill C2
5 Xerri's Grotto A2

Activities, Courses & Tours
6 Lino's Stables B2

Eating
7 D-Venue B2
8 Oleander B2

Drinking & Nightlife
9 73 in the Square B2

Nadur

POP 3970

Nadur is Gozo's 'second city', spreading along a high ridge to the east of Victoria. In Malti, Nadur means 'lookout', and a 17th-century watchtower overlooks the Comino sea lanes from the western end of the ridge. There's a large **market** every Wednesday from around 7am to 11am near the church. The town is famous for its bakeries, and a few new openings around its recently restored main square make it an excellent destination for drinks and dinner.

Sights

Church of Saints Peter & Paul CHURCH

(Pjazza San Pietru u San Pawl) Nadur's ornate Church of Saints Peter and Paul was built in the late 18th century – the entrance is framed by white statues of the two saints, giving the church its local nickname of *iż-Żewġ* (the pair). The interior is richly decorated with marble sculptures, and the vault is covered with 150 paintings. The surrounding square has recently been revitalised.

★ **San Blas Bay** BEACH

San Blas, a tiny, rock-strewn bay with some patches of coarse, rust-coloured sand, is backed by steep, terraced fields with prickly-pear hedges. There's parking space for only a handful of cars at the beginning of the very narrow track above the bay. It's a steep walk down to it, but you can take a jeep down or up (€2.50 per person).

Bring a picnic lunch and a mask and fins for **snorkelling** as the water is quite shallow and very clear. You can walk to San Blas from Nadur in about 30 minutes; it's just over 2.5km from town (take Triq San Blas off Triq it-Tiġrija, two blocks north of Nadur's church). Bus 303 heads here hourly from Victoria (18 minutes), via Nadur (five minutes). Alight at the Weraq bus stop then walk 600m to the beach.

Ħondoq ir-Rummien BEACH

From the village square of nearby Qala, head east along Triq il-Kunċizzjoni, which leads down to the coast at Ħondoq ir-Rummien, a popular swimming cove with a scrap of sand, bathing ladders on the rocks, and benches with a view across the water to Comino. There are toilets here and a kiosk catering to sunbathers. Snacks and drinks are available.

Qala Windmills WINDMILL

Built in the 19th century, these windmills in the village of Qala (pronounced 'a-la') were in use until the 1970s. From Nadur's main square it is 2km east to the windmills.

Daħlet Qorrot BEACH

Attractive Daħlet Qorrot is popular with local weekenders. There's a tiny gravel beach, but most of the swimming is off the rocks beside the rows of little boathouses (carved out of the rock, and with brightly painted doors); there's usually plenty of space to park. It's within walking distance of Nadur: from Triq it-Tiġrija, head north for about 300m on Triq San Blas, then take the Triq Daħlet Qorrot turn-off; the bay is just over 2km away.

Eating & Drinking

Maxokk Bakery PIZZA, BAKERY €

(☎2155 0014; www.maxokkbakery.com; Triq San Ġakbu; pizza/ftira from €4/6; ⊙10.30am-7pm Mon-Sat, 1-7pm Sun) An excellent bakery, open since the 1930s, selling traditional *ftira* (Maltese bread) and pizza, freshly baked in a bread oven and with a wide range of toppings. It also serves craft beer from Gozo, and there are a few seats nearby to enjoy an outdoor feast.

Good luck keeping your Gozitan sausage from the friendly dogs often mooching around.

Mekrens Bakery PIZZA, BAKERY €

(☎2155 2342; Triq tal-Hanaq; pizza from €4.50; ⊙4.30am-8pm) This is a great traditional bakery, serving up *ftira* (traditional Maltese bread) and delicious varieties of pizza.

★ **Osteria Scottadito** ITALIAN €€

(☎2733 3000; www.osteriascottadito.com; 20 Triq Madre Ġ Camilleri; mains €9-24; ⊙7-11pm Tue-Sun) Energetic owners from northern Italy run this excellent restaurant tucked behind Nadur's church. Cuisine influenced by the Emilia-Romagna region of Italy is the focus, but many local and sustainable ingredients are used. Try the Scottadito lamb chops with a pecorino and wild fennel crust. It's an old shepherds' dish apparently, and it's best eaten with your hands. Tuck in.

★ **Gebuba** CRAFT BEER

(☎7947 0141; www.facebook.com/gebuba; Triq il-Knisja; ⊙6pm-late) With more than 300 brews from around Malta and the world, the team at Gebuba are big beer fans. Seating is either on Nadur's pretty main square or amid Gebuba's cosy interior, and friendly owner Giovanni can also recommend local Gozitan wines and liqueurs. He's all over what's happening in Malta's nascent craft-beer scene, so ask him what's new.

Getting There & Away

To get to Nadur, take bus 322, which runs from Mġarr (seven minutes), and goes on to Ramla Bay (eight minutes), Xagħra (18 minutes) and Marsalforn (21 minutes).

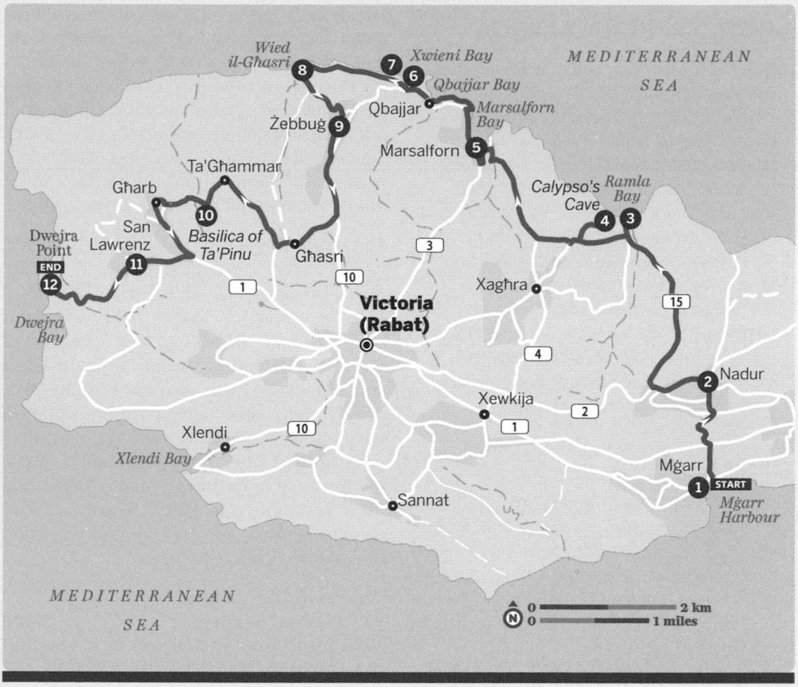

Driving Tour
Gozo

START MĠARR
END DWEJRA
LENGTH 20KM; 1½ HOURS

This drive takes in some of Gozo's loveliest scenery. Begin at the port of ❶ **Mġarr** (p135), then take Triq Sant Antnin uphill towards ❷ **Nadur** (p145), perched on a hilltop and with great views from its modified watchtower. Nadur's town square has recently been restored and is framed by the ornate Church of Saints Peter & Paul.

From Nadur, take the road through lovely countryside towards ❸ **Ramla Bay** (p144). When you reach the bay, stop for a look and perhaps a swim, then take the first right-hand turn. You'll drive through a landscape of terraced fields and copper-coloured walls. At the next junction, if you take the right-hand fork you can drive round to ❹ **Calypso's Cave** (p144) for great views over the bay.

Gozo's largest (yet still low-key) resort, ❺ **Marsalforn** (p141), with its compact harbour, is a good spot to stop for lunch. After dining, drive along the seafront and then take the coastal road. This will lead you to ❻ **Xwieni Bay** (p141), which is overlooked by the fabulously wild coast, where ❼ **salt pans** (p140) are scooped out from the cliffs and still in use. Exploring the rugged landscape of the salt pans is a fascinating experience, especially when ocean breezes are whipping up a salty spray along Gozo's northern coast.

Follow the coast road around to visit the breathtaking gorge and bay of ❽ **Wied il-Għasri** (p144), then continue inland to the village of ❾ **Żebbuġ** (p141) (the name means 'olives'), which is famous for the onyx found locally (check out the elaborate decoration of the Parish Church) and for lace-making. Continue on through Għasri village towards Għarb, passing the dramatically isolated pilgrimage centre ❿ **Basilica of Ta'Pinu** (p139). From here, take the road towards the pretty village of ⓫ **San Lawrenz** (p139) before finishing your drive at ⓬ **Dwejra** (p140), an area featuring some of Gozo's most stunning coastal formations.

PROTECTING THE GARNIJA

Due to rubbish being left on the island overnight, Comino has a significant problem with rats. You won't see them during the day, but at night they raid the rubbish bins to feed. Unfortunately they have also been known to feed on the eggs and chicks of the *garnija* (Yelkouan shearwaters) that inhabit the island. As Comino also has a large population of wild rabbits, it's not possible to poison the rats. BirdLife Malta (see www.birdlifemalta.org/arcipelagugarnija) is lobbying for daily rubbish removal, but visitors can do their bit by taking all rubbish with them when they leave.

COMINO

Comino (Kemmuna in Malti) is a small, barren chunk of limestone wedged smack-bang between Malta and Gozo. It was once reportedly the hideout of pirates and smugglers, and its remoteness saw it used as a place of isolation for cholera and plague victims in the early 19th century.

The almost empty island – there's just one hotel here – is a breathtakingly beautiful place, ringed by caves and sea cliffs. It's home to the Blue Lagoon, one of Malta's loveliest and most-visited natural attractions. In summer, hordes of day trippers descend from Malta and Gozo, but in spring, autumn and winter you'll have a better chance of enjoying the turquoise waters.

Comino is only 2.5km by 1.5km. It's a nature reserve and bird sanctuary, and free of cars. A walk along the rough tracks affords some great views of northern Malta and of Gozo. It's impossible to get lost here.

Sights & Activities

Blue Lagoon LAGOON

Comino's biggest draw is the Blue Lagoon, a sheltered cove between the western end of the island and the uninhabited islet of **Cominotto** (Kemmunett in Malti). It's incredibly beautiful and inviting, with a white-sand seabed and clear waters.

The southern end of the lagoon is roped off to keep boats out; there is top-notch **swimming** and **snorkelling** here, plus you can swim over to Cominotto. In summer the bay gets super busy, particularly between 10am and 4pm. Try to time your visit for later in the day.

Take care in the unrelenting summer heat – there is no shade, and most sunbathing is done on the exposed rocky ledges surrounding the cove; also be careful of currents here on windy days. There are public toilets and a few kiosks selling cool drinks, ice creams and snacks (burgers, hot dogs and sandwiches). Deckchairs and umbrellas can be hired for extended luxurious lazing about.

St Mary's Tower FORTRESS

(☎2122 5952; www.dinlarthelwa.org; €2.50; ⏲10.30am-3pm Wed, Fri, Sat & Sun Apr-Oct & when flag is flying) St Mary's Tower was built by the Knights in 1618. It was once part of the chain of signal towers between Gozo and Mdina, and was also used by the British. It may have served as an isolation hospital at some point, and was definitely used to house livestock. Restored in 2004, the tower is open to the public. Climb the steps and enjoy the views. Nearby, explore an 18th-century gun battery that was used to guard the Gozo Channel.

Church of Our Lady's Return from Egypt CHURCH

(Santa Marija Bay) This simple but beautiful chapel was built by the Knights in 1618.

Diveshack Comino DIVING

(☎2134 5671; www.divemalta.com; Comino Hotel; introductory dives from €60) Specialises in diving around Comino; has another PADI five-star branch in Sliema.

Getting There & Away

Numerous companies operate trips to Comino from Mġarr on Gozo. Return tickets for adults/children are around €10/5. Usually the trip includes a quick whiz around the island's caves.

Sightseeing trips to the Blue Lagoon leave from tourist towns such as Sliema, Buġibba and Golden Bay in Malta, and Xlendi and Marsalforn in Gozo.

If you'd like to visit the Blue Lagoon from Malta without the crowds, take advantage of the trip leaving at 4pm from Golden Bay with Charlie's Discovery Speedboat Trips (p90).

Getting Around

The main part of the Comino Hotel is on San Niklaw Bay, and the Comino Hotel Bungalows are on Santa Marija Bay, 500m to the east. Triq Congreve, a rough track lined with oleander trees, runs from Santa Marija Bay south to St Mary's Tower.

Side tracks lead to the Blue Lagoon and San Niklaw Bay.

Understand Malta & Gozo

History

Inhabited for millennia, the Maltese Islands have a rollicking history and some of the world's most sophisticated prehistoric architecture. The islands' destiny has been shaped by geography, with their natural harbours and prime location attracting a series of masters – the Phoenicians, Romans, Arabs and Normans among them. However, the most influential settlers were the Knights of St John, who held sway until Napoleon's arrival. Under British rule, Malta showed incredible bravery during WWII, and finally achieved independence in 1964.

The Mystery of the Temple Builders

About 1000 years before the construction of the Great Pyramid of Cheops in Egypt, the people of Malta were manipulating megaliths that weighed up to 50 tonnes and creating elaborate buildings that appear to be oriented in relation to the winter solstice sunrise. The Maltese megalithic temples, built between 3600 and 2500 BC, are the oldest surviving free-standing structures in the world. It's thought that their builders were descended from the islands' neolithic inhabitants, rather than being new settlers, yet it appears they started building these structures quite suddenly.

Renowned British archaeologist and scholar David H Trump wrote *Malta Prehistory & Temples,* the definitive guide to Malta's prehistory. This comprehensive book includes detailed visual treatment of 30 key sites.

It was a seemingly peaceful era, perhaps due to the islands' then geographical isolation, as no evidence of defensive structures remain. The society that built the temples must have been sophisticated, as indicated by the scale and complexity of the buildings and the evidence of delicate sculpture and decoration, mostly displayed in Valletta's National Museum of Archaeology (p52). The builders were also significantly wealthy enough to pay for the materials and extra labour beyond the needs of everyday life. Although the materials were mainly local, they often were transported from a distance of around 1km. It's thought that the massive slabs of stone were moved by rolling them on ball-shaped rocks - such stones have been discovered at the sites.

The buildings have been termed 'temples' but, while there is evidence of ritual activity, it is still not known definitively what they were used for.

TIMELINE

c 5200 BC

Arrival of first known inhabitants, by primitive boats or rafts from Sicily. The Maltese Islands are more wooded, fertile and richer in animal life at this time.

c 3600–2500 BC

Megalithic temples are built. Some of the most important of these are the temple complexes at Ġgantija and Ħaġar Qim.

c 2000 BC

Bronze Age culture develops. The most well-known Bronze Age site in Malta is the Tarxien Temple complex a short distance south of Valletta.

TAKE THE CAR TO SICILY

Escaping north to Sicily is a popular weekend activity for the people of Malta, and it's an easy 90-minute journey on the Virtu car ferry north to the southeast Sicilian port of Pozzallo. University of Malta research from 2013 indicates that just 20,000 years ago, during the last ice age, the sea level was around 130m lower than today, and a 40km-wide land bridge stretched north linking Malta to Sicily.

The present-day capital of Valletta was 10km inland, and the Dingli Cliffs, now a spectacular 220m high, soared almost 400m from sea level. Most tellingly, Malta, Gozo, Comino and the tiny islet of Filfla were all part of a contiguous land mass that was around 450 sq km larger, making ice-age Malta more than twice the surface area of today's Maltese archipelago.

It's a mystery why this population died out: some theories are drought and famine, an epidemic or an attack from overseas – or perhaps a combination of these afflictions. Whatever the reason, temple building appears to have come to a sudden stop around 2500 BC. The temples fell into disrepair, and the Bronze Age culture that followed was completely different in its practices (for example, cremation rather than burial) and its artworks, which were heavier and rougher than the fine work of the mysterious temple builders.

A Trading Post

Phoenicians & Romans

As sea travel developed, so did Malta's significance. It was impossible for ancient vessels to sail overnight or attempt long, continuous trips, so Malta was the ideal place to stop on a journey between mainland Europe and Africa.

From around 800 to 218 BC, Malta was ruled by the Phoenicians and, for around the last 250 years of this period, by Phoenicia's principal North African colony, Carthage. There is a direct legacy of this period visible in contemporary Malta: with watchful eyes painted on their prow, the colourful Maltese fishing boats – the *luzzu* and the *kajjik* – seem little changed from the Phoenician trading vessels that once plied the Mediterranean.

During the Second Punic War (218–201 BC) Rome took control of Malta before finally crushing Carthage in the Third Punic War (149–146 BC). The island was then given the status of a *municipium* (free town), with the power to control its own affairs and to send an ambassador to Rome. However, there is evidence that Malta retained a Punic influence. The 1st-century-BC historian Diodorus Siculus described the island as a

800–480 BC

Malta is occupied by the Phoenicians, a seafaring people based in present-day Lebanon. A significant Phoenician influence lingers in Malti, the country's modern language.

480–218 BC

Malta is controlled by the Carthaginian Empire, based in present-day Tunisia. Under yet another ruling civilisation, it is a further reminder of Malta's strategically important location.

218 BC – AD 395

The Romans take over Malta, having destroyed Carthage in the Punic Wars. In less than 750 years, the islands of Malta and Gozo have had three different rulers.

41 BC

The Romans make Malta a *municipium* (free town). As an outpost of Roman Sicily, the islands prosper through trade – a forerunner to modern Malta's focus on online international business.

The Great Siege: Malta 1565, by Ernle Bradford, is a page-turning account of the epic battle between the Ottoman Turks and the Knights of St John.

Phoenician colony, and the biblical account of St Paul's shipwreck on Malta in AD 60 describes the islanders as 'barbarous' (ie they did not speak the 'civilised' languages of Latin or Greek). St Paul's shipwreck was also particularly significant because he brought Christianity to the islands.

Malta seems to have prospered under Roman rule. The main town, called Melita, occupied the hilltop of Mdina but also spread over an area around three times the size of the later medieval citadel. The excavated remains of townhouses, villas, farms and baths suggest that the inhabitants enjoyed a comfortable lifestyle and occupied themselves with the production of olives, wheat, honey and grapes.

Arabs

The rapid expansion of Islam in the 7th to 9th centuries saw an Arab empire extend from Spain to India. Arab armies invaded Sicily in 827 and finally conquered it in 878; Malta fell into Arab hands in 870. Both Malta and Sicily remained Muslim possessions until the end of the 11th century though the Arab rulers tolerated the Christian population. They had a strong influence on the Malti language – apart from the names Malta and Gozo, which are thought to have Latin roots, most Maltese place names date from after the Arab occupation.

The Knights Arrive

For 400 years after the Norman conquest of Malta and Sicily (1090–91), the histories of these two Mediterranean islands were linked – their rulers were a succession of Normans, Angevins (French), Aragonese and Castilians (Spanish). Malta remained a minor pawn on the edge of the European chessboard, and its relatively small population of downtrodden islanders paid their taxes by trading, slaving and piracy, and were repaid in kind by marauding Turks and Barbary corsairs. This was the scene when the Knights of St John arrived, having been given the islands (much to the islanders' dismay) by the Holy Roman Emperor Charles V. The Knights were to rule the islands until the arrival of the French in the 18th century.

East Versus West

Swapped for a Falcon

In 1479 the marriage of Catholic monarchs Fernando II of Aragon and Isabella of Castile led to the unification of Spain. Under their grandson, the Holy Roman Emperor Charles V, Malta became part of the vast Spanish Empire. One of the greatest threats to Charles' realm was the expanding Ottoman Empire of Süleyman the Magnificent in the East. Sultan Süleyman had driven the Knights of St John from their island stronghold of Rhodes between 1522 and 1523. When the Knights begged Charles V to

AD 60

St Paul is shipwrecked on Malta and introduces Christianity to the population. His arrival lives on in place names including St Paul's Bay.

395–870

After the Roman Empire split in AD 395, Malta is believed to have fallen under Byzantine rule from Constantinople (modern-day Istanbul).

870–1090

North African Arabs occupy Malta, introducing irrigation and the cultivation of cotton and citrus fruits. Many modern Maltese surnames also date from these times.

1090–1530

Normans take over. During their rule, a Maltese aristocracy is established, and the architectural style referred to as Siculo-Norman developed.

find them a new home, he offered them Malta along with the governorship of Tripoli, hoping that they might help to contain the Turkish naval forces in the eastern Mediterranean. The nominal rent was to be two falcons a year – one for the emperor and one for the viceroy of Sicily. Malta consequently found itself at the heart of a struggle between two religious philosophies, Islam and Christianity, and became the location for one of the mightiest clashes between East and West, which was to shape the nation's future and the landscape of the island as we see it today.

The Great Siege of 1565

Grand Master Philippe Villiers de L'Isle Adam (1530–34) of the Knights of St John was not particularly impressed by the gift of the Maltese Islands, which seemed to him barren, waterless and poorly defended. Equally unimpressed were the 12,000 or so local inhabitants, who were given no say in the matter, including the aristocracy, who remained aloof

WHO WERE THE KNIGHTS OF ST JOHN?

The Sovereign and Military Order of the Knights Hospitaller of St John of Jerusalem had its origins in the Christian Crusades of the 11th and 12th centuries.

A hospital for poor pilgrims in Jerusalem was founded by some Italian merchants from Amalfi in 1070. The hospital, operated by monks, won the protection of the papacy in 1113 and was raised to the status of an independent religious order known as the Hospitallers. The Order set up more hospitals along the pilgrimage route from Italy to the Holy Land, and the knights who had been healed of their wounds showed their gratitude by granting funds and property to the growing Order.

When the armies of Islam recaptured the Holy Land in 1291, the Order sought refuge in the Kingdom of Cyprus. In 1309 they acquired the island of Rhodes, planning to stay close to the Middle East in the hope of reconquering Jerusalem. And there they remained for more than 200 years, building fortresses, auberges and a hospital, and evolving from a land-based army into the medieval world's most formidable naval fighting force.

The Order consisted of European noblemen who lived the lives of monks and soldiers. Their traditional attire was a hooded monk's habit emblazoned with a white Maltese cross. This eight-pointed cross is said to represent the eight virtues the Knights strove to uphold: to live in truth; to have faith; to repent of sins; to give proof of humility; to love justice; to be merciful; to be sincere and whole-hearted; and to endure persecution. The Order comprised eight nationalities or langues (literally 'tongues' or languages) – Italian, French, Provencal, Auvergnat, Castilian, Aragonese, German and English.

The hospitals created by the Order – first in the Holy Land, then in Rhodes and finally in Malta – were often at the forefront of medical development. Ironically, although the Knights had sworn to bring death and destruction to the 'infidel' Muslims, much of the Order's medical knowledge was gleaned from the study of Arabic medicine.

1530

The Knights of St John arrive in Malta having been gifted the islands by Emperor Charles V. A nominal rent of two falcons is to be paid.

1565

The Knights defeat Turkish invaders in the Great Siege of Malta. Historians claim the victory of the Knights was vital in eroding the European perception of Ottoman invincibility.

1566

Valletta is founded, and is the first planned city in Europe. Utilising a grid pattern for its streets, it is a historical precedent for modern settlements like Manhattan.

1798

Napoleon's fleet calls at Malta and captures the island with hardly a fight. Under the French, nobility, slavery and the feudal system are all abolished.

MALTA'S WATCHTOWERS

The Knights of St John concentrated their defences on the Three Cities and Valletta. Up to the 19th century, only the two old capitals – Mdina on Malta and Victoria on Gozo – were fortified, and even their defences were not particularly robust. Farmers on the outskirts of the capitals could shelter within the cities, but villages elsewhere were left to fend for themselves.

Malta had long had watchtowers, but Grand Master Juan de Lascaris-Castellar of the Knights of Malta commissioned five towers from 1637 to 1640; another knight, Grand Master Martin de Redin, subsequently built a string of 13 towers around the perimeters of the islands from 1658 to 1659. These were strong enough to withstand a small attack, but not a long siege. They were positioned so Gozo and Malta could signal to each other – with fire, gunfire and flags – if Turkish invaders were sighted off the coast. The towers still stand today, and range from simple, small watchtowers, to larger mini-fortresses.

in their palazzi in Mdina. However, determined to make the best of a bad job and hoping one day to return to Rhodes, in 1530 the Knights settled in the fishing village of Birgu (now Vittoriosa), on the south side of Grand Harbour, and set about fortifying their defences.

While in Rhodes, the Knights had been a constant thorn in the side of the Ottoman Turks. In Malta their greatest adversary was Turkish admiral Dragut Reis, who invaded Gozo in 1551 and carried off almost the entire population of 5000 into slavery. Not much later, in 1559, the Knights lost half their galleys in a disastrous attack on Dragut's lair on the island of Djerba (Tunisia). With the power of the Knights at a low ebb, Süleyman the Magnificent saw an opportunity to polish off this troublesome crew, while at the same time capturing Malta as a base for the invasion of Europe.

Jean Parisot de la Valette, Grand Master between 1557 and 1568, was a stern disciplinarian and an experienced soldier. He foresaw the threat of a Turkish siege and prepared for it well, renewing Fort St Angelo and building Fort St Michael and Fort St Elmo. The Knights' galley fleet was taken into the creek below Birgu, and a great chain was stretched across the harbour entrance between Fort St Angelo and Fort St Michael to keep out enemy vessels. Food, water and arms were stockpiled, and la Valette sent urgent requests for aid to the emperor, the pope and the viceroy of Sicily. No help came. In May 1565, when an Ottoman fleet carrying more than 30,000 men arrived to lay siege to the island, la Valette was 70 years old and commanded a force of only 700 Knights and around 8000 Maltese irregulars and mercenary troops.

The Turkish force, led jointly by Admiral Piali and Mustafa Pasha, dropped anchor in the bay of Marsaxlokk, and its soldiers set up camp on the plain of Marsa. The entire population of Malta took refuge within

The Order of Malta website (www.orderofmalta.int) covers the long, illustrious history of the Knights, as well as information about present-day knightly activities.

1800

The Maltese rebel against the French garrison and ask the British for assistance. Following a naval blockade, the French surrender in September.

1814

Malta becomes a prosperous trading port and entrepôt; after the 1814 Treaty of Paris it is formally recognised as a Crown Colony of the British Empire.

1814–1964

The British rule Malta, allowing varying levels of Maltese self-government. Local activists continue to press for full independence from the islands' colonial powers.

1853–56

Malta is the headquarters of the British Mediterranean Fleet, and is used as a base and supply station for the Royal Navy during the Crimean War.

the walls of Birgu, Isla and Mdina, taking their livestock with them and poisoning the wells and cisterns they left behind. The Turks began their campaign with an attack on Fort St Elmo, which guarded the entrance to both Grand and Marsamxett Harbours. The fort was small, holding a garrison of only 60 Knights and a few hundred men – Mustafa Pasha was confident that it would fall in less than a week.

Despite continuous bombardment and repeated mass assaults on its walls, Fort St Elmo held out for over four weeks, and cost the lives of 8000 Turkish soldiers before it was taken. When the fort finally fell, not one of the Christian defenders survived.

Looking across at the looming bulk of Fort St Angelo from the smoke and rubble of St Elmo, Mustafa Pasha is said to have muttered, 'Allah! If so small a son has cost us so dear, what price shall we have to pay for so large a father?'

Hoping to intimidate the already demoralised defenders of Fort St Angelo, Mustafa Pasha ordered that several of the leading Knights be beheaded and their heads fixed on stakes looking across towards Birgu. The Turks nailed the decapitated bodies to makeshift wooden crucifixes and sent them floating across the harbour. La Valette's response was immediate and equally cruel: all Turkish prisoners were decapitated and their heads used as cannonballs, fired across the harbour to St Elmo.

Then began the final assault on the strongholds of Birgu and Isla: the Turks launched at least 10 massed assaults, but each time they were beaten back. Turkish morale was drained by the long hot summer, increasing casualties and the impending possibility of having to spend the entire winter on Malta (the Mediterranean sailing season traditionally ended with the storms of late September). The ferocity of their attacks decreased. On 7 September, the Knights' long-promised relief force from Sicily finally arrived – 28 ships carrying some 8000 men landed at Mellieħa Bay and took command of the high ground around Naxxar as the Turks scrambled at Marsamxett.

Seeing the unexpectedly small size of the relief force, Mustafa Pasha ordered some of his troops to land again at St Paul's Bay, while the rest marched towards Naxxar from Marsamxett. But the tired and demoralised Turkish soldiers were in no mood to fight these fresh and ferocious soldiers, and turned and ran for the galleys now anchored in St Paul's Bay. Thousands were hacked to pieces in the shallow waters of the bay as they tried to escape. That night the banner of the Order of St John flew once again over the battered ruins of St Elmo.

The part played in the Great Siege by the ordinary people of Malta is often overlooked, but their courage and resilience was a deciding factor in the Turkish defeat. Besides the defence force made up of 5000 or so Maltese soldiers, the local women and children contributed by repairing

Didier Destremau, former French ambassador to Malta, wrote *Malte Tricolore – The Story of a French Malta 1798–1964*, a lighthearted, satirical history of Malta 'as it might have happened', had Napoleon not got the boot.

While the Royal British Navy was in Malta, the traditional *dgħajsa* boats were a popular way for naval officers to cross Grand Harbour.

1887
For the first time in its history, Malta acquires representative government through a legislative council, composed of a majority of Maltese elected members. This is later revoked in 1903.

1914–18
Malta serves as a military hospital during WWI. After treating more than 136,000 soldiers, it was dubbed the 'Nurse of the Mediterranean'.

1919
There is a growing desire for Maltese self-government. Tension comes to a head on 7 June when riots break out.

1921
The British respond to Maltese unrest by granting a new constitution that provides for a limited form of self-government. Joseph Howard becomes the first prime minister of Malta.

walls, supplying food and ammunition and tending the wounded. The date of the end of the siege, 8 September, is still commemorated in Malta as the Victory Day public holiday.

After the Siege

The Knights of St John, previously neglected, were now hailed as the saviours of Europe. Money and honours were heaped on them by grateful monarchs, and the construction of the new city of Valletta – named after the hero of the siege – and its enormous fortifications began. Although sporadic raids continued, Malta was never again seriously threatened by the Turks.

The period following the Great Siege was one of building – not only massive new fortifications and watchtowers, but also churches, palaces and auberges. The military engineer Francesco Laparelli was sent to Malta by the pope to design the new defences of Valletta, and Italian artists arrived to decorate its churches, chapels and palazzi. An influx of new Knights, eager to join the now prestigious Order, swelled the coffers of the treasury. The pious Grand Master Jean de la Cassière (1572–81) oversaw the construction of the Order's new hospital, the Sacra Infermeria, and the magnificent St John's Co-Cathedral.

In later years, with the Turkish threat removed, the Knights occupied themselves less with militarism and monasticism, and more with piracy, commerce, drinking and duelling.

Following their 1798 expulsion from Malta by Napoleon and the loss of their French estates, the Knights sought refuge first in Russia and later in Italy. After several years of uncertainty, they finally made their headquarters in the Palazzo di Malta (the former Embassy of the Hospitallers) in Rome. The Order continues to this day; since 2008 the Grand Master has been Englishman Fra' Matthew Festing. See www.orderofmalta.org/english for more details.

While her husband Prince Philip was stationed with the Royal British Navy, Queen Elizabeth II lived in Malta intermittently from 1949 to 1951. Reputedly she learned to dance the samba in the boardroom of the Phoenicia Hotel.

A Military Linchpin

Napoleon in Malta

In the aftermath of the French Revolution, Grand Master Emmanuel de Rohan (1775–97) provided money for Louis XVI's doomed attempt to escape from Paris. By the late 18th century around three-quarters of the Order's income came from the Knights of the French langue, and when the revolutionary authorities confiscated all of the Order's properties and estates in France, the Order was left in dire financial straits.

In 1798 Napoleon Bonaparte arrived in Malta aboard his flagship *L'Orient,* at the head of the French Navy, on his way to Egypt to counter the British influence in the Mediterranean. He demanded that he be allowed to water his ships, but the Knights refused. The French landed

1930s–50s

Economic depression and political turmoil result in large numbers of Maltese emigrating to the USA, Australia, Canada and the UK.

1940

Mussolini's Italy enters WWII on 10 June. On 11 June Italian bombers strike at Malta's Grand Harbour. Three ageing biplanes take to the air to defend the islands.

1940–43

Malta assumes huge strategic importance as a WWII naval and air force base; the country experiences heavy bombing and great hardship.

1942

King George VI awards the George Cross, Britain's highest award for civilian bravery, to the entire population of Malta.

and captured the island with hardly a fight – many of the Knights were in league with the French, and the Maltese were in no mood for a battle. On 11 June 1798 the Order surrendered to Napoleon.

Napoleon stayed in Malta for only six days (in the Palazzo de Parisio in Valletta), but when he left, *L'Orient* was weighed down with silver, gold, paintings and tapestries looted from the Order's churches, auberges and infirmary. (Most of this treasure went to the bottom of the sea a few months later when the Royal Navy under Admiral Nelson destroyed the French fleet at the Battle of the Nile.) The French also abolished the Maltese aristocracy, defaced coats of arms, desecrated churches and closed down monasteries.

Napoleon left behind a garrison of 4000 men, but they were taken unawares by a spontaneous uprising of the Maltese and had to retreat within the walls of Valletta. A Maltese deputation sought help from the sympathetic British, who enforced a naval blockade.

The French garrison finally capitulated in September 1800 – but the British government, having taken Malta, was somewhat unsure what to do with it.

It wasn't until 1934 that Malti became the co-official language of Malta (alongside English), and the use of Italian was officially dropped. The first-ever grammar of the Maltese language was published at this time.

Crown Colony

The Treaty of Amiens (March 1802) provided for the return of Malta to the Order of St John, but the Maltese, not wanting the Order back, petitioned the British to stay. Their pleas fell on deaf ears, and arrangements were made for the return of the Order. But when war between Britain and France broke out again in May 1803, leaving the British government faced with the blockade of European ports against British trade, they soon changed their mind regarding the potential usefulness of Malta.

While the latter stages of the Napoleonic Wars wore on, Malta rapidly became a prosperous entrepôt, and with the Treaty of Paris in 1814 it was formally recognised as a Crown Colony of the British Empire.

The end of the Napoleonic Wars brought an economic slump to Malta as trade fell off and little was done in the way of investment in the island. But its fortunes revived during the Crimean War (1853–56), when it was developed by the Royal Navy as a major naval base and supply station. With the opening of the Suez Canal in 1869, Malta became one of the chief coaling ports on the imperial steamship route between Britain and India.

The early 19th century also saw the beginnings of Maltese political development. In 1835 a Council of Government made up of prominent local citizens was appointed to advise the governor and a free press was established. In the second half of the 19th century vast sums were spent on improving Malta's defences and dockyard facilities as the island

1943

In July Malta serves as the operational headquarters and air support base for the Allied invasion of Sicily. Captured Italian warships are anchored in Marsaxlokk Bay.

1947

A measure of self-government is restored with a general election, but a postwar economic slump creates more political tension.

1958

The pivotal and pugnacious Dom Mintoff resigns as prime minister following a clash with the British and the Maltese Churches.

1964

On 21 September Malta finally gains its independence from Great Britain, but Queen Elizabeth II remains the head of state.

became a linchpin in the imperial chain of command. The Victoria Lines and several large dry docks were built during this period. Commercial facilities were also improved to cater for the busy trade route to India and the Far East. In 1883 a railway was built between Valletta and Mdina (it closed in 1931).

Malta suffered 154 days and nights of nonstop bombing in 1942. By comparison, at the height of London's Blitz there were 57 days of continuous bombing.

During WWI Malta served as a military hospital, providing 25,000 beds for casualties from the disastrous Gallipoli campaign in Turkey. But prices and taxes rose during the war and the economy fell. During protest riots in 1919, four Maltese citizens were shot dead by panicking British soldiers and several more were injured.

The British government responded to the unrest by giving the Maltese a greater say in the running of Malta. The 1921 constitution created a diarchic system of government, with a Maltese assembly presiding over local affairs and a British imperial government controlling foreign policy and defence.

Fortress Malta

The outbreak of WWII found Britain undecided about the strategic importance of Malta. The islands' need for defence did not seem crucial at a time when Britain was itself poorly armed, and the Italian threat was remote until the Fall of France in June 1940. Thus Malta was unprepared and undefended when on 11 June, the day after Mussolini entered the war, Italian bombers attacked Grand Harbour.

The only aircraft available on the islands at this time were three Gloster Gladiator biplanes – quickly nicknamed Faith, Hope and Charity – whose pilots fought with such tenacity that Italian pilots estimated the strength of the Maltese squadron to be in the region of 25 aircraft. The Gladiators battled on alone for three weeks before squadrons of modern Hurricane fighters arrived to bolster the islands' air defences. The remains of the sole surviving aircraft, Faith, can be seen at Valletta's National War Museum (52).

Malta effectively became a fortified aircraft carrier, a base for bombing attacks on enemy ships and harbours in Sicily and North Africa. It also harboured submarines that preyed on Italian and German supply ships. Malta's importance was clear to Hitler too, and crack squadrons of Stuka dive bombers were stationed in Sicily with the objective of pounding the Maltese Islands into submission.

The day after Mussolini's Italy entered WWII, one of that country's first acts of war was to bomb Malta.

Malta's greatest ordeal came in 1942, when the country came close to starvation and surrender. In April alone some 6700 tonnes of bombs were dropped on Grand Harbour and the surrounding area. On 15 April, King George VI awarded the George Cross – Britain's highest award for civilian bravery – to the entire population of Malta.

1974

Under returned Prime Minister Dom Mintoff, Malta becomes a republic, with a parliament-appointed president now the head of state.

1980

The USSR opens an embassy on Malta as Mintoff forges strong political links with North Korea, the USSR and Libya.

1984

Dom Mintoff again resigns as prime minister, but continues to play an important backbench role in Maltese politics until 1998.

1989

Neutral Malta hosts an important summit between Mikhail Gorbachev and George Bush Sr, marking the end of the Cold War.

Just as Malta's importance to the Allies lay in disrupting enemy supply lines, so its major weakness was the difficulty of getting supplies to the island. At the height of the siege in the summer of 1942, the governor made an inventory of remaining food and fuel, and informed London that Malta would only last until August without further supplies. A massive relief convoy known as Operation Pedestal, consisting of 14 supply ships escorted by three aircraft carriers, two battleships, seven cruisers and 24 destroyers, was dispatched to run the gauntlet of enemy bombers and submarines. It suffered massive attacks, and only five supply ships made it into Grand Harbour – the crippled oil tanker *Ohio,* with its precious cargo of fuel, limped in on 15 August, lashed between two warships.

Malta was thus able to continue its vital task of disrupting enemy supply lines. The aircraft and submarines based in Malta succeeded in destroying or damaging German convoys to North Africa to the extent that Rommel's Afrika Korps was low on fuel and ammunition during the crucial Battle of El Alamein in October 1942, a situation that contributed to a famous Allied victory and the beginning of the end of the German presence in North Africa.

In July 1943 Malta served as the operational headquarters and air support base for Operation Husky, the Allied invasion of Sicily. The Italian Navy finally surrendered to the Allies on 8 September, after which Malta's role in the war rapidly diminished.

The Malta Story (1953), starring Alec Guinness and Jack Hawkins, involves men in spiffy uniforms fighting dangerous battles, performing heroic acts and winning hearts (of course). Surprisingly, it's the only movie made about the dramatic WWII events in Malta.

Independent Republic

WWII left the islands with 35,000 homes destroyed and the population on the brink of starvation. In 1947 the war-torn island was given a measure of self-government and a £30-million war-damage fund to help rebuilding and restoration. But Britain's reductions in defence spending and the loss of jobs in the naval dockyard led to calls either for closer integration with Britain or for Malta to go it alone. Malta's prime minister from 1955 was the Labour Party's Dominic (Dom) Mintoff, a politician who never shied from controversy. He took on the Roman Catholic Church, which he saw as hampering progress, and proposed not independence but that the Maltese government should integrate with that of the UK, with Maltese MPs at Westminster and the islanders given British citizenship. The British Government refused and Mintoff resigned in 1958. His clash with the Church was instrumental in his subsequent electoral defeats in 1962 and 1966.

On 21 September 1964, with Nationalist Prime Minister Dr George Borg Olivier at the helm, Malta finally gained its independence. It remained within the British Commonwealth, with Queen Elizabeth II as the head of state represented in Malta by a governor-general.

During WWII, the flying time to Malta by German and Italian bombers based in Sicily was less than 15 minutes.

2003–04

In a 2003 referendum with a voter turnout of 92%, just over half the electorate votes to join the EU. On 1 May 2004 Malta joins the EU, along with nine other states.

2008

On 1 January Malta kisses goodbye to the Maltese lira, its currency since 1972, and adopts the euro. Maltese euro coins proudly display the Maltese cross.

2012

Former prime minister Dom Mintoff dies, aged 96. Also an architect and engineer, he was leader of the Labour Party from 1949 to 1984.

2015

Malta votes to retain the tradition of spring bird hunting in a nationwide referendum. The issue remains very divisive in Maltese society.

Dom Mintoff took over once again in 1971, and Malta became a republic in 1974. In 1979 links with Britain were reduced further when Mintoff expelled the British armed services, declared Malta's neutrality and signed agreements with Libya, the USSR and North Korea. His government brought in measures on housing, nationalised many industries and made all schools comprehensive. He forged a strong, if erratic, relationship with Colonel Muammar Gaddafi, and in 1980 the USSR opened an embassy on the island. In 1984 Mintoff stood down as prime minister but continued as an influential backbencher. When he died in 2012, thousands of Maltese united in mourning and assessed the legacy of their most prominent contemporary politician.

It's no small feat to cover a country's past in fewer than 300 pages, but *A Concise History of Malta*, by Carmel Cassar, is an entertaining introduction to Maltese history.

In the 1987 election, the conservative Nationalists achieved a majority and retained power for most of the next 26 years. In 1989 Malta was the scene for the historic summit between USSR and US leaders Mikhail Gorbachev and George Bush Sr that signalled the end of the Cold War. The meetings took place on-board the Soviet cruise ship TS *Maxim Gorkiy,* anchored off the coast of Marsaxlokk, in choppy seas.

In 2004 Malta joined the EU, and in 2008 became part of the Eurozone, which brought much inward investment and helped diversify the local economy. More recently the islands have been buffeted by, but largely rode out, the European financial crisis, experiencing reasonably steady growth. From 2013, the government policies of the Maltese Labour Party have produced continued economic development, but this is balanced by concern for the environment and its impact on Malta's established traditions.

Murder and political turmoil

In October 2017, Malta was shocked by the car-bombing death of Maltese investigative journalist and anti-corruption campaigner Daphne Caruana Galizia. Ongoing investigations throughout 2019 resulted in the arrest of Maltese businessman Yorgen Fenech as a 'person of interest' in the murder of Caruana Galizia, and Fenech's court statement subsequently implicated Keith Schembri, Chief of Staff to Maltese Prime Minister Joseph Muscat, as being complicit in planning the murder.

When Malta gained independence in 1964 it was the first time since prehistory that the country had been ruled by the native Maltese and not by an outside power.

During the ongoing trial of three other men for the actual murder, Schembri continued to refute Fenech's claims, but fallout resulted in mass protests in Maltese streets from November 2019, and the eventual resignation of both Schembri and Prime Minister Muscat in early 2020.

Caruana Galizia was a harsh critic of the Maltese government, partially triggering an early election in 2017 by publishing allegations linking the government to the Panama Papers scandal, and many in Malta continue to believe her murder was ordered by leading figures in the Maltese establishment.

2017

During a particularly severe storm at the end of winter, Gozo's famed Azure Window crashes into the ocean.

2018

Valletta enjoys cultural and infrastructural development as a European Capital of Culture. Projects include art galleries and museums.

2020

Fallout from the trial following the 2017 murder of journalist Daphne Caruana Galizia escalates to include the 2020 resignation of the Maltese Prime Minister.

2021

With a journey time of around 45 minutes, Malta's long-awaited passenger ferry linking Valletta and Gozo begins operating in June.

The Maltese Way of Life

The Maltese have many passions: Roman Catholicism, band clubs, sport, cars, fireworks, swimming, sailing, food and family. And almost as many cultural influences from the nation's string of occupiers: the Phoenicians, Carthaginians, Romans, Byzantines, Arabs, Normans, Sicilians, Knights of St John, French and British. This is a society with a unique, powerful identity that harbours numerous contradictions – it's old-fashioned yet forward-thinking, bureaucratic yet rule-bending, and a defensive small island that extends a warm welcome.

Psyche

The Maltese are friendly and warm, yet it can take a long time for outsiders to feel integrated into society, despite the many different nationalities who've made their home here over millennia. Malta has one of the highest per-capita refugee acceptance rates in the world, but the issue of migrants from North Africa is fiercely debated and Malta was rated 33rd out of 38 countries in the 2015 Migrant Integration Policy Index.

Church buildings and parish activities remain at the core of village life, and the Catholic Church still exerts a strong influence. If you're here during an important religious festival such as Holy Week or any of the festas (celebrating villages' patron saints, from June to September), you'll experience firsthand how people of all ages take part, from young children in costume to the frailest elderly locals lined up in wheelchairs to watch the procession pass.

Family values are held in high regard, as is the love of socialising common to southern European countries – Sunday in particular is the day to gather with family and friends, and enjoy good food and company. In some ways Malta feels wedded to tradition, but it also embraces the new – it's an important iGaming centre, for example. There are strong class divisions, perhaps a hangover from British rule, and the elite tend to speak English and attend English schools. The south is more Maltese and slightly looked down upon by the more cosmopolitan north but, on such a small island, everyone mingles in any case.

The Maltese are justifiably proud of their small country's historical importance and the local grit and determination (well demonstrated during WWII). The vast majority of the population take great interest in political matters and love discussing politics – the accessibility of politicians in this small population probably plays a large part. The locals also put their money where their mouth is: voter turnout is among the highest in the world (over 90%) but, interestingly, margins are usually close – the country seems fairly evenly split on major issues. In the 2015 hunting referendum the pro-hunting side won 50.44% to 49.56%. The Maltese relish taking sides in other areas too: there is fierce competition between the local band clubs, the local football teams, and about who has the best local festa.

Aspiring anthropologists should seek out Tarcisio Zarb's book *Folklore of an Island – Maltese Threshold Customs*, which covers Maltese traditions related to all of life's big occasions, including birth, puberty, marriage and death.

Malta is among the most densely populated countries in the world, with 1368 people per sq km, slightly more than Bangladesh, which has 1252.

The Church

Malta's Roman Catholic Church plays a significant role, and the important events of people's lives are all celebrated in church: christenings, first communions, weddings and funerals. One indicator of the Church's strength is the fact that divorce only became legal here in 2011 (it's been legal in Italy since 1974). Under the Maltese constitution, Roman Catholic Christianity is the official state religion and must be taught in state schools, though the constitution guarantees freedom of worship.

It is estimated that there are as many Maltese living abroad as there are in Malta. Australia and Canada have significant populations.

Though the Roman Catholic Church plays a major role in everyday life, there is evidence that its influence is waning. Around 95% of Maltese are Catholic, but the Church estimates that only around 40% now attend Sunday Mass – a drop of around 20% in 20 years (but still larger than in Italy, where the figure is more like 20% to 30% attendance).

Religious occasions are celebrated with food and drink, socialising, music, processions and fireworks, and the most important event in the calendar is the annual parish festa, which is held on the day of the village's patron saint.

Women in Malta

Women have been traditionally expected to stay at home to look after their children or elderly parents, or to be supported by their husbands – it's still thought of as unusual for women to be completely financially independent. Malta's gender employment gap is the largest in the EU, with around 60% of women not employed. The government has been trying to address this issue, introducing lots of incentives for women to work; for example, tax incentives for married women over 40 who return to work, and free childcare centres.

The costs of childcare appear low compared with the UK or other European countries, but so are many of the rates of pay. After-school clubs, which most schools have, cost €0.80 per hour, while a childminder costs around €3 per hour (the minimum wage is €4.31 per hour). There are lots of free or inexpensive sports-centred courses for children over the long summer months (school holidays run from June to September) as the government tries to address the child obesity problem: one in four Maltese children are judged to be obese.

Much of Malta's immigration over recent years has been due to other Europeans moving to work in the online gaming industry.

Locals talk of low official wages spurring the creation of a parallel economy of cash work on the side. Taking on two to three jobs is common, and many qualified women work from home, in jobs such as hairdressing and dressmaking, which is another contributor to the low official percentage of women in employment.

Interestingly, the birth rate is fairly low at around 1.4 children per woman of child-bearing age, which is a little higher than its famously non-procreative and Roman Catholic neighbour Italy, but not much.

THE MALTESE NAME GAME

Spend just a short time wandering the streets of Valletta and the city's faded heritage shopfronts soon reveal many of the same names. Surnames like Borg, Grech, Camilleri, Azzopardi, Zammit and Micallef all feature, showcasing a provenance from Arabic, Italian, French, Spanish or Sicilian.

In fact, Maltese census data indicates around a quarter of the total population has one of the country's top 10 surnames, and looking at the top 100 family names, more than 75% of the population is covered. Across on traditionally more insular Gozo, having a particular surname is enough to guarantee roots in a specific village. It's a telling indicator of Malta's location in the centre of the Mediterranean with historical links stretching north and west to Europe, south to Africa, and east to Arabia and the Levant.

A LINGUISTIC MELTING POT

The native language of Malta is Malti (also called Maltese). Some linguists attribute its origins to the Phoenician occupation of Malta in the 1st millennium BC, but most link it to North African Arabic dialects. The language has an Arabic grammar and construction but is formed from a morass of influences, laced with Sicilian, Italian, Spanish, French and English loan words. Until the 1930s, Italian was the official language of the country, used in the Church and for all administrative matters, even though only the aristocracy could speak it. Malti only became an official language in 1934 (alongside English).

Music

The Maltese are great music lovers and the *għana* (*ah*-na; folk song) is Maltese folk music at its most individual and traditional. A tribute to Malta's geographic location, *għana* verses are a mixture of the Sicilian ballad and the rhythmic wail of an Arabic tune, and were traditionally viewed as the music of the farmers, labourers and working classes. In the genre's truest form, lyrics are created fresh each time and tell stories of village life and events in local history. The verses are always sung by men with guitar accompaniment.

The Malti language is rich in proverbs. *'Ghidli ma' min taghmilha u nghidlek x'int'* translates to 'Tell me who you're friends with, and I'll tell you what you are'.

The St James' Cavalier Centre for Creativity (p65) in Valletta organises *għana* nights, as do other venues across Malta, especially in the centre and south. You might see performances at various heritage events, or even chance upon an impromptu *għana* performance in a rural bar. Għanafest takes place in mid-June in Floriana, with three days of live concerts.

Etnika is one traditional folk group that has revived ethnic Maltese musical forms and instruments. Its style of music, using traditional bagpipes, horns and drums, was once part of Malta's daily life, and was used in a variety of social contexts, including weddings and funerals. Etnika reinterprets this musical heritage for a contemporary audience and sometimes fuses it with *għana*, jazz and flamenco for a unique sound.

Traditional band music is one of the most popular traditions on the islands, with bands playing a vital role in the village festa and other open-air events. Every town and village has at least one band club and they are often engaged in strong rivalry.

There's a great deal of live music in Malta over the spring and summer months, with gigs at pubs and bars, and the Jazz Festival, Arts Festival, Music Week, **Isle of MTV** (www.isleofmtv.com; ⌚late Jun) and **Lost & Found** (www.lostandfoundfestival.com; ⌚early May).

Crafts

Malta is noted for its fine crafts, especially its handmade lace, hand-woven fabrics and silver filigree.

Lace-making probably arrived with the Knights in the 16th century. It was traditionally the role of village women. Although the craft has developed into a healthy industry, you still occasionally see women making lace in villages around Gozo.

For Rozina...a Husband, by playwright and novelist Francis Ebejer (1925–93), is a collection of short stories (in English) that seeks to capture the essence of Maltese village life.

The art of producing silver filigree was probably introduced to the islands in the 17th century via Sicily, which was then strongly influenced by Spain. Malta's silversmiths still produce beautiful filigree by traditional methods, yet it's mostly created in quantities to meet tourist demand.

Other handicrafts include weaving, knitting and glass-blowing; the latter is an especially healthy small industry that produces glassware exported throughout the world. Head to Ta'Qali Crafts Village (p110) near Rabat or its smaller Gozitan equivalent, Ta'Dbieġi Crafts Village (p139), for the opportunity to see locals practising their craft and to buy souvenirs. Malta Artisan Markets (www.maltaartisanmarkets.com) are regular events held in locations such as Palazzo Parisio (p114), where you can find contemporary crafts made by artisans around the islands.

The annual Eurovision Song Contest is hugely popular in Malta. The country's best results were when it came second in 2002 and 2005.

Sport

Football (Soccer)

The Maltese are staunch, passionate football fans and follow the fortunes of local sides and international teams (especially British and Italian) with equal fervour – countless bars televise matches. The local and Maltese Premier League season runs from October till May; league and international matches are held at the 20,000-seat **Ta'Qali National Stadium** (☎2143 6137; www.mfa.com.mt), which is situated between Mosta and Rabat, and results are reported in the local newspapers. The Malta Football Association (www.mfa.com.mt/en/home.htm) and Malta Football (www.maltafootball.com) are good resources.

Water Polo

As the heat of summer increases, football gives way to water polo. Between July and September, the fans who were once shouting on the terraces now yell from the pool side. Games are fierce and physical – it's worth trying to take in a match during your stay. The important clashes are held at the Tal-Qroqq National Swimming Pool Complex on Triq Maria Teresa Spinelli in Gżira. Further information is available from the Aquatic Sports Association (www.asaofmalta.org).

The Events section of www.visitmalta.com is a great starting point for information about forthcoming cultural events, including literary recitals, traditional folk music performances and lunchtime concerts.

Racing

Another of Malta's much-loved spectator sports is horse racing. Race meetings are held at the Marsa Racecourse (part of the Marsa Sports Club outside Valletta) every Sunday, and sometimes on Friday and Saturday, from January to July. Races are mostly harness racing – and the betting is frantic. In season, some tour operators offer a day trip to the races. For more information see www.maltaracingclub.com.

In car-loving Malta, motor racing is also hugely popular; the Mdina Grand Prix Classic Car Event (www.maltaclassic.com) takes place annually in October, with a challenging 2.2km circuit outside the city walls.

BIRD HUNTING

One of Malta's favourite traditional sports is bird hunting; there are around 14,000 registered hunters and trappers in the country. Most birds are shot or trapped while migrating between Africa and Europe; Malta is one of the major flyways for migrating birds and more than 384 species have been recorded here.

The spring hunting season is open between 12 and 30 April; the autumn season runs from 1 September to 31 January. Two species of bird – turtle dove and quail – may be legally hunted; shooting at any other bird is illegal. There has been a decline in illegal shootings but they do happen, and in 2015 the spring hunting season was closed three days early by the prime minister after a kestrel – a protected bird of prey – was shot by a hunter and landed in a school playground.

Malta is the only EU member state that still allows hunting during the spring season. In 2015 there was a national referendum to decide whether spring hunting should be banned completely. Polls prior to the vote showed the conservationists with a strong lead, but the pro-hunting camp won by a slim majority of 2220, to maintain the tradition.

In 2018, the European Court of Justice ruled the live trapping of seven species of wild finches was banned under European Law in Malta, adjudicating on a lengthy legal battle that had been ongoing since 2015.

Above Easter Sunday procession, Valletta (p22)

Right Maltese lace (p163)

KRZYSZTOF_JANKOWSKI/SHUTTERSTOCK ©

5000 Years of Architecture

Malta's architectural history kicked off in spectacular fashion with some of the world's most extraordinary prehistoric architecture, great temple-like buildings both above and below ground. The next inhabitants to leave such a powerful mark on the islands were the Knights of St John, with their stately 16th- and 17th-century fortified towns and baroque cathedrals. You won't just be astounded by the buildings of the past but also by those of today, most notably Renzo Piano's dramatic additions to new-look Valletta.

The architecture on Malta and Gozo is partly shaped by geology: the islands are predominantly made up of layers of limestone. This type of stone, with its natural faults, allows rocks to be levered out with simple tools. Prehistoric builders exploited the weaknesses in the rock to carve out their mammoth slabs. The stone, while soft when first quarried, becomes harder when it dries out, making it ideal for carving and moulding.

Malta's prehistoric temples predate the Egyptian pyramids by around 1000 years. Especially ancient are the megalithic temple complexes at Ġgantija.

Historical context is also of huge importance. Grand defensive structures are abundant, signalling how often the islands were fought over throughout their history. There are the great forts and walled cities constructed by the Knights of St John; the Victoria Lines, built by the British, running across the Maltese hills; and castellated watchtowers, which stalk the coastline like sentinels.

Prehistoric Innovation

The islands are home to a series of extraordinary megalithic monuments constructed between the 4th and 3rd millennia BC. A model made by the temple builders has been discovered, which shows the corbelled roof of a temple made of stone, indicating the extraordinary sophistication of the ancient builders.

The Hal Saflieni Hypogeum (p67), a multi-level underground burial complex hewn out of Globigerina limestone, dates from 5000 years ago. The builders carved out the stone in such a way as to imitate structures above ground, with rock-cut decoration, smoothed walls and curved ceilings. The well-preserved forms of this underground complex have also cast light on the less enduring monuments above ground, such as the Tarxien Temples (p67) and Ħaġar Qim (p124) on Malta and Ġgantija (p143) on Gozo. Where the roofs of the above-ground temples have collapsed, the Hypogeum's parallel subterranean architecture provides an invaluable reference point.

Read *Malta: Phoenician, Punic & Roman,* by Maltese archaeologist Anthony Bonanno, to learn about the island's early history. Numerous colour photographs are excellent.

Early Prosperity

Malta's urban architecture developed during prosperous times. The Carthaginians built Malta's first towns, although little remains from this period. Some significant Roman relics have been preserved, including the grand villa complex at Rabat in central Malta, a typically Roman structure centred on a peristyle courtyard. Although the cultural impact of the later Islamic period was extremely significant, it left little architectural trace.

For over 2000 years Mdina was the island's major town. Originally a Phoenician settlement, it was enlarged and built upon by the Romans, and developed further by the Byzantines, Arabs, Normans and Aragonese. Mdina reached its current form in the 15th and 16th centuries, though the 1720s saw major redevelopment as the fortifications were bolstered.

Best Prehistoric

- *Hal Saflieni Hypogeum (Malta)*
- *Tarxien Temples (Malta)*
- *Ħaġar Qim & Mnajdra (Malta)*
- *Ġgantija Temples (Gozo)*

Military Might

When the Knights of St John arrived in Malta in the 16th century they set about building defences, particularly around Birgu (Vittoriosa); they also rebuilt the fortifications around Mdina. They based themselves at Birgu, and here constructed splendid hostels, or auberges, where the members of the Order lived.

After the Knights fought off the Ottoman threat in the Great Siege of 1565, grateful European allies poured money into Malta. With this largesse the Knights built Valletta, surrounding it with huge bastions. Because the island is so rocky, the fortifications were often carved into the rock, rather than built upon it, which helped increase their strength. The well-connected Knights had access to all the leading courts of Europe, so were able to call on the great military engineers of the era to create cutting-edge defences, which remain vastly impressive today. These constructions are not merely intimidating, but also beautiful, with delicate decorative elements that exalt their builders – intricacies that helped reinforce the power of the Order.

However, the extent of the building was vastly expensive, and by the late 1600s the order was bankrupted by its cost. Built for conflict but untested, these fortifications were the nuclear weaponry of their day, acting as a deterrent to potential invaders.

Baroque Splendours

Together, the Knights of St John and the Church created a distinctive variation of baroque, the ornate style that dominated Europe from the 16th to the 18th centuries. This frenzy of decoration was a visual form of propaganda, exalting god, Christianity and the nobility of its builders.

MALTA'S CHURCHES

The Maltese claim to be one of the earliest Christian peoples in the world, having been converted by St Paul after his shipwreck on Malta in AD 60, and ecclesiastical architecture certainly dominates the landscape.

There are 64 Catholic parishes and 313 Catholic churches on Malta, and 15 Catholic parishes and 46 Catholic churches on Gozo. The main period of church-building in Malta took place after the arrival of the Knights of St John, in the 16th, 17th and 18th centuries; the oldest surviving church is the tiny medieval Chapel of the Annunciation (p123) at Ħal Millieri near Żurrieq, which dates from the mid-15th century.

In the 16th century the Knights imported the Renaissance style from Italy. This was supplanted by the more elaborate forms of Maltese baroque, which evolved throughout the 17th century and culminated in the design of St Paul's Cathedral (p106) in Mdina. The 19th and 20th centuries saw the addition of several large churches in the neo-Gothic style, including St Paul's Anglican Cathedral in Valletta and the Church of Our Lady of Lourdes (p135) in Mġarr, Gozo. Two huge rotundas were also built by public subscription: the vast Mosta Dome (p112) and the Rotunda (p137) at Xewkija, Gozo, which has space to seat 4000 people.

The greatest Maltese architect of the 16th century was Gerolamo Cassar (1520–86). He was born in the fishing village of Birgu 10 years before the Knights of St John arrived from Rhodes, and worked as an assistant to Francesco Laparelli, the military engineer who designed the fortifications of Valletta. Cassar studied architecture in Rome and was responsible for the design of many of Malta's finest buildings, including the Grand Master's Palace (p172), the facade of St John's Co-Cathedral (p51) and many of the Knights' auberges.

At the Ġgantija temples, the fine interior work was created from Globigerina limestone, dragged from quarries more than a kilometre away.

Prolific architect Tommaso Dingli (1591–1666) created many of Malta's parish churches. His masterpiece is the Church of St Mary (p115) in Attard, which he designed when he was only 22 years of age. Lorenzo Gafa (1630–1704) designed many of the finest examples of Maltese baroque, among them the cathedrals of Mdina and Gozo.

Valletta's Manoel Theatre (p57) is an architectural treasure, with a magnificent auditorium. Founded by the Portuguese Grand Master Antonio Manoel de Vilhena in 1731, it was used regularly by the Knights for their productions, and is one of the oldest working theatres in Europe.

Great Mansions

Malta is not only rich in ecclesiastical and military architecture, but has some splendid noble houses, several of which are open to the public. These include Casa Rocca Piccola (p57) in Valletta, Palazzo Falson (p106) in Mdina, and Villa Bologna (p115) in Attard, which provide a glimpse into the gilded world of the Maltese aristocracy. The grandest of them all is the largely 19th-century Palazzo Parisio (p114) in Naxxar, once a summer house belonging to Maltese-Sicilian gentry, and later transformed by a wealthy Maltese marquis, who added extravagant murals and a mirror-lined ballroom to create a mini Versailles.

5000 Years of Architecture in Malta, by Leonard Mahoney, provides comprehensive coverage of Malta's archaeological history, from Neolithic temples to the auberges of the Knights and beyond.

Contemporary Style

Malta has been blighted in the modern period by over-development in many places, though building in its historical centres has remained strictly controlled. While the contemporary scene is not all bad news, every new major development has been dogged by controversy.

One of Malta's foremost architects is Richard England (www.richardengland.com), whose work has included transforming Valletta's St James Cavalier (originally designed by military engineer Laparelli de Cortona) into its contemporary guise as the Centre for Creativity (p65). England is also responsible for the striking design of St Joseph's Church in Manikata on the outskirts of Mellieħa, for which he used the *girna* (a small circular building farmers construct in the middle of fields) as inspiration.

Another well-known contemporary local architect is the prolific Chris Briffa, who has been responsible for many architectural projects around Malta in recent years, and has won plaudits for his sympathetic approach

THE MALTESE BALCONY

The first recorded *gallarija* in Valletta was the long gallery that lines the Grand Master's Palace (p51), built in the late 17th century. When the city of Valletta was first built in the 16th century, open balconies were very popular, but this palatial enclosed gallery sparked a trend that everyone began to copy. At first people merely enclosed the top part of their existing balconies, but then they started to add lower panels to match, resulting in the unique Maltese style of balcony we see today.

CARAVAGGIO IN MALTA

The Italian painter Michelangelo Merisi (1571–1610) is better known by the name of his home town, Caravaggio, in northern Italy. His realist depictions of religious subjects and dramatic use of light shocked and revolutionised the 16th-century art world.

He made his name in Rome with a series of controversial works, but was also notorious for his volatility and violence. Numerous brawls culminated in Caravaggio murdering a man during an argument over a tennis game. He fled Rome and went into hiding in Naples for several months. Then, towards the end of 1607, he moved to Malta.

Here, Caravaggio was welcomed as a famous artist and produced several works for the Knights of St John, including the famous *Beheading of St John the Baptist* for the Oratory of St John's Co-Cathedral (p51). In July 1608 he was admitted into the Order as a Knight of Justice, but only two months later he was arrested for an unspecified crime, and imprisoned in Fort St Angelo.

He escaped to Sicily, but was expelled from the Order and spent the next two years on the run. He created some of his finest paintings – ever darker and more twisted – during this period. He died in Italy; the cause of his death remains unknown.

to converting historic buildings. One of his architectural innovations has been to open up the traditional *gallarija* (Maltese balcony) in such a way that none of the view is obscured. He's also converted **Casa Ellul** (Map p54; ☎2122 4821; www.casaellul.com; Triq it-Teatru l-Antik; d from €250; ❄📶) and the Harbour Club (p62), designed the stylish Ġgantija Temples (p143) visitor centre and worked on projects to develop a row of bars in Valletta's Strait St.

There have been a remarkable number of architectural developments in Malta in recent years, including the sleekly remodelled Valletta, Cottonera (Vittoriosa), Senglea and Qawra waterfronts; Tigné Point (p79); the Mdina Ditch Garden (p106); the starfish-shaped Malta National Aquarium (p97); and the huge Xghajra Smart City (p68) development, an entire town to house Malta's emerging tech industry. All of these projects have provoked debate as they are seen by some to be at odds with Malta's traditional heritage architecture.

Without doubt the most high-profile and controversial project is that of Italian architect Renzo Piano in Valletta. Piano's City Gate (p53) consists of a breach in the city walls, replacing the 1960s development that previously framed the entrance. Just inside the gate and forming part of a harmonious ensemble, his modernist Parliament Building (p57) supports huge golden-stone blocks on a steel structure, and uses the latest ecological architectural innovations to heat and cool the building. Alongside the Parliament Building is Piano's Opera House (p58), an open-air auditorium above the ruins of the former building, which had been destroyed in WWII and left as a ruin as a reminder of the past. Like the islands' prehistoric builders, Piano has been inspired by the local stone, and the complex includes piazzas, staircases and walkways that have turned the area into a dynamic public space.

A more recent project linked with Valletta's status as a European Capital of Culture for 2018 was the transformation of the Auberge d'Italie into MUŻA (p56), a stunning community-focused reimagining of Malta's Museum of Fine Arts. Looking ahead, future plans include the redevelopment of Valletta's Ditch Gardens in a style similar to the successful rehabilitation of similar areas in Mdina and Il-Kastell on Gozo.

Best Baroque

St John's Co-Cathedral (Valletta)

Church of St Paul's Shipwreck (Valletta)

St Paul's Cathedral (Mdina)

Cathedral of the Assumption (Victoria)

Above City Gate, Valletta (p53)

Left Palazzo Parisio, Valletta (p61)

Survival Guide

Directory A–Z

Accessible Travel

Maltese government policy is to improve access for people with disabilities, but many of Malta's historic places – notably the steep, stepped streets of Valletta – remain difficult, if not impossible, to negotiate for those with restricted mobility. Several sights are accessible, however, including Fort St Elmo & National War Museum (p52), the Grand Master's Palace (p51) and the National Museum of Archaeology (p52).

A good number of the more expensive hotels have wheelchair access and some have rooms specially designed for guests with disabilities. Sliema, with its long promenade, is a good place to be based. The Malta and Gozo bus services have wheelchair-accessible buses.

The Nautic Team (p27) on Gozo is equipped for divers with disabilities, offering courses and equipment hire.

The **Malta Tourism Authority** (www.visitmalta.com) can provide information on hotels and sights equipped for wheelchair users.

General information is available from the **National Commission for Persons with Disabilities** (Centru Hidma Socjali; ☎2226 7600; www.crpd.org.mt; Triq Salvu Psaila, Birkirkara; ⊙8.15am-noon Mon-Fri).

Lonely Planet has a Travel for All community on Google+, as well as the Thorntree community at www.lonelyplanet.com/thorntree/forums/travellers-with-disabilities. Download Lonely Planet's free Accessible Travel guides from https://shop.lonelyplanet.com/categories/accessible-travel.com.

Climate

Valletta

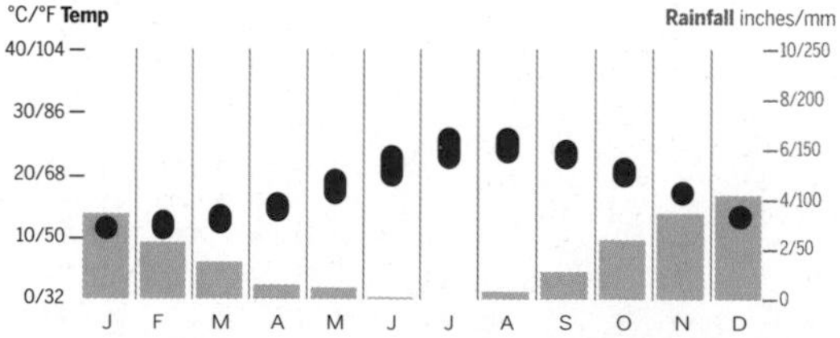

Customs Regulations

No restrictions if you're travelling from another EU country, though you're likely to be questioned if amounts seem excessive. If you're entering Malta from outside the EU, the duty-free allowance per person is 1L of spirits, 4L of wine, and 200 cigarettes or 100 cigarillos or 50 cigars or 250g of tobacco.

Discount Cards

If you're planning to visit more than a few of Malta and Gozo's cultural treasures, consider a multisite pass from Heritage Malta, which covers 23 Heritage Malta sites plus the Citadel Visitor Centre and the National Malta Aquarium. Admission fees can mount up, considering that a single adult ticket to the Armoury and State Rooms in Valletta costs €10, the Ħaġar Qim and Mnajdra Temples cost €10, and most other sites cost €5 or €6.

The pass offers 30 days of admission to most Heritage Malta sights (the Hypogeum is an exception; see www.heritagemalta.org for a full list). An adult/child pass costs €50/25, while a family ticket (two adults and two children) is an even better bargain at €110.

Other discounts include the following:

➡ **Malta Pass** (www.maltapass.com.mt; 1/2/3 days €24.95/39.95/49.95) allows admission to more than 40 attractions, plus a harbour cruise and open-bus tour. Buy online.

- People over 60 years of age are entitled to discounted admission to all government-owned museums.
- A valid ISIC card (www.isic.org) or European Youth Card (www.eyca.org) will get you discounts.
- The **National Student Travel Service** (NSTS; ☎2558 8000; www.nsts.org; 220 Triq San Pawl) can provide information about where you can get student reductions. Admission to state-run museums is discounted for card-carrying students.

PLAN YOUR STAY ONLINE

For more accommodation reviews by Lonely Planet authors, check out www.lonelyplanet.com. You'll find independent reviews, as well as recommendations on the best places to stay.

Electricity

Type G
230V/50Hz

Embassies & Consulates

Full lists of Maltese embassies abroad and foreign embassies in Malta can be found at www.foreignaffairs.gov.mt.

Health

Availability of Health Care in Malta

High-standard health and dental care is readily available in Malta, and for minor illnesses pharmacists can give valuable advice and sell over-the-counter medication. They can also advise when more specialised help is required and point you in the right direction.

There are pharmacies in most towns; these are generally open from 9am to 1pm and 4pm to 7pm Monday to Saturday. On Sundays and public holidays they open by roster in the morning – the local Sunday newspapers print details of the roster, and it can be found online at www.ehealth.gov.mt.

Malta's public general hospital is **Mater Dei Hospital** (☎2545 0000, emergency 112; www.deputyprimeminister.gov.mt/en/MDH; Triq Dun Karm), 2km southwest of Sliema and accessible by bus 75 from Valletta. Gozo's smaller **General Hospital** (☎2156 1600; Triq l-Arċisqof Pietru Pace) may also be of use. General practitioner service is available at a network of health centres (at Floriana, Gżira, Qormi, Paola, Cospicua, Mosta, Rabat and on Gozo) as well as some pharmacies. English is spoken at all pharmacies, hospitals and health centres.

Consultation is usually free for EU nationals at most health centres, but residents of other countries pay around €15 for an initial visit.

Medical Insurance

Citizens of the EU, Iceland, Liechtenstein, Norway and Switzerland receive free or reduced-cost state-provided health care with the European Health Insurance Card (EHIC) for medical treatment that becomes necessary while in Malta. The EHIC will not provide cover for non-emergencies or emergency repatriation home. Each family member will need a separate card. The EHIC is free; full details are online at www.ehic.org.uk.

Malta has reciprocal health agreements with Australia and the UK. Australians are eligible for subsidised health care for up to six months from their date of arrival in Malta; UK residents for up to 30 days. Details of these arrangements and various health services can be found on the website of the Maltese Ministry of Health (www.deputyprimeminister.gov.mt/en/Pages/health.aspx).

If you need health insurance, strongly consider a policy covering the worst possible scenario, such as an accident requiring an emergency flight home.

Insurance

A travel insurance policy to cover theft, loss and medical problems is always a good idea. Some insurance policies specifically exclude 'dangerous activities', which can include scuba diving. Note that policies don't usually cover dental work, only pain relief. Check the small print before signing up.

You may prefer to have an insurance policy that pays doctors or hospitals directly rather than you having to pay on the spot and claim later. If you have to claim later, make sure you keep all documentation.

Some policies ask you to call (reverse charges) a centre in your home country, where an assessment of your problem is made.

Internet Access

Malta has extensive wi-fi coverage – most towns and even some of the sleepiest villages have a wi-fi hot spot in their main square. Many establishments, including hotels, cafes, bars and restaurants, also offer wi-fi. The wi-fi at most guesthouses, hostels and hotels is usually free. Signals are of varying quality.

If you're visiting from outside Europe, you may need a voltage converter to adjust the current in Europe (240V) to one your electronic device can handle. You do not usually need these for laptop computers and digital-camera battery chargers.

Language Courses

The Maltese Islands are renowned as an enjoyable place to study English, and young people flock to the more than 40 language schools across the islands. Schools are mainly clustered in Valletta, St Julian's and Paceville. For a list, see www.visitmalta.com.

Legal Matters

All towns and most villages have their own police station; the smaller ones are staffed by a single officer and often marked by a traditional British-style blue lamp.

If you are arrested or detained by the police you have the right to be informed, in a language that you understand, of the reasons for your arrest or detention, and if the police do not release you they must bring you before a court within 48 hours.

You also have the right to inform your consulate and to speak to a lawyer.

For an emergency requiring help from the police (*pulizija* in Malti), call 112.

Gozo Police Headquarters (☎2156 2040; Triq ir-Repubblika) Gozo's main police station is located near the corner of Triq ir-Repubblika and Triq Putirjal.

Malta Police Headquarters (☎2122 4001; www.pulizija.gov.mt; Pjazza San Kalċidonju) Located in Floriana.

LGBTIQ+ Travellers

Homosexual sex was legalised in Malta in 1973. In 2014 the government passed a bill approving same-sex civil unions and gay adoption. Gay marriage was subsequently approved in 2017, and getting married in Malta is an increasingly popular option for gay couples from overseas. Gay marriages contracted abroad are also recognised by the state. However, Malta is a conservative, very Catholic country and public affection (straight or gay) is generally frowned upon.

Still, while Malta is not a very 'out' destination, it is gay-friendly. For more information see www.visitmalta.com/en/gay-friendly-malta and www.gayguidemalta.com.

Malta Gay Rights Movement (www.maltagayrights.org) staged its first Gay Pride march in Valletta in July 2004, and the marches have been held annually ever since. Although the march and surrounding festivities are tiny in comparison to the large gatherings elsewhere in

PRACTICALITIES

Newspapers & Magazines

- The *Times of Malta* (www.timesofmalta.com) Good mix of local, European and world news; English-language daily newspaper.
- The *Independent* (www.independent.com.mt) Coverage of domestic social issues; English-language daily newspaper.
- *Malta Today* (www.maltatoday.com.mt) Online source of local and international news.

Radio & TV

- More than 20 local radio stations broadcast, mostly in Malti but occasionally in English.
- TVM is the state-run TV channel.
- Most of the Italian TV stations, such as RAI-1, RAI-2 and RAI-3 can be received in Malta.
- Satellite and cable TV are widely available in hotels and bars.

Weights & Measures

- Metric system, like elsewhere in Europe, though pint glasses are still used in some pubs.

Smoking

- Banned in any enclosed private or public premises open to the public except in designated smoking rooms. People can smoke freely outside.

Europe, they're a chance for Malta's LGBTIQ+ community to gather, celebrate diversity and push for an end to discrimination.

Money

Malta abandoned the Maltese lira and adopted the euro (€) on 1 January 2008. To prevent retailers from rounding up prices, the rate of exchange was fixed at Lm1 to €2.33, which is why you'll still sometimes see euro prices in fractions or multiples of 2.33.

The reverse sides of Maltese coins feature a uniquely Maltese design (a Maltese cross, for example), but are legal tender in all countries in the Eurozone.

ATMs

There are plentiful ATMs at Malta International Airport, Valletta's waterfront and in all the main towns in Malta, where you can withdraw euros using a credit or debit card and PIN.

ATM withdrawals may incur a transaction charge of around 2.75% and an ATM charge of around 1.5% to 2% of the amount withdrawn – check with your bank before departing. You may also need to inform your bank before you travel, to avoid your card being blocked.

Cash

Cash can be changed at hotels, banks, exchange bureaux and some tourist shops. There are also 24-hour exchange machines at banks in the main tourist towns, including Valletta, Sliema and Buġibba, where you can feed in foreign banknotes and get euros back.

You'll need to carry cash because some smaller restaurants and hotels don't accept cards.

Credit Cards

Visa, MasterCard and Amex credit cards and charge cards are widely accepted in larger hotels, restaurants and shops, though smaller places only deal in cash. Travel and car-hire agencies accept cards.

Taxes & Refunds

VAT (value-added tax) was reintroduced to Malta in 1999, with two rates: accommodation is charged at 5% (and is usually included in the rates quoted) and other items at 18%. Visitors to Malta can reclaim VAT on their purchases provided they are residents outside the EU, and will be taking the goods outside the EU when they depart from Malta.

Tipping & Bargaining

Hotels Baggage porters should get about €1 per piece of luggage; car-park attendants around €1.

Restaurants In restaurants where no service charge is included, leave 10% for good service.

Bars Not expected but good to leave loose change if paying by cash.

Taxis Drivers don't expect a tip, but it's nice to round up a fare in order to leave a small tip (up to 10%) if warranted.

Opening Hours

The following are high-season opening hours; hours are sometimes shorter in the low season.

Banks 8.30am–12.30pm Monday to Friday, sometimes to 2pm Friday, 8.30am–noon Saturday

Bars 8pm–4am

Cafes 9am–10pm

Restaurants noon–3pm and 7–11pm, usually closed Sunday or Monday

Shops 9am–1pm and 4–7pm Monday to Saturday

Photography

Memory cards and camera equipment are easily obtained at photographic shops in all the main towns.

For tips on taking the perfect holiday snaps, look out for Lonely Planet's *Travel Photography* book.

Post

for Malta Post (www.maltapost.com) operates a reliable postal service. Post office branches are found in most towns and villages (in some towns the local newsagent/souvenir shop acts as a branch agent).

Local postage costs €0.26 up to 50g; a 20g letter or postcard sent airmail to the UK or Europe costs €0.59, to the USA €0.91 and to Australia €1.12. Stamps are frequently available from hotels and souvenir shops as well as from post offices.

Safe Travel

Hunting

If you go walking in the countryside, be aware of the common pastime of shooting and trapping birds – the little stone shacks that pepper the cliff tops are shooters' hides. You will hear the popping of shotguns before you see the shooters. There are usually two hunting seasons, in spring and autumn.

Road Conditions & Driving

Much of the road network in Malta is badly in need of repair, which means that driving is often an uncomfortably bumpy experience. Rules of the road are rarely observed, which adds to the stress of driving in unfamiliar territory, especially during rush-hour conditions around Sliema and St Julian's.

Take special care on roundabouts and always wait to see what other drivers are doing, even if it's your right of way (never assume they will stop for you!). A satnav will also enormously reduce the stress of driving, particularly as signposting can be erratic.

Swimming

Malta and Gozo's waters are not really tidal, and when the weather is calm it's usually completely safe to swim. However, the Maltese often repeat the saying, 'The sea has a soft belly, but a hard head', a warning to be wary of the sea around the islands because of its powerful undercurrents in windy weather. Locals advise never to swim in rough sea.

Major beaches have lifeguards patrolling and a flag system operating from June to September. If there's no flag system operating and if you're in doubt, ask a local about whether it's safe and where to swim.

Theft & Violence

Malta has a low rate of violent crime, and crimes against visitors are a rarity. Incidents involving pickpockets and purse-snatchers are uncommon, but in past years there have been increasing reports of thieves breaking into cars parked in quiet areas including Marfa and Delimara Point. Lock your car and don't leave anything of value in it. There have been occasional incidents of drunken violence in Paceville late at night; exercise caution.

Telephone

Mobile Phones

Mobile-phone numbers begin with either 79 or 99. Malta uses the GSM900 mobile phone network, which is compatible with the rest of Europe, Australia and New Zealand, but not with the USA and Canada's GSM1900.

If you have a GSM phone, check with your service provider about using it in Malta and beware of calls being routed internationally (expensive for a 'local' call).

You may consider buying a Maltese SIM card, which gives you a Maltese mobile number. (Your mobile may be locked to the local network in your home country, so ask your home network for advice before going abroad.) Prepaid vouchers for topping up credit are available at many stores and kiosks throughout Malta.

Phone Codes

The international direct dialling code is ☎00, followed by the relevant country code and then the number. To call Malta from abroad, dial the international access code, ☎356 (the country code for Malta) and then the number.

There are no area codes in Malta; all phone numbers are eight-digit numbers.

Public Phones & Phonecards

Public telephones are widely available, and most are card-operated (there are also coin-operated phones, but these are not as common). You can buy phonecards from Easyline or Hello at many kiosks and post offices.

Time

Malta is in the same time zone as most of Western Europe: one hour ahead of GMT/UTC on standard time, and two hours ahead from the last Sunday in March to the last Sunday in October (the daylight-saving period).

Toilets

Malta is well equipped with public toilets, often at the entrance to a public garden or near the village square. They are usually clean and in good order. If there is an attendant, it is good manners to leave a tip of a few cents in a dish by the door.

Tourist Information

Local Tourist Offices

As well as the useful and comprehensive Malta Tourism site (www.visitmalta.com), there are tourist information offices in Valletta, near the Valletta bus station, Mdina, Buġibba, at Malta International Airport, and in Victoria and at the Ferry Terminal in Mġarr on Gozo.

The specialist site www.visitgozo.com is an excellent resource.

Visas

Everyone is required to have a valid passport (or ID card for EU citizens) to enter Malta. EU citizens are entitled to travel freely around the member states of the EU, and settle anywhere within its territory.

Malta is part of the Schengen area. Citizens from some non-EU countries are required to hold a visa when travelling to the Schengen area. Generally, a short-stay visa issued by one of the Schengen states entitles its holder to travel throughout the 25 Schengen states for up to three months within a six-month period. Visas for visits exceeding that period are at the discretion of the Malta authorities. Citizens of Australia, Canada, Israel, Japan, New Zealand and the US can stay for up to 90 days without a visa; other nationalities can check their visa requirements online at www.identitymalta.com/schengen.

If you wish to stay for more than 90 days, you will have to apply for a Temporary Residence Permit via the Department for Citizenship and Expatriates Affairs (eresidence.mhas@gov.mt). You will need two photographs, a letter regarding your reasons for staying (an English-language course, employment, self-employment etc), a completed application form, evidence of your means of support, and documents showing your health insurance. More information is available at www.identitymalta.com/citizenships-expatriates.

Transport

GETTING THERE & AWAY

Almost all visitors to Malta arrive by plane, but the country also has car ferry links to southern Italy and Sicily. Flights, cars and tours can be booked online at lonelyplanet.com/bookings.

Entering Malta & Gozo

For virtually all travellers, entering Malta is a very straightforward procedure. In many cases, flights into the country will be from other Schengen countries, further reducing the complexity of the process.

Passport

Citizens of most EU member states can travel to Malta with their national identity cards. All other travellers must have a full valid passport.

Air

Malta is well connected to Europe and North Africa, but there are no direct flights into Malta from places further afield. If you're flying from elsewhere, it's best to travel to a major European hub, such as London, Amsterdam or Brussels, then join a direct connecting flight to Malta.

Airports & Airlines

All flights arrive and depart from **Malta International Airport** (MLA; ☎2124 9600; www.maltairport.com; Luqa), 8km south of Valletta. The airport has good facilities, including ATMs and currency exchange, internet access, a tourist office (open daily), left luggage, and regular, inexpensive bus connections to Malta's major towns and to the Gozo ferry. There is also an office of Malta Public Transport selling travel cards for buses and ferries throughout Malta.

The Maltese national airline is **Air Malta** (KM; ☎2166 2211; www.airmalta.com), a small airline with a good safety record.

Departure Tax

Departure tax is included in the price of a ticket.

Land

You can travel by bus from most parts of Europe to a port in Italy and catch a ferry from there to Malta. Eurolines (www.eurolines.com) is a consortium of coach companies that operates across Europe, with offices in all major European cities.

With your own vehicle, you can drive to southern Italy and take a car ferry from Salerno or from Pozzallo or Catania (Sicily) to Malta. From northern Europe the fastest road route is via the Simplon Pass to Milan, from which Italy's main highway, the Autostrada del Sole,

CLIMATE CHANGE & TRAVEL

Every form of transport that relies on carbon-based fuel generates CO_2, the main cause of human-induced climate change. Modern travel is dependent on aeroplanes, which might use less fuel per kilometre per person than most cars but travel much greater distances. The altitude at which aircraft emit gases (including CO_2) and particles also contributes to their climate change impact. Many websites offer 'carbon calculators' that allow people to estimate the carbon emissions generated by their journey and, for those who wish to do so, to offset the impact of the greenhouse gases emitted with contributions to portfolios of climate-friendly initiatives throughout the world. Lonely Planet offsets the carbon footprint of all staff and author travel.

stretches all the way to Reggio di Calabria. From London the distance is around 2200km.

Car drivers and motorbike riders will need the vehicle's registration papers, a Green Card, a nationality plate and their domestic licence. Contact your local automobile association for details about necessary documentation.

Sea

Ferry

Malta has regular sea links with Pozzallo and Catania in southern Sicily, and also Salerno in southern Italy. Ferries dock at the Sea Passenger Terminal beside the Valletta Waterfront in Floriana, underneath the southeast bastions of Valletta.

Virtu Ferries (☎2206 9022; www.virtuferries.com) runs the Malta–Sicily crossing with its catamaran service (carrying cars and passengers) to/from Pozzallo, with bus transfers to Catania (two hours).

For less frequent summer-only ferry transport from Salerno (Italy) or Catania (Sicily) consult **Grimaldi Lines** (www.grimaldi-lines.com; per person with vehicle from €189). One-way journeys with a vehicle cost around €189.

The Pozzallo–Malta crossing takes 1½ hours and operates year-round, with daily sailings from June to August, dropping to four or five days a week in September, weather permitting. The return passenger fare in high/low season is €153/89 (day return €139/84).

Tickets for children under four years are free but there is a charge of €10 for local transport where applicable; children aged four to 14 years pay 50% of the adult fares.

Public transport links from the ferry terminal at Valletta's waterfront have vastly improved with the **Upper Barrakka Lift**, which connects the waterfront with Upper Barrakka Gardens in Valletta. However, if you have luggage you'll probably prefer to catch a taxi to your destination. Set fees are established – head to the information booth at Valletta Waterfront (to Valletta is €15, to Sliema/St Julian's €25).

Yacht

Malta's excellent harbour and its strategic location at the hub of the Mediterranean has led to its development as a major yachting centre.

There are berths for 720 yachts (up to 22m length overall) in the Msida and Ta' Xbiex marinas (www.marinamalta.com) near Valletta; Mġarr Marina (www.gozomarina.net) on Gozo has space for more than 200 boats. There are also marinas at the Portomaso complex (www.portomasomarina.com) in St Julian's, and the Grand Harbour Marina (https://en.cnmarinas.com/grand-harbour-marina) in Vittoriosa.

For more information on these marinas and details of the logistics and formalities of sailing to Malta, contact **Transport Malta** (☎2122 2203; www.transport.gov.mt).

Malta's popularity with the yachting fraternity means that it is possible to make your way there as unpaid crew. Yachts tend to leave Gibraltar, southern Spain and the Balearics in April and May to head towards the popular cruising grounds of the Greek Islands and the Turkish coast. It's possible to just turn up at a marina and ask if there are any yachts looking for crew, but there are also agencies that bring together yacht owners and prospective crew (for a fee). One such agency is UK-based **Crewseekers** (☎0238-115 9207; www.crewseekers.net), which charges £75/99 for a six-/12-month membership.

EXCURSIONS TO SICILY

Virtu Ferries (☎2206 9022; www.virtuferries.com) runs 90-minute passenger catamaran services to Pozzallo that enable travellers to make a day trip to the Italian island of Sicily. You take the boat at 6.30am and return at 9.30pm. The itinerary takes in Mt Etna and the town of Taormina; Syracuse, the Marina di Ragusa and Modica; or Mt Etna and Modica (adult/child four to 14 years €127/95). Other themed excursions include a culinary tour, a quad-bike adventure, and a tour exploring the towns and countryside featured in the popular *Inspector Montalbano* television series.

Prices include taxes but exclude lunch; transfers in Malta cost €10. You can book a trip online or through most hotels and travel agents in Malta.

GETTING AROUND

Bicycle

Cycling on Maltese roads can be nerve wracking – the roads are often narrow and potholed, there's lots of traffic, and drivers show little consideration for cyclists. However, things are considerably better on the back roads and also on Gozo – the roads can still be rough, but there's far less traffic, and more and more visitors are opting to cycle around the island rather than rely on the buses.

You can rent bikes from **Magri Cycles & Spares** (☎2141 4399; www.magricycles.com; Triq Geronimo Abos, L-Iklin; ⏲9am-12.30pm & 4-7pm) and **Victoria Garage**

(☎2155 6414; www.victoriagaragegozo.com; Triq Putirjal; bicycle per day from €5, car per day from around €22). Electric bikes can be rented from **Eco Bikes** (Map p98; ☎9947 1627; www.ecobikesmalta.com; Triq il-Imsell; tours from €45, bike/e-bike per day from €15/20; ⏲9am-1pm & 5-7pm Mon-Sat). A handy pick-up/drop-off service for using bicycles around Malta's main tourist destinations is **nextbike** (☎2099 6666; www.nextbike.com.mt; from €1.50).

KARROZZIN

The *karrozzin* – a traditional horse-drawn carriage with seats for four passengers – has been in use in Malta since 1856. Many of the carriages are treasured family possessions passed down through generations, and are cared for with obsessive pride.

You can catch a *karrozzin* at Valletta's City Gate, Marsamxetto Ferry, Fort St Elmo, Valletta Waterfront and Mdina's Main Gate. There is an unfortunate tendency in some drivers to overcharge unwitting tourists. Haggle with the driver and be sure to agree on a fare before getting in. The fixed fare is €35 for 35 minutes.

Boat

To/from Valletta

Valletta Ferry Services operates regular ferries between Valletta's Marsamxett Harbour and **Sliema** (Map p54; ☎2346 3862; www.vallettaferryservices.com; single/return daytime adult €1.50/2.80, child €0.50/0.90, after 7.30pm adult €1.75/3.30; ⏲7.15am-7.15pm Oct-May, to 12.45am Jun-Sep), as well as from near Valletta Waterfront to the **Three Cities** (Map p54; ☎2346 3862; www.vallettaferryservices.com; single/return daytime adult €1.50/2.80, child €0.50/0.90, after 7.30pm adult €1.75/3.30; ⏲half-hourly 7am-7pm Oct-May, to midnight Jun-Sep).

To get from Valletta to the Three Cities, another option is on a traditional wooden *dgħajsa*. A one-way journey is €2 per person, and for €8 you can also go on a short harbour cruise.

To/from Gozo & Comino

Gozo Channel (☎2155 6114; www.gozochannel.com; foot passenger day/night €4.65/4.05, child €1.15, car & driver day/night €15.70/12.80) operates the car ferry that shuttles between Malta's Ċirkewwa and Gozo's Mġarr every 45 minutes from 6am to around 6pm (and roughly every 1½ hours throughout the night). If travelling by vehicle you pay on your return leg, when leaving Mġarr (Gozo), so there's no need to buy a ticket in Ċirkewwa on the way out.

A new fast ferry is planned to link Mġarr with Valletta's Grand Harbour, providing a more convenient transport link for students and commuters between the islands.

Bus

The bone-shaking, charming, brightly painted vintage buses that were so characteristic of Malta were taken out of service in 2011, replaced by boring-looking but more efficient modern buses, which have disabled access. These are operated by Malta Public Transport (www.publictransport.com.mt), which is presently run by the Spanish company Autobuses Urbanos de León.

Many bus routes on Malta originate from the Valletta Bus Station and radiate to all parts of the island, but there are also many routes that bypass the capital; bus timings range from every 10 minutes to hourly for less-visited places. Punctuality is a challenge, however, and many buses run considerably late, especially in the afternoon and evening. Patience is a traveller's friend. On Gozo the bus system is much more efficient than previously, though some places are only served by an hourly bus.

Tickets

You can buy single tickets as you board the bus or from ticket machines, which are found near numerous bus stops. Blocks of tickets and seven-day passes must be bought in advance from ticket offices or Agenda bookshop outlets. There's also a convenient Public Transport Malta office and electronic kiosk selling Explorer and ExplorePlus passes in the arrivals hall at the airport.

If you're caught travelling without a ticket, there's a penalty charge of €10. Fares:

- Single tickets (valid two hours) cost €2/1.50 July to September/October to June. They may be bought on the bus.
- €3 night fare (on night buses) are available year-round.
- Block of 12 tickets €15. This is a multi-user option, so if two people are travelling together, they can scan the ticket twice. A ticket is valid for two hours from when it's scanned. On night buses, you pay double (ie scan two tickets for one journey).
- Explorer seven-day tickets cost adult/child €21/15 and are valid on both Malta and Gozo, unlimited journeys, day or night
- ExplorePlus Card (€39) Valid for seven days and provides unlimited transport on public buses, two ferry trips with **Valletta Ferry Services** (Map p54; ☎2346 3862; www.vallettaferryservices.com; single/return daytime adult

€1.50/2.80, child €0.50/0.90, after 7.30pm adult €1.75/3.30; ⏲7.15am-7.15pm Oct-May, to 12.45am Jun-Sep), one day's travel with **CitySightseeing Malta** (☎2346 7777; www.citysightseeing.com.mt; adult/child €20/12; ⏲half-hourly 9am-3pm Mon-Sat, to 1pm Sun), and a trip to Comino with **Captain Morgan Cruises** (☎2346 3333; www.captainmorgan.com.mt; adult/child harbour cruise €16/13, around Malta €30/15, Blue Lagoon €25/10, underwater safari €16/10, jeep safari Malta €80/65, Gozo €80/65).

➡ Tallinja stored-value card. For this you need to register at Valletta Bus Station, at the airport, or online two weeks in advance to allow for delivery. You have to provide an ID card number, but this can be Maltese, a foreign ID, or your passport number. You also have to give your Malta address, which may be the address of your hotel in Malta – the card will be delivered there. With the Tallinja card, a single journey costs €0.75/0.25 per adult/child. Night buses cost €2.50. It is most relevant if you're staying in Malta for an extended period. There is a one-off €10 registration fee.

Routes & Timetables

To see up-to-date, full bus timetables and route maps, check online at www.publictransport.com.mt. The website also has a handy online journey planner. If you're staying in Malta for an extended period, download Malta Public Transport's Tallinja app, which provides real-time information about bus arrivals and departures.

There are six different express services running between the airport and various parts of the island, including St Julian's, Sliema and Ċirkewwa. The X4 runs between Valletta and the airport, and takes just over 20 minutes. For Sliema and St Julian's, catch the X3 from the airport.

Most buses run from around 5.30am to 11pm, and frequency varies depending on the popularity of the route. In towns and villages the bus terminus is usually found on or near the parish church square.

Car & Motorcycle

The Maltese love their cars. On weekends (Sunday in particular) they take to the road en masse, visiting friends and family or heading for the beach or a favourite picnic site. This means that there is often serious congestion on the roads around Valletta, Sliema and St Julian's. Friday and Saturday night in Paceville is one big traffic jam. However, renting a car gives you more flexibility, particularly to discover out-of-the-way beach coves.

Distance isn't a problem – the longest distance on Malta is 27km and the widest point is around 15km. On Gozo the longest distance is about 14km and the widest only 7km.

Automobile Associations

If you're renting a car, you'll be provided with a telephone number to contact in the event of mechanical difficulties or breakdown. If you're bringing your own vehicle, it's a good idea to take out European breakdown cover (offered in the UK by both the RAC and the AA). For roadside assistance in Malta, contact **RMF** (☎2124 2222; www.rmfmalta.com) or **MTC** (☎2143 3333; www.mtctowingmalta.com).

Bringing Your Own Vehicle

Tourists are permitted to use their vehicles for a maximum of six months in any given year without the need to apply for a permit. A motor vehicle entering a foreign country must display a sticker identifying its country of registration.

BIG YELLOW BUSES

Malta's old buses were a tourist attraction in themselves, and it's a shame in terms of local colour and photo opportunities that they're no longer rattling around the islands' potholed roads at unsettling speeds. Run as independent businesses by their drivers, they were lovingly customised with handmade parts and decorations. They were known as *xarabank*, a derivation of *charabanc* (a carriage or an old-fashioned term for a motor coach).

On the other hand, they probably also contributed to Malta being the most car-dense country in Europe. Quaintness of buses is not necessarily an endearing quality when you have to use them day to day, and the bus system is more efficient nowadays. You will very occasionally see an old bus on the road: the classic Bedfords, Thames, Leylands and AECs dating from the 1950s, '60s and '70s, brightly painted in a livery of yellow, white and orange, have not completely disappeared. A few are now used for wedding transport and photographs, and on the Sliema waterfront near the Valletta ferry, one has been repurposed as a colourful souvenir shop.

The Malta Buses by Michael Cassar and Joseph Bonnici is an illustrated history of the islands' celebrated public transport.

Driving Licences

All EU member states' driving licences are fully recognised throughout Europe. For those with a non-EU licence, an International Driving Permit (IDP) is a useful adjunct, especially if your home licence has no photo or is in a language other than English. Your local automobile association can issue an IDP, valid for one year, for a small fee. You must carry your home licence together with the IDP.

Fuel

The price of fuel is set by the government and at the time of research was €1.31/1.18 a litre for unleaded/diesel. Petrol is dispensed by attendants, and garages are generally open from 7am to 7pm (6pm in winter) Monday to Saturday; most are closed on Sunday and public holidays – though a few are open from 8am to noon on a roster system.

Larger stations have a self-service, cash-operated pump (€5, €10 and €20 notes accepted) for filling up outside opening hours.

Hire

Car rental rates in Malta are among the lowest in Europe. If you hire a car on Malta you can take it over to Gozo on the ferry without a problem. Rental rates on Gozo are lower (but with an extra charge for taking the car to Malta), but if you're visiting both islands the inconvenience of hiring a car in both places would outweigh any benefits. Supply is limited on Gozo so for July and August you'll need to book in advance to be assured of a vehicle.

Most of the car-hire companies have representatives at the airport, but rates vary so it's worth shopping around. Make sure you know what is included in the quoted rate – many of the local agencies quote very low rates that do not include full insurance against theft and collision damage.

Obviously rates will vary with season, length of rental period and the size and make of car (plus extras like air-con). Rates for the smallest vehicles start at around €25 a day (for rental of seven days or longer) in the high season. A child seat costs around €4 per day – but confirm whether it's a booster seat or full child seat.

The age limit for rental drivers is generally 21 to 70 years, but drivers between 21 and 25 years may be asked to pay a supplement of up to €10 a day. You will need a valid driving licence that you have held for at least one year. Rental rates often include free delivery and collection, especially in the Valletta-Sliema-St Julian's area.

Many accommodation providers offer car-rental arrangements – it pays to ask when you're making a booking. Most will drop off and collect cars (usually for a small fee). As well as all the major international companies, such as Avis, Budget and Hertz, there are dozens of local car-hire agencies.

Billy's (☎2152 3676; www.billyscarhire.com; 113 Triq Ġorġ Borg Olivier, Mellieħa) Excellent option on Malta.

Mayjo Car Rentals (☎2155 6678; www.mayjocarhire.com; Triq Fortunato Mizzi; per day around €22; ⏰8.30am-4.30pm Mon-Fri, to 12.30pm Sat) Gozo's widest range of cars.

Wembleys (☎2137 4141, 2137 4242; http://wembleys.com; 50 Triq San Ġorġ) Malta-based and also a good taxi service.

Insurance

Car-hire companies offer collision damage waiver (CDW) and/or theft damage protection insurance at extra cost (usually charged per day). Be sure to read the fine print and understand what you're covered for, and what excess charges you'll be up for in the event of an accident.

If you are bringing your own car, check with your local insurance company before you leave to make sure you are covered.

Parking

Parking can be tricky in the Sliema-St Julian's and Buġibba-Qawra areas. While there are car parks available, it's far more difficult to find parking in the high season. There's a large car park next to the Malta National Aquarium (from €2). In Valletta you can park within the city walls in the blue parking bays, but those delineated in green are reserved for residents.

If you can't find parking within the walls, you can use the large MCP underground **car park** (www.mcpcarparks.com.mt/mcp-floriana) near the bus terminus, close to the Phoenicia Hotel, which is only a short walk from Valletta's City Gate and sights.

Parking in the MCP costs €3 for up to two hours and €6 for over four hours. Alternatively, you can use the Park & Ride facility, just south of Floriana, where parking costs €0.40 per day and free shuttle buses run to the City Gate in Valletta. Parking elsewhere costs around €2 per hour.

Road Rules & Conditions

Unlike most of Europe, the Maltese drive on the left. Speed limits are 80km/h on highways and 50km/h in urban areas, but are rarely observed. Wearing a seat belt is compulsory for the driver and front-seat passenger. Any accidents must be reported to the nearest police station (and to the rental company if the car is hired); don't move your vehicle until the police arrive, otherwise your insurance may be nullified.

Road signs and regulations are pretty much the same as the rest of Europe, with one important difference – in Malta no one seems to pay attention to any of the rules. Be prepared for drivers overtaking on the inside, ignoring traffic lights, refusing to give way at junctions and hanging on your rear bumper if they think you're going too slowly. All rental cars have registration numbers ending in K, so tourists can be spotted easily. Vehicles coming from your right are supposed to have right of way at roundabouts, but don't count on vehicles on your left observing this rule.

You should also be aware that many of the roads are in pitiful condition, with cracks and potholes, and there are very few road markings. In winter, minor roads are occasionally blocked by wash-outs or collapsed retaining walls after heavy rain. Signposting is variable – some minor sights are easy to find, while major towns remain elusive. Often places seem to be well signposted, and then the signposts peter out. A satnav or a detailed road map will help ease the way.

The maximum allowable blood-alcohol concentration in drivers in Malta is 0.08%.

Taxi

Official Maltese taxis are white (usually Mercedes, with a taxi sign on top; www.maltataxi.net). To combat regular complaints of overcharging, taxi drivers must by law use the meter to determine the fare (except from the airport and sea port, where there are set fares). At the time of writing, Uber was not available in Malta, but a local company **eCABS** (☎2138 3838; www.ecabs.com.mt) offers a similar app-based service.

Details of the fixed fares from the airport are available at the taxi desk in the arrivals hall, where you can pay in advance and hand a ticket to the driver. These were the fares at the time of research:

- Valletta or Floriana €20
- Three Cities area €22
- Mdina or Rabat €22
- Sliema or St Julian's €25
- Buġibba or St Paul's Bay €30
- Golden Bay area €30
- Mellieħa €30
- Ċirkewwa €35

There are taxi ranks at City Gate and outside the Grand Master's Palace in Valletta, and at bus stations and major hotels in the main tourist resorts. Within Valletta, **Smart Cabs** (Map p54; ☎7741 4177; 3 people within city perimeter/to cruise-ship terminal €5/8) provides an electric-powered taxi service for a flat fare of €5/8 for three people inside/outside the city walls.

As an alternative to the official Maltese white taxis, unsigned black taxis are owned by private companies and usually offer cheaper set fares (similar to the UK's minicabs). To order a taxi, it's best to ask your hotel reception for the name and number of their preferred service. There are several 24-hour companies.

Belmont Garage (☎2155 6962; www.gozo.com/belmontgarage; Nadur)

Wembley's (Map p82;☎2137 4141, 2137 4242; www.wembleys.com; 115 Triq San Gorg, St Julian's) Reliable 24-hour radio taxi service offering both cars and minivans. Prices are often slightly less than other companies.

Tours

There are loads of companies offering tours around the islands by boat, bus, 4WD or a combination of the three. Prices vary (as does what's included), so shop around. If you're pushed for time these trips can be a good way to see the highlights, but itineraries can be rushed, with little free time.

Tours include half-day tours to the Blue Grotto or Valletta's Sunday market; full-day trips to the Three Cities, Mosta and Mdina; or evening trips to take in festa celebrations. Day trips to Gozo and Comino are also common. Tours can be arranged through most hotels and travel agents.

Captain Morgan Cruises (☎2346 3333; www.captainmorgan.com.mt; adult/child harbour cruise €16/13, around Malta €30/15, Blue Lagoon €25/10, underwater safari €16/10, jeep safari Malta €80/65, Gozo €80/65) Provides a range of cruises, including the Grand Harbour, around Malta and day trips to the Blue Lagoon.

CitySightseeing Malta (☎2346 7777; www.citysightseeing.com.mt; adult/child €20/12; ⌚half-hourly 9am-3pm Mon-Sat, to 1pm Sun) Operates tours of Malta in open-top buses: hop on and off any of the buses at any of the 20 or so stops. You can board and buy a ticket at any stop.

City Sightseeing Gozo (www.city-sightseeing.com; adult/child €18/10; ⌚every 45min 9.45am-6.30pm) Hop-on-hop-off bus tours of Gozo. The full circuit takes two hours.

Hera Cruises (Map p79; ☎2133 0583; www.heracruises.com; Sliema Waterfront) Boat tours in a Turkish *gulet* (old-style sailing boat) leave from Sliema waterfront. Options include an all-day cruise right around Malta (adult/child €50/25) and the three-bay trip to Comino and Gozo (€45/25). Prices include lunch, and good discounts are sometimes offered during quieter months. Check the website or ask at the Hera Cruises kiosk at Sliema.

Luzzu Cruises (☎7906 4489; www.luzzucruises.com; 2-harbour cruise adult/child €16/13, Gozo, Comino & Blue Lagoon €40/20, Comino, Blue Lagoon & caves €25/15, Marsaxlokk Sun market €17.50/12.50) A range of tours, including a two-harbour cruise and day-long trips taking in Gozo, Comino and the **Blue Lagoon**. Also arranges boat trips to Marsaxlokk for the Sunday market.

Language

Malti – the native language of Malta – is a member of the Semitic language group, which also includes Arabic, Hebrew and Amharic. It's thought by some to be a direct descendant of the language spoken by the Phoenicians, but most linguists consider it to be related to the Arabic dialects of western North Africa. Malti is the only Semitic language that is written in a Latin script.
Both Malti and English are official languages in Malta, and almost everyone is bilingual. Travellers will have no trouble at all getting by in English at all times. This chapter provides a basic introduction to Malti.

PRONUNCIATION

Most letters of the Maltese alphabet are pronounced as they are in English, with the following exceptions:

ċ	as the 'ch' in 'child'
ġ	soft, as the 'j' in 'job'
għ	inaudible; lengthens the preceding or following vowel
h	inaudible, as in 'hour'
ħ	as the 'h' in 'hand'
ij	as the 'ai' in 'aisle'
j	as the 'y' in 'yellow'
q	a glottal stop, which is similar to the pause in the middle of 'uh-oh'
x	as the 'sh' in 'shop'
z	as the 'ts' in 'bits'
ż	soft, as in 'zero'

BASICS

Hello.	*Merħba.*
Good morning/day.	*Bonġu.*
Good evening.	*Bonswa.*
Goodbye.	*Saħħa.*
Yes.	*Iva.*
No.	*Le.*
Please.	*Jekk jogħġbok.*
Thank you.	*Grazzi.*
Excuse me.	*Skużani.*
How are you?	*Kif inti?*
I'm fine, thank you.	*Tajjed, grazzi.*
Do you speak English?	*Titkellem bl-ingliż?*
What's your name?	*X'ismek?*
My name is ...	*Jisimni ...*
I love you.	*Inħobbok.*

ACCOMMODATION

Do you have any rooms available?	*Għad fadlilkom xi kmamar vojta?*
Can you show me a room?	*Tista' turini kamra?*
How much is it?	*Kemm hi?*
I'd like a room ...	*Nixtieq kamra ...*
with en suite	*bil-kamra tal-banju*
with one bed	*b'sodda waħda*
with two beds	*b'żewġ sodod*

SIGNS

Dħul	Entrance
Ħrug	Exit
Magħluq	Closed
Miftuħ	Open
Nisa	Women
Rġiel	Men
Sqaq	Lane/Alley
Twaletta	Toilet
Vjalq	Avenue

DIRECTIONS

Where is a/the ...?	*Fejn hu ...?*
Go straight ahead.	*Mur dritt.*
Turn left.	*Dur fuq ix-xellug.*
Turn right.	*Dur fuq il-lemin.*

far	*il-bogħod*
near	*il-viċin*
left luggage	*hallejt il-bagalji*

EMERGENCIES

Help!	*Ajjut!*
Police!	*Pulizija!*
Call a doctor!	*Qibgħad ghat-tabib!*
I'm lost.	*Ninsab mitluf.*

ambulance	*ambulans*
hospital	*sptar*

SHOPPING & SERVICES

At what time does it open/close?	*Fix'ħin jiftaħ/jagħlaq?*
How much?	*Kemm?*

bank	*bank*
... embassy	*ambaxxata ...*
hotel	*hotel/il-lukanda*
market	*suq*
pharmacy	*ispiżerija*
post office	*posta*
public telephone	*telefon pubbliku*
shop	*ħanut*

TIME & DATES

What's the time?	*X'ħin hu?*

morning	*fil-għodu*
afternoon	*wara nofs in-nhar*
yesterday	*il-bieraħ*
today	*illum*
tomorrow	*għada*

Monday	*it-tnejn*
Tuesday	*it-tlieta*
Wednesday	*l-erbgħa*
Thursday	*il-ħamis*
Friday	*il-gimgħa*
Saturday	*is-sibt*
Sunday	*il-ħadd*

January	*Jannar*
February	*Frar*
March	*Marzu*
April	*April*
May	*Mejju*
June	*Ġunju*
July	*Lulju*

NUMBERS

0	*xejn*
1	*wieħed*
2	*tnejn*
3	*tlieta*
4	*erbgħa*
5	*ħamsa*
6	*sitta*
7	*sebgħa*
8	*tmienja*
9	*disgħa*
10	*għaxra*
11	*ħdax*
12	*tnax*
13	*tlettax*
14	*erbatax*
15	*ħmistax*
16	*sittax*
17	*sbatax*
18	*tmintax*
19	*dsatax*
20	*għoxrin*
30	*tletin*
40	*erbgħin*
50	*ħamsin*
60	*sittin*
70	*sebgħin*
80	*tmienin*
90	*disgħin*
100	*mija*
1000	*elf*

August	*Awissu*
September	*Settembru*
October	*Ottubru*
November	*Novembru*
December	*Diċembru*

TRANSPORT

I'd like a ticket.	*Nixtieq biljett.*
When does the boat leave/arrive?	*Meta jitlaq/jasal il-vapur?*
When does the bus leave/arrive?	*Meta titlaq/jasal il-karozza?*
I'd like to hire a car/bicycle.	*Nixtieq nikri karozza/rota.*

GLOSSARY

AFM – Armed Forces of Malta
auberge – the residence of an individual langue of the Knights of St John
bajja – bay
bastion – a defensive work with two faces and two flanks, projecting from the line of the rampart
belt – city
bieb – gate
cavalier – a defensive work inside the main fortification, rising above the level of the main rampart to give covering fire
ċimiterju – cemetery
curtain – a stretch of rampart linking two bastions, with a parapet along the top
daħla – creek
dawret – bypass
demi-bastion – a half-bastion with only one face and one flank
dgħajsa – a traditional oar-powered boat
festa – feast day
fortiżża – fort
foss – ditch
għajn – spring (of water)
għar – cave
ġnien – garden
Grand Master – the title typically given to the head of an order of knights, including the Knights of Malta
kajjik – fishing boat
kappillan – parish priest
karrozzin – traditional horse-drawn carriage
kastell – castle
katidral – cathedral
kbira – big, main
knisja – church
kwartier – quarter, neighbourhood
langue – a division of the Knights of St John, based on nationality
luzzu – fishing boat
marsa – harbour
medina – fortified town, citadel
mina – arch, gate
misraħ – square
mitħna – windmill
mużew – museum
palazzo – Italian term for palace or mansion
parroċċa – parish
passeggiata – evening stroll (Italian term)
pjazza – square
plajja – beach, seashore
pont – bridge
pulizija – police
rabat – town outside the walls of a citadel
ramla – bay, beach
ras – point, headland
razzett – farm, farmhouse
sqaq – alley, lane
suq – market
sur – bastion
taraġ – stairs, steps
telgħa – hill
torri – tower, castle
triq – street, road
trulli – cone-shaped buildings that echo the traditional architecture of Puglia in Southern Italy
vedette – a lookout point, watchtower
vjal – avenue
wied – valley
xatt – wharf, marina

Behind the Scenes

SEND US YOUR FEEDBACK

We love to hear from travellers – your comments keep us on our toes and help make our books better. Our well-travelled team reads every word on what you loved or loathed about this book. Although we cannot reply individually to your submissions, we always guarantee that your feedback goes straight to the appropriate authors, in time for the next edition. Each person who sends us information is thanked in the next edition – the most useful submissions are rewarded with a selection of digital PDF chapters.

Visit **lonelyplanet.com/contact** to submit your updates and suggestions or to ask for help. Our award-winning website also features inspirational travel stories, news and discussions.

Note: We may edit, reproduce and incorporate your comments in Lonely Planet products such as guidebooks, websites and digital products, so let us know if you don't want your comments reproduced or your name acknowledged. For a copy of our privacy policy visit lonelyplanet.com/privacy.

ACKNOWLEDGEMENTS

Climate map data adapted from Peel MC, Finlayson BL & McMahon TA (2007) 'Updated World Map of the Köppen-Geiger Climate Classification', *Hydrology and Earth System Sciences*, 11, 163344

Cover photograph: Malta traditional fishing boats in Marsaxlokk; Maurice Tricatelle/Shutterstock ©

THIS BOOK

This 8th edition of Lonely Planet's *Malta & Gozo* guidebook was researched and written by Brett Atkinson. The previous edition was also written by Brett. The 6th edition was written by Abigail Blasi. This guidebook was produced by the following:

Destination Editor Anna Tyler

Senior Product Editor Dan Bolger

Product Editor Pete Cruttenden

Senior Cartographer Mark Griffiths

Book Designer Gwen Cotter

Assisting Editors Ronan Abayawickrema, Michelle Bennett, Helen Koehne, Charlotte Orr, Simon Williamson

Cover Researcher Ania Bartoszek

Thanks to Imogen Bannister, Mireille Bord, Hannah Cartmel, Katie Connolly, Alexander Dels, Kate Kiely, Karen Henderson, Andi Jones, Kate Matthews, Monique Perrin, Genna Patterson, Martine Power, Rachel Rawling, Kirsten Rawlings, Neil Stopforth.

Index

Map Pages **000**
Photo Pages **000**

Map Pages **000**
Photo Pages **000**

Map Legend

Sights
- Beach
- Bird Sanctuary
- Buddhist
- Castle/Palace
- Christian
- Confucian
- Hindu
- Islamic
- Jain
- Jewish
- Monument
- Museum/Gallery/Historic Building
- Ruin
- Shinto
- Sikh
- Taoist
- Winery/Vineyard
- Zoo/Wildlife Sanctuary
- Other Sight

Activities, Courses & Tours
- Bodysurfing
- Diving
- Canoeing/Kayaking
- Course/Tour
- Sento Hot Baths/Onsen
- Skiing
- Snorkelling
- Surfing
- Swimming/Pool
- Walking
- Windsurfing
- Other Activity

Sleeping
- Sleeping
- Camping
- Hut/Shelter

Eating
- Eating

Drinking & Nightlife
- Drinking & Nightlife
- Cafe

Entertainment
- Entertainment

Shopping
- Shopping

Information
- Bank
- Embassy/Consulate
- Hospital/Medical
- Internet
- Police
- Post Office
- Telephone
- Toilet
- Tourist Information
- Other Information

Geographic
- Beach
- Gate
- Hut/Shelter
- Lighthouse
- Lookout
- Mountain/Volcano
- Oasis
- Park
- Pass
- Picnic Area
- Waterfall

Population
- Capital (National)
- Capital (State/Province)
- City/Large Town
- Town/Village

Transport
- Airport
- Border crossing
- Bus
- Cable car/Funicular
- Cycling
- Ferry
- Metro station
- Monorail
- Parking
- Petrol station
- S-Bahn/Subway station
- Taxi
- T-bane/Tunnelbana station
- Train station/Railway
- Tram
- U-Bahn/Underground station
- Other Transport

Routes
- Tollway
- Freeway
- Primary
- Secondary
- Tertiary
- Lane
- Unsealed road
- Road under construction
- Plaza/Mall
- Steps
- Tunnel
- Pedestrian overpass
- Walking Tour
- Walking Tour detour
- Path/Walking Trail

Boundaries
- International
- State/Province
- Disputed
- Regional/Suburb
- Marine Park
- Cliff
- Wall

Hydrography
- River, Creek
- Intermittent River
- Canal
- Water
- Dry/Salt/Intermittent Lake
- Reef

Areas
- Airport/Runway
- Beach/Desert
- Cemetery (Christian)
- Cemetery (Other)
- Glacier
- Mudflat
- Park/Forest
- Sight (Building)
- Sportsground
- Swamp/Mangrove

Note: Not all symbols displayed above appear on the maps in this book

OUR STORY

A beat-up old car, a few dollars in the pocket and a sense of adventure. In 1972 that's all Tony and Maureen Wheeler needed for the trip of a lifetime – across Europe and Asia overland to Australia. It took several months, and at the end – broke but inspired – they sat at their kitchen table writing and stapling together their first travel guide, *Across Asia on the Cheap*. Within a week they'd sold 1500 copies. Lonely Planet was born.

Today, Lonely Planet has offices in Tennessee, Dublin and Beijing, with a network of over 2000 contributors in every corner of the globe. We share Tony's belief that 'a great guidebook should do three things: inform, educate and amuse'.

OUR WRITERS

Brett Atkinson

Brett is based in Auckland, New Zealand, but is frequently on the road for Lonely Planet, covering areas as diverse as Vietnam, Sri Lanka, New Zealand, Morocco, California and the South Pacific. He's a full-time travel and food writer specialising in adventure travel, unusual destinations and surprising angles on more well-known destinations. Craft beer and street food are Brett's favourite reasons to explore places, and he is featured regularly on the Lonely Planet website and in newspapers, magazines and websites across New Zealand and Australia.

Published by Lonely Planet Global Limited
CRN 554153
8th edition – Oct 2021
ISBN 978 1 78701 7139

10 9 8 7 6 5 4 3 2 1
Printed in China